No Comment!

No Comment!

An Executive's Essential Guide to the News Media

DONALD W. BLOHOWIAK

PRAEGER

New York
Westport, Connecticut
London

Library of Congress Cataloging-in-Publication Data

Blohowiak, Donald W.
  No comment!

  Bibliography: p.
  Includes index.
  1. Mass media and business. 2. Mass media and
business—United States. I. Title.
HD59.B57 1987   659.2   87-15831
ISBN 0-275-92820-9 (alk. paper)

Library of Congress Catalog Card Number: 87-15831
ISBN: 0-275-92820-9

First published in 1987

Praeger Publishers, One Madison Avenue, New York, NY 10010
A division of Greenwood Press, Inc.

Printed in the United States of America

∞
The paper used in this book complies with the Permanent
Paper Standard issued by the National Information Standards
Organization (Z39.48-1984).

10 9 8 7 6 5 4 3 2 1

For Susan,
my best friend

Contents

PART III
MEDIA BIAS

PART IV
HALF-TRUTHS, SMOKE SCREENS,
AND OTHER CORPORATE POLICIES

PART V
MEETING THE MEDIA

PART VI
CRISIS!

PART VII
FIGHTING BACK:
WHEN PUBLIC WRONGS NEED RIGHTING

Acknowledgments

This work would not have been possible were it not for the help of hundreds of cooperative colleagues in journalism, public relations, and business management. I am grateful to the companies and organizations that provided documents, studies, position papers, and other materials that allowed me to validate (or radically revise) the ideas that have been dancing in my head for years. I'm indebted to many, many people who gave freely of their time, experiences, insights, and themselves. Many of their thoughts are represented on these pages; some without attribution, in keeping with the wishes of the candid for anonymity. You know who you are and I thank you.

I am grateful to the following people: Hank Ackerman of the Associated Press, Robert Clark, Ph.D., and Fred Polner, Esq., for their encouragement when this book was in its early stages, and Jeannie Wilson, who typed early drafts in Detroit. For their help and moral support during the later versions of the book, I'd like to thank Alison Podel Bricken at Praeger Publishers for believing in the project, John Stephen Crowley for his suggestions and friendship, my friend and associate Thomas J. Rizzo, and friends Rick and Nancy Mitchell, Nanci Rosen, Pete Holzman, and Al Brauer. My thanks also to some people whose help goes back many years: John Schaller and Capps B. Sutherland, who actually paid me to join the professional media fraternity back in West Bend, Wisconsin, when I was barely 17; Donald B. Badgley, who encouraged me when I got there (often at the crack of dawn, with recorders rolling); and Tony Rizzo, George Otwell, Jay Bowles, and Roy Steinfort, who brought me into the Associated Press, which was the perfect launching point for this discussion of business and media issues.

My deepest thanks to Benjamin and Aaron who were patient and understanding while their dad seemed eternally attached to the computer in the den. I owe a special debt of gratitude to Susan, their mother, who cheerfully took up all the burdens my preoccupation created and charitably endured reading and editing every word of every rewrite. Finally, I want to thank Tom Jonas, who has more letters of academic achievement behind his name than anyone else I've ever met. Tom, by his example, taught me it was possible to move beyond cynicism to constructive criticism.

Introduction

To some business people, "news" is a dirty four-letter word. To many others, "news" represents a potential threat to their businesses and livelihoods.

Anytime, anywhere, any organization can find itself engulfed in a fiery public information disaster, the flames of which are fueled by an eager press. Damaging accusations—regardless of merit—can be detailed without compassion on the front page of the local newspaper or the *Wall Street Journal*, as the lead story on a network or local radio or television news program, or as the cover story in a trade journal or weekly news magazine.

An accident, a strike, a lawsuit, a boycott, a government action, an unkind stroke of fate can force any company (union, organization, individual) in America into the public eye. Few corporations choose to expose their shortcomings or vulnerability in open public display. But every day, the news media thrust companies into the spotlight of negative publicity. Some find themselves there because of events they could not control, others because they lacked the foresight and finesse to manage a potentially dangerous situation.

The list of companies caught in a snare of unwanted and damaging media publicity is endless. It's easy to recall notorious examples involving some of the most prominent names in corporate America (and what were some of the least): from Union Carbide for the world's worst industrial accident; to Coca-Cola for its "new Coke" flop; to Morton Thiokol for space shuttle O-rings; to E. F. Hutton, General Electric, GTE,

Rockwell, and others for fraud; to J. P. Stevens for protracted labor problems; to Bank of America for running afoul of banking laws; to Cattle King for selling tainted meat; to Johnson and Johnson for poisoned Tylenol; and so on, ad infinitum.

There are thousands of companies, large and small, to which one could point for news stories concerning a litany of misfortunes and alleged transgressions such as bankruptcies, government investigations, unfriendly corporate takeovers, product recalls, declining market shares, increasing prices, and charges of price fixing, violating safety rules, unfair labor practices, tax evasion, false advertising, questionable accounting practices, and executive improprieties.

In today's information-intensive and competitive environment, the integrity of a company's reputation is vital. A 1985 survey (by Sales Consultants International) asked consumers what most influences their buying decisions. They found that the *image* of a company or its product was the number one factor.[1] Any damage to the public image of a company or its products, therefore, seriously threatens its success, even survival. "Consumer confidence in a brand or a company *is* the franchise. The loss of [public] confidence can destroy a business," concludes ad man Tony Wainwright.[2]

News media attention to a firm's troubles—real or perceived—multiplies them. Short of destruction, negative publicity threatens to diminish profits and stock prices, shrink market share, spawn lawsuits, force executives and other workers to lose their jobs, encourage government regulations, and otherwise impair a company.

Regardless of how an organization finds its way into the clutches of probing reporters, its executives must know how to deal effectively with what popularly is called "the media." Ronald Rhody, senior vice-president with Bank of America, told *Fortune* that managing press coverage is "as important as any force we have to deal with—as important to senior managers as capital and labor."[3]

If that strikes you as an exaggeration, consider this. Unlike a court of law, the court of public opinion, conducted by the press, features no presumption of innocence. It appoints no one as counsel to the accused. There is no right to a fair hearing in a trial by media. No rules govern "testimony" or "evidence." There's no provision for confronting your accusers (who may never be identified to you), much less cross-examining them. In fact, you may be denied entirely a platform on which to present a defense to the charges leveled against you. The press may act unilaterally as prosecutor and judge as it tries your case before the public jury. If the press does concede to airing arguments defending you, the accused, it subjects those statements to the editorial control of the news media prosecutors. If the same rules were applied in a court of law, the defense would be forced to have its arguments edited and then presented to the jury by the prosecution. Would anyone ever be found not guilty under those circumstances?

Free press and free enterprise are not mutually exclusive concepts. But the press does not view its role as that of cheerleader for corporate America.

Despite the tremendous impact news coverage can have on an organization, most business executives are poorly prepared to encounter the unsympathetic news media. Business schools do not prepare their students to confront this dynamic and powerful force in U.S. free enterprise. Management books ignore the subject.

Until now, many business people who found themselves subjected to media scrutiny were left to ignorantly and fearfully fend for themselves (trial by fire, with the world watching) or to blindly hand off media relations to public relations experts (who harbor a vested interest in promoting the media mystique). When meeting the press, one needs to know the rules of the high-stakes news media game—as well as the power tactics and the winning strategies—to emerge from the interaction intact.

In *NO COMMENT!* you will gain a keen insight into what the news media are and how you can effectively and advantageously deal with them. The book reveals the goals, motivations, and thinking of the people who shape the news accounts of your firm, whose work can magnify your troubles by bringing them to the minds of millions of people (like customers, employees, investors, competitors, legislators, and regulators). These potential adversaries are journalists, who've appointed themselves the nation's watchdogs, information gatekeepers, and guardians of truth. Understanding them and the news process is key to your effectively negotiating with the press.

Within these pages you'll come to understand why the press stalks business, why bad news is good news for the news business, why reporters are accused of having a leftist bias, why there seems to be an undeniable antibusiness slant in the press, why millions of dollars spent on public relations are often not only wasted but actually counterproductive. And you'll learn how to prevent unfair media coverage; how to avoid self-defeating PR blunders; how to improve your company's reputation; how to maintain your integrity and cool under media fire; how to take and keep control of even a combative interview; how to prevent out-of-context quotes; what to say even when you want to say nothing; how to plan for, survive, and manage a public information crisis; what to do when you feel victimized by the news media or find them ignoring your point of view on important matters; and how to generate and keep momentum for positive press.

The book is not a "how to gain publicity" primer. To the contrary, it focuses on reacting to unsolicited (and thus potentially dangerous) publicity. I firmly believe that one can be effective in dealing with a potential adversary only when one understands the other side. With that in mind, *NO COMMENT!* is filled with a solid grounding of the "why" behind the business/media relationship. This puts a context around the book's practical tactical information that you can put to work protecting your organization's image before, during, and after it's trained in the press's gun sights.

You need not read *NO COMMENT!* from first chapter to last. But I believe you will derive the greatest benefit from this book if you read all its chapters. They are typically short and to the point.

I sincerely hope you bought this book before needing it to cope with a public information crisis. If the media gun is to your head at the moment, you might do well to jump to parts V, VI, and VII.

I offer *NO COMMENT!* to assist anyone who could be accused of having a dirty hand in the world's cookie jar.

PART I
THE BUSINESS/MEDIA PRIMER

Since the media have often been the scrutinizers and the bearers, if not the originators, of criticism, business has been wont to blame the media for the decline of its standing in the public mind.

Craig Aronoff

Businessmen have alternately feared and hated news people.

Tom Murray

OmniMedia

All the world's a stage,
And all the men and women merely players.
William Shakespeare

The media. We use the term in conversation as if it were some single, massive monolith. As in, "It's all because of the media. The media is blowing this whole thing out of proportion."

The media are the mediums. Medium is a noun meaning something in the middle position (an ideal place for a news report to be). Medium also is defined as a means of transmitting or conveying something, as in words or pictures. The media are conduits, channels of information dissemination. They're employed as means of distributing news reports (which may or may not be in the middle of where they should be).

The media are everything from the *Wall Street Journal* to *Ladies' Home Journal* to the *Milwaukee Journal, Playboy* to *Plastics Weekly, The Nation* to *Nation's Business* to *National Geographic* to the National Broadcasting Company to the *National Law Review* to *Newsweek,* the *Washington Post* to *Women's Wear Daily* to WXYZ (ABC owns it in Detroit). There are thousands and thousands of media outlets in this country.

The media are ubiquitous. Virtually no U.S. home is without several radios and one or more TVs; most subscribe to one or more newspapers and magazines; tens of millions subscribe to cable television. Most of our waking hours are spent consuming some form of the news media.

Americans' appetite for information seems insatiable; we monitor all-news radio and television stations, read magazines and books in record numbers. We consume information and follow that with digestion of more information.

Virtually everything we know about the world outside our own homes and offices derives from news reports. If it were not for the news media, what would most of us know of the Supreme Court or our local school board; Japan, the Soviet Union or any other country; developments in medicine; the arts; or even the industry in which we work?

The news media know few spatial barriers, and they aren't much bound by time either. The modern technology of news gathering—satellites, videotape, portable cameras, and computers—allows for constant, worldwide news collection and immediate distribution to end consumers, us. Today, from virtually any corner of the planet, we learn of news not just seconds after it's occurred but actually as it's happening. This is true whether it's a news conference in Washington, Moscow, or Reykjavik, Iceland; riots in Miami, Paris, Tokyo, or Tehran; or disasters in New Orleans, New Delhi, or Newfoundland. Just about everywhere is readily accessible.

The world's news organizations constantly monitor each other. Almost no news outlet anywhere on the globe can publish or broadcast a news account without many other media immediately having access to the information. News organizations have cooperative agreements to share their resources. Wire services, radio and TV networks, cable TV services—they all work together, blanketing the planet with probing eyes and ears. What's reported in Pretoria can be news in Peoria (and vice versa) literally within seconds. We live in an age of *OmniMedia*, when an occurrence judged newsworthy by any news organization presently becomes news on all seven continents.

This can have tremendous implications for any business whose reach extends beyond the borders of the smallest town in America.

American Edwards, a medical products company, saw the effect of OmniMedia in the fall of 1986. The company markets a gastric bubble, a device to be inserted into the stomach of severely obese patients. When a woman in Florida who had an Edwards bubble implant died, a local newspaper did a story on the incident. A national wire service picked up the story. Within a day's time and across the country, I personally saw or heard related stories on a TV newscast in Los Angeles, in *USA Today*, on Paul Harvey's noon news and comment program, and on a medical talk show broadcast over ABC's TalkRadio network. Those and subsequent reports focused national attention on, and sparked a national debate over, the efficacy of the weight-loss treatment.[1]

A small business in a small town is no more immune to media inspection than a monolithic multinational corporation headquartered in

New York City. Through the globally connected OmniMedia, the world's eyes can be upon you instantly.

Let's say you run a 200-employee manufacturing plant in South Dakota that makes mood rings. A reporter for the local paper hears about your new labor contract giving hourly workers gift certificates for travel and luxury items as a performance incentive. She thinks it's novel and newsworthy.

Without your seeking any publicity, the paper prints a story about your company's new program. An editor at the state office of a national wire service sees the story in the local paper, rewrites it and sends it over the news wire. The news service's national editor comes across the story, finds it interesting and puts it on the national circuit of the news wire. From there, newspapers and broadcasters around the nation have access to the story about your company. You may get calls from the *New York Times*, CBS radio, business journals, NBC TV, other local newspapers, radio and TV stations, and in a day or so, from news organizations in Europe, Australia, Taiwan, and other ports.

All that attention from a story you didn't seek to publicize and that you didn't think was anybody else's business!

Marshall McLuhan's global village concept *is* reality. The media pervade our society with their omnipresence. Given current technology, nothing happens beyond the immediate grasp of OmniMedia. Business and other institutions are captive to OmniMedia's long reach.

A leader in our society has a responsibility, an obligation, to his organization and to himself to understand how the news media work, how they might threaten the organization, and how they may be used to its advantage. Executives must prepare themselves to face, even battle, the men and women of the news media who'd gladly invade the sacrosanct halls of corporate America.

Corporate America: Under the Microscope

I am responsible for my actions, but who is responsible for those of General Motors?

Ralph Nader

The main trouble with business is businessmen.

Howard K. Smith

Private enterprise has been and continues to be thought of as a private affair by many who engage in it. But for a multitude of reasons, the media try (and not often enough, some argue) to make private transactions public business.

The press *is* watching business closely. One page from a metropolitan newspaper can tell the story. The *Orange County Register*, a southern California daily with a circulation of over 300,000, reported stories under these headlines one day in early 1987: "GM plans to lay off 2,000 in Kansas City"; "Ford exec asks cut in Japanese Imports"; "SEC chief says more big news is coming"; "Guiness director quits over scheme"; "People/Continental to offer 2-for-1 tickets"; "GE to lay off 3,000 workers at Northeast plants"; "Lyng says stricter farm subsidy limits coming"; "Loral buys Goodyear Aerospace." The page featured other stories about energy stocks, the falling price of the dollar in Europe, President Reagan's trade plans, and a few other odds and ends. A large picture showed striking Lockheed Shipbuilding workers crossing a picket line in Seattle.[1]

All that business news, good and bad, on one page of one newspaper one Tuesday! Clearly, OmniMedia are watching.

PUBLIC INTEREST IN PRIVATE ENTERPRISE

As our society grows increasingly complex, as powerful multinational corporations dominate more and more of our daily lives, private enterprise becomes an increasingly public affair. Joseph F. Awad, corporate director of public relations for Reynolds Metals, observes, "You cannot really fix the point at which the rest of society leaves off and a business begins."[2]

Because the business of business is the business of the nation, the public, and thus the news media, demand accountability from the barons of business. This is true not only for tax-supported defense contractors and multi-billion-dollar multinational public companies, but most every commercial enterprise with potential impact on the public welfare.

The justification for this interest is complex. Partly, it's because so many people, through Individual Retirement Accounts, mutual funds, and the like, now own stock in publicly traded companies. The number of Americans owning stock, according to the New York Stock Exchange, more than doubled between 1965 and 1985. Some 47 million of us now own shares of companies; there's a stockholder in almost one of every three households.[3] Not surprisingly, there is great public interest in the day-to-day affairs of the business world. The press has a role as intelligence gatherer for its vast audience of investors.

Interest in business news also finds roots in the public's fear of business, fear that stems from a perception of "us little citizens versus you goliath corporations." Business, meaning any enterprise of any size, is more powerful than any individual, and thus many people believe that business takes heartless advantage of the populace in the name of profit. A 1985 Roper poll conducted for *U.S. News and World Report* asked people across the country their feelings about the power of institutions in the United States. The rankings for "too powerful" were quite telling: big business led government, labor unions, and TV networks. Better than half the people surveyed thought big business wielded too much power.[4]

The news media, prying into private commercial matters, play a role in which they're acting on behalf of the public's right to know what business might be doing *to* the citizenry. Within this mentality, the very foundation of American free enterprise—the profit motive itself—is suspect. The theory holds that profit is the province of used car salespeople (who allow no moral scruples to come between them and making money) and cold-hearted capitalists (who regard people as either chattel laborers, enriching corporate coffers with their meagerly rewarded sweat, or suckers, buying goods and services at prices far in excess of their worth).

Such a negative, even destructive, attitude is in part a remnant of the consumer movement of the 1960s and 1970s (a la Nader's Raiders) and in part a lingering distrust of powerful institutions, a leftover from the Vietnam war and Watergate experiences. As we shall see later in this chapter, this antibusiness sentiment also grows from the increasing size of big business, its indifference, misconduct, and the direct threat business activities pose to our individual health and well-being.

A 1970s HANGOVER

In the early 1970s, a demoralizing retreat from war and the infamous Watergate affair tarnished the United States. The hallowed presidency of the United States was debauched by ugly suspicions of criminal wrongdoing. America and her press lost innocence. Journalists vowed, Never again will we trust anyone in power without questioning, investigating, challenging. If the presidency were not pure, then, certainly, lesser institutions were dirty. Moral blemishes, wherever they lay, would be discovered and publicly exposed.

A post-Watergate distrust of, and disappointment in, all institutions pervaded homes and newsrooms alike.

The energy crises of the 1970s accentuated such suspicious thinking. Many people presumed that big oil companies were manipulating the flow of petroleum products. While supplies dwindled, demand remained abundant, creating the classic capitalist scenario for raising prices and profits. Whether anybody manipulated anything, oil prices and oil company profits did go up. The press noted such events with accusing tones in reports laced with innuendo. Despite loud denials by oil industry and government officials, the public, aided by the news media, went right on believing that the oil crises were carefully orchestrated hoaxes.

Around the same time, consumer confidence in business was rocked by chemical spills, spiraling inflation, critically high unemployment, unaffordable interest rates for home loans (and everything else), and dismal economic news from every quarter.

During this period, the press found it was capable of challenging the establishment. The news media had the resources, clout, and moxie to stick their noses where they really hadn't been before. It became quite fashionable for journalists to question private enterprise loudly and boldly. As a 1983 Mobil Corporation advertisement postulated, "Watergate ushered in a new era of investigative journalism, and crusading reporters quickly turned their sights on business."[5]

This trend was found not only in big-time media like the *Washington Post* and CBS but in their imitators at the local level as well. This is why today most newspapers and radio and television stations offer consumer hotline services (e.g., "Seven On Your Side," "Consumer Help Line," "Action Line"). Through these, a reporter may investigate allegations that a retailer refuses to refund the purchase price of defective merchandise, that a gas station is selling leaded gasoline as unleaded, or that a local high-tech assembly plant is dumping contaminated waste into a creek.

The news media are watching out for the interests of a vulnerable public. And we are vulnerable, caveat emptor notwithstanding. Few of us grow our own food, build our own homes, make our own clothes, or generate our own electricity. For the necessities of life, we are entirely dependent on, and vulnerable to, profit-seeking enterprises. There is nothing perverse or radical about the press holding business publicly accountable for its actions. More than a generation ago, Robert Wood Johnson, who was chairman of Johnson and Johnson from 1939 to 1963 (and who was son of its founder), observed in a company policy statement, "The day has passed when business was a private matter—if it ever really was. In a business society, every act of business has social consequences and may arouse public interest. Every time business hires, builds, sells, or buys, it is acting for the . . . people as well as for itself, and must be prepared to accept full responsibility."[6]

In other words, operating in the public arena means accepting responsibility in the public spotlight. Today, the public demands that business officials publicly announce what's in their products; proclaim products' hazards and shortcomings, explain how those products are made, stored, and shipped; justify company personnel practices; reveal where they make their investments; divulge the taxes they paid—or didn't—and disclose how they make their profits. (For example, the Council on Economic Priorities compiled a widely available book called *Rating America's Corporate Conscience*. The group ranked businesses and their brands according to company ethics, which included the number of managerial positions held by women and minorities, the percent of pretax profits donated to charities, and other measures.)[7] Media coverage mirrors this public interest.

While most companies still conduct their business quite privately behind closed doors, there's little about business that can be considered private anymore. American business can no longer hide under the shelter of "free and private enterprise."

LAND OF THE GIANTS

Press interest in—or distrust of—corporations is amplified by the perceived bigness, and resulting moral distance, of modern business. Like most people, reporters don't really distinguish between big business and small business. A firm with 50 employees and $1 million in sales frequently is thought of in the same terms as one with 50,000 employees and several billion dollars in sales.

Statistically, most firms aren't giant companies yet. But America's big businesses are getting bigger, and their economic clout is approaching the incomprehensible. A top news story of the 1980s is merger mania, the apparently insatiable drive of megacorporations to copulate with other capitalist behemoths.

There were 32 corporate mergers in 1985 alone with values of over $1 billion. Some of the biggest involved firms that touch consumers directly: for $5.7 billion Philip Morris ate General Foods; similarly, R. J. Reynolds smoked out Nabisco for almost $5 billion; General Electric zapped RCA, which owns NBC, at a cost of almost $6.3 billion to create a $38-billion bureaucracy. Additional megamergers included General Motors and Hughes Aircraft; Allied Corporation and Signal Companies; Capital Cities Communications and ABC; Procter and Gamble and Richardson-Vicks; and others. There were some 3,000 major corporate mergers in 1985, about double the rate of 1980.[8]

This rampant urge to merge led columnist Ellen Goodman to predict in early 1986, "Following a spring fever of corporate mergers, the Fortune 500 will announce that they are now the Fortune 50."[9] By year's end, her prediction practically came true, as there were about 3,000 other major mergers or corporate sales in 1986. Some of those were big, multi-billion-dollar deals, like Burroughs plugging into Sperry, the sales of Safeway stores and R. H. Macy and Company, Campeau Corporation's purchase of Allied Stores Corporation, Unilever's cleanup of Chesebrough-Pond's, and many other big deals.[10] In early 1987, *Business Week* estimated that, "If mergers and acquisitions were to continue at 1986's rate, every public company could be turned over to new owners by the year 2001."[11]

All over this country there must be legions of people who work for what they think is a small company, totally unaware that the company they serve is really only a division beholden to a much larger corporate monstrosity. While most people don't work for the biggest companies, it's virtually impossible for them not to send their dollars to the gargantuans. The consumer can have any soap he wants, but they all seem to be made by one or two firms. The government can contract with any vendor in the USA, but only a handful seem get the lion's share of our tax dollars.

Some of the biggest companies in this country (some of which are owned by private or foreign concerns) are either not household names or the extent of their prevalence in our daily lives escapes our notice. Their multi-billion-dollar economic tentacles are often imperceptible to the unaided consumer eye. Take, for example, ARA Services, Amfac, B. A. T., Bechtel, and Cargill (who knows how this privately held $30-

billion-a-year mammoth grain trader influences the cost of our daily bread?). Add, as well, Continental Grain, Cyanamid, Farley Industries, Foremost McKesson, Gulf and Western, Halliburton, IC Industries, ITT, Loews Corporation, Mocatta Metals, Northwest Industries, Rockwell International, Schlumberger, Tenneco, Transamerica, TRW, Unilever, and so on.[12]

The long reach of big business into our day-to-day lives goes undetected by most people. But the media, themselves increasingly part of the billion-dollar corporate establishment, are cognizant of big business, and they demand accountability from it.

WITHOUT COMMITMENT OR COUNTRY

Big commercial institutions tend to draw cold, impersonal attention from journalists, who tend to see the character of those companies in a light of the same color.

With the notable exception of enterprises led by Lee Iacocca and Ted Turner, most modern business entities lack personality; they are lifeless. Unlike their corporate ancestors, they are not run by people who own a large stake in the business, who grew up in the town where the firm is based, or who assume personal responsibility for the company's good citizenship.

To the contrary, today's modern big business is run by professional managers. These elite men and women may crisscross the country several times while riding the corporate fast track. Unlike the company's hourly workers, these managers often know little or no sense of community. Their current residence isn't a place for roots, it's but a stepping stone. The professional manager's job is to make quarterly profits, expediently, efficiently, and consistently. The reward for big earnings is to step up to the next rung on the career ladder, often with another move to another corporation in another state. Such motivation leads to shorter-term outlooks, with diminished regard for corporate responsibility to the economic, social, or physical welfare of a community. (In fairness, I must admit to living in five time zones in the past ten years while chasing the corporate brass ring.)

The insipid commitment individual managers make to their temporary communities extends to business's attitude toward the nation as a whole. While many U.S. firms—in transportation, electronics, and other industries—have merged or joined forces with foreign companies, a frightening disparity has been created in our balance of trade with other nations. In the face of serious domestic un- and underemployment, many companies move manufacturing operations abroad, forsaking U.S. jobs. Oil companies still import much of our energy from politically unstable governments, placing us all economically at risk. Some U.S.

corporations import steel from abroad while the domestic steel industry struggles for its very survival. Corporations, big and small, import everything from consumer electronics and motorcycles to tobacco, clothing, and cars, damaging or crushing domestic producers in the process.

Thomas Jefferson, in colonial America, observed, "The merchant has no country." And this certainly rings true in 20th-century America. In late 1986, famed corporate acquirer Irwin Jacobs declared, "The world is one market today."[13]

Coupled with our trade imbalance and world market orientation, foreign investment in the United States is escalating. It touches all segments of American life: consumer and industrial goods, real estate, financial services, and so on. Foreign investment in U.S. manufacturing, according to the Commerce Department, had increased to nearly $60 billion in 1985, of which $12 billion was infused in 1984 alone.[14] In early 1987, *Business Week* reported that foreign companies spent another $18 billion buying U.S. companies in 1986.[15] Not long after that report, *Fortune* postulated that in order to "finance the trade deficit, the U.S. will have to continue attracting large amounts of foreign capital."[16] While the absolute numbers are still relatively small, more and more Americans are going to work for European, Asian, and Middle Eastern economic masters.

The theme of a strong United States being rooted in a strong industrial base was once embodied in the slogan, "What's good for General Motors is good for America." But today, the truth is that what's good for $95-billion General Motors and its brother conglomerates is only good for the company. A modern corporation loves no nation; its loyalty is to profitable markets. All else is peripheral (including, as we have seen, employees and their families, homes, and communities).

One journalist put it to me this way, "The influence large multinational companies can exert is incredible. Their allegience is not to the people of the United States but to the bottom line. Profit means more than people. Look at how the steel companies abandoned the people of Youngstown, Ohio."

Even a strong dollar, seemingly good for the United States, can be very bad news for U.S.-based multinational firms. It can cost a company its foreign sales. This lowers profits and threatens a company's international viability, which may then endanger the jobs of U.S. workers.

As the U.S. economy shifts from a homegrown industrial base to a service base without a nationality, who's to say what business or economic developments are really good for U.S. citizens? Are America's best interests parochial or planetary?

These difficult questions elude answers and only provoke many more questions from average citizens and their watchdogs, the nation's journalists.

FELONIOUS FAILURE, ETHICAL LAPSES

Big is not necessarily bad, but big corporations do raise big issues of morality. Suspicions about the moral deficiency of big business are confirmed regularly. The news media detail stories of business corruption and lawbreaking—from defense contract fraud by Rockwell, GE, GTE, and others (the Defense Department announced in February 1987 it was investigating 59 of its top 100 contractors for over 300 cases of suspected corruption[17])—to wire fraud by E. F. Hutton, to failure to report billions in cash transactions ("most of it suspected drug money," claimed the *Washington Post*[18]) at Crocker National Bank, to other incidents of obstructing justice, fixing prices, making improper campaign contributions, and so on.

In late 1985, Amatai Etzioni, author and sociologist at George Washington University, claimed that "roughly two-thirds of our 500 largest corporations have been involved to some extent in illegal behavior over the last 10 years. . . . [T]he top 100 corporations were involved in more incidents (55 percent) than all the others combined."[19]

Not surprisingly, only 32 percent of Americans surveyed by a 1985 CBS-*New York Times* poll believed that most corporate executives are honest.[20] Just as bad, "49% of the public think ethical standards [in business] have declined in the past decade, while only 9% think they have risen," according to the *Wall Street Journal*, which commissioned a 1983 Gallup poll.[21]

Illegal activities aside, business gives its critics plenty of other ammunition for pot shots. U.S. companies export to other countries drugs that can't pass review in the United States and ship products to poor nations that, critics say, don't need the goods and would be better off without them.

Here at home, tobacco companies continue producing and through advertising (about $875 million worth a year)[22] continue encouraging people to consume habit-forming killer products. Children, through seductive ads, are enticed to consume breakfast cereals that are up to 55 percent sugar. Via political action committees, business is assembling the best Congress money can buy. Examples abound. The news media have ample rationale to keep their eyes trained on business.

THE SPECTER OF TECHNOLOGY

Issues of morality or economic clout aren't the only ones that pique the interest of the news media in corporate America. The technology developed by modern business to meet the needs of our modern society also spurs news media attention. More specifically, the perils that modern technology present to mankind give rise to intense interest in the corporations controlling the technology.

One threatening technology is nuclear science, which creates both military devices capable of eradicating the human species and energy-generating systems capable of poisoning significant human populations with radiation emissions.

We also fear the technology of synthetic and natural chemicals that business adds to our foods to make them more attractive, longer lasting, or lower in calories. Such additives may slowly poison us. We fear the technology of plastics and other synthetic materials for clothes, toys, homes, appliances, and furnishings; they can cause waste disposal problems, and they emit deadly gases when burned.

People are afraid of hazardous substances, discarded by manufacturers, that contaminate water supplies or leak poison gases into the air; and they're scared of acid rain created by air pollutants emitted by heavy industry. They threaten to damage irreparably the environment for generations to come.

We distrust the technology that built automobiles with new, light-weight, fuel-saving materials because the cars still accelerate beyond 70 MPH but offer scant protection to people riding in them. We're leery of technology that builds marvelous products but at the same time creates workplaces that expose employees to immediate bodily harm or that may cause workers to suffer serious health disorders decades from now.

Commercial concerns produce technology that leaves by-products of air pollution, water pollution, food pollution, and personal pollution. Modern business, endeavoring to meet the needs of modern America, is exposing modern man to many potentially life-threatening maladies. The modern press intends to hold the responsible enterprise accountable.

ALARM AND JUSTIFICATION

Changes in the U.S. economy and way of life, brought about by a global economic system and high technology, spook most of us (at least occasionally), and the news media reflect our fears and concerns. With its coverage of international corporate oligarchies and all their, however tiny, missteps, the press is quietly sounding an alarm. (Though not to the degree of its turn-of-the-century media forebears, the muckrakers, who loudly decried bully industrialists.) The alarm summons us to think about the frightening implications of the sweeping changes taking place in our society.

Perhaps, one could argue, any such alarm is, well, alarmist. Americans still enjoy one of the highest standards of living in the world. No other country offers the variety of goods and services to its citizens that ours

PART II

UNDERSTANDING THIS BUSINESS OF NEWS

To the press alone, checquered as it is with abuses, the world is indebted for all the triumphs which have been gained by reason and humanity over error and oppression.
Thomas Jefferson

does. A contemporary capitalist, looking at the same trends in U.S. business that give some journalists and others the intellectual equivalent of hives, could suggest that they result from the free enterprise system's natural market forces and that the resulting economic and technical developments bring great improvements to the lifestyle of most Americans.

Further, one could argue, there can be no sinister plot by corporations—who are just collections of ordinary folk themselves—to squash individual citizen consumers or small competitors. After all, the capitalist retorts, it's the individual consumer that the large companies exist to serve. In a free market, citizens vote with their dollars. If the megacompanies don't do the job, they will be replaced by smaller, more market-sensitive competitors.

This may be true. But the economic power, the moral concerns, the potential threat to public health and safety that business represents to America are all issues that mandate press oversight. Whenever, wherever, and however business lapses or violates the public trust, the news media, watchdogs of America's institutions, rightfully will be there to hound the evildoers.

Action News: The Life of Journalists

Time and tide wait for no man.

English Proverb

Imagine this. You walk in to work one day, your boss hands you a pen, a pad of paper, a tape recorder, and tells you, "Jones, I want you to go out there and find all there is to find that's important, pertinent, and topical. Overturn every rock, peek around every corner. Ferret out human drama, uncover life's tragedies, ironies, and joys. Write about what you discover, reducing it all to terms any twelve-year-old can understand. Be thorough but not boring, objective but not sterile, interesting but not melodramatic. Have your copy ready in four hours."

That scenario, while admittedly exaggerated, does represent the charge of U.S. journalists. Their function is to view the world, record as best they can their observations—suppressing personal opinion and political inclinations—digest the essential, discard the rest, and report their findings in the simplest but most interesting way possible. It's a tough job.

In this chapter and a few that follow, we'll paint a picture of the people who paint pictures of the world for you. We'll try to answer that age-old question, "Who are these guys, anyway?"

THE SKILLS

The public doesn't elect the people who shape our perceptions of the world. Journalists are hired by their news media employers for a variety of reasons. They may bring an expertise (economics, law, medicine, education, science, religion, business, or labor, for example) to the reporting staff or they may be good writers or have other attributes that win them a place in the journalistic fraternity (like name recognition or connections in high places).

No laws require formal training for one to become a journalist. There's no licensing of reporters or editors, though licensing has been proposed on occasion, much to the chagrin of journalists, who fight such suggestions vehemently. (Business executives, we should point out, also are not licensed to ply their trade.) Ted Koppel, ABC's brilliant interviewer and anchor, suggests that journalism isn't a profession (as those employed in the field would like to think of it), but rather it's more of a trade. Journalists don't pass a state board exam or any other competency test, they have no continuing education requirements, and they generally lack other trappings of a profession. The U.S. Labor Department classifies journalists as nonexempt (nonprofessional) workers, subject to overtime pay and other rules governing hourly employees.[1]

To practice journalism, one need only find a medium in which to report. Technical skills required of a journalist are those taught to every youngster in grammar school: reading and writing. Also helpful are a strong sense of curiosity and an aggressive disposition.

It's not difficult to find journalists who aren't college graduates or indeed to find some who didn't graduate from high school, such as ABC anchorman Peter Jennings.[2] The requisites for entering the field of journalism are not unlike those for entering business: determination, native intelligence, and an aptitude for the skills necessary to meet the demands of the occupation.

ROMANCE, PRESSURE, ADDICTION

Popular fiction in books, TV shows, and movies portrays reporters as living glamorous lives, pursuing the powerful, rubbing elbows with the elite, seeking truth, justice, and the American way. Mythic journalists take up worthy causes. They uncover corruption, injustice, and the abuse of power. They expose scoundrels and salute unsung heroes. A day's work (according to the mythology) takes them to exotic places, exposes them to the high and mighty, and is always psychically satisfying.

The romance attributed to journalism has some foundation in fact. A reporter can arrive at the office for a day's work and not know where she'll spend the next eight hours practicing her craft. The reporter goes where the news happens. One day she's in federal court covering a kidnapping trial; the next day the reporter is at the scene of a five-alarm fire and a meeting of the local water board; the day after that she's off to cover a convention of hypnotists and a struggle for power in your company. Some days a reporter may cover nearly all those things before heading home. The uncertainty, the excitement, the status, the constant change of scenery, the access to exclusive places—all of these draw people into reporting.

Many reporters share a common trait with executives, cops, salespeople, fire fighters, and skydivers. They're adrenalin addicts. They like to get charged up on their own juices. The general assignment reporter (of which there are still many, though there's a trend toward specialized beats in many newsrooms) just can't wait for major news to break so he or she can dash to the incident's scene. The event generates its own excitement, but on top of that, the reporter is always under deadline pressure.

Reporters are eternally locked in a perverse game of Beat the Clock. News goes out on schedule no matter what. This holds true for radio, TV, newspapers, magazines, newsletters, everything. Deadline means deadline; reporters constantly push to meet the always-looming deadline.

Time is a reporter's greatest adversary. It takes time to get to the scene of a news event, time to surmise the news value of what's happening, time to locate the principals of the story, time to interview them, time to get back to the newsroom to file the story, time to get opposing viewpoints for a balanced story, time to edit the story, time to double-check the facts, time to answer an editor's questions or objections about the story. Time, time, time. There's no way to recapture it once it's elapsed, no way to stretch it when you need more of it. With every tick of every second, the reporter's day is shorter and the deadline closer. It is the stuff of ulcers.

Competition exerts additional pressure on the reporter. The news business is as competitive as any industry in the United States. The profits of the news industry, among the highest in the nation, exacerbate the pressure. A reporter must not only get the story before deadline, but get it quickly and uniquely so that competitors have no edge with which to draw viewers or readers from the reporter's outlet. In the news business, news is not news if it's a day (sometimes minutes or even seconds) late or if the competition scoops the story.

There's pressure to be fast, accurate, engaging, and better than the next guy. It is a potboiler environment. And it's addictive; it gets in one's blood. I've had the good fortune to meet literally thousands of journalists, but not one who wished he or she were doing something else. Journalists complain about pay and stingy management, but never about wanting a different occupation. Of those who leave the business, most try to get back in somehow—volunteering for the local public station, working on a charity's publications, something that brings back a little of the thrill.

While I was the news director for a Milwaukee radio station, a college professor asked if I could find a job in some local newsroom for a friend of his. The friend was working in public relations for a large insurance company in Chicago. She sent me her résumé and some very good writing samples. I called her to express my surprise that she was looking for work.

She said she was well paid, worked in a low-pressure environment, and in a nice office. But, she lamented, "This job is so boring, so *corporate*. I miss the excitement of the newsroom." She confessed she was willing to take a cut in pay to return to the high-pressure environment of the news business.

Another acquaintance of mine traded the pressure-cooker life of a news producer at a network-owned television station for a sedate role as public relations manager at a large utility. "It's different and I like it," he said, "but sometimes I look up at three o'clock in the afternoon and I see the accountants working at their desks, and secretaries working, and I notice how *quiet* it is. That takes some getting used to!"

Because the pressures that reporters work under are constant and so stressful, many of the people who make their livelihood reporting are young. Old reporters are a special breed of survivors. As a reporter grows older, the hectic life of chasing fire trucks, politicians, and scofflaws grows tiresome. The reporter is likely to move into an editor's or producer's role (almost all news executives come out of the ranks) or into something less chaotic, like teaching or public relations.

Good, Bad News!

> The labor crisis settled at the negotiating table is nothing compared to the confrontation that results in a strike—or better yet, violence along the picket lines. Normality has become the nemesis of the network news.
>
> **Spiro Agnew**

> If you are traveling around the world and want to know where you are, pick up a newspaper.... If you read a newspaper with good news, you're in a dictatorship; if you see a newspaper filled with bad news, you're in a democracy.
>
> **Daniel Patrick Moynihan**

> Real news is bad news.
>
> **Marshall McLuhan**

Business, labor, and consumers all seem to agree on one thing: The news media are preoccupied—some would say obsessed—with reporting bad news. When the Gallup Organization interviewed 4,300 Americans during 1985, it found that 60 percent of them believed the media paid too much attention to bad news.[1] Reporters do focus most of their effort on tragedy, conflict, and controversy. A George Washington University study of news reports found that the ratio of bad news to good was 20 to 1.[2]

Bad news supersedes good news not because journalists are bloodthirsty voyeurs but because negativity is the nature of news. The classic definition of news goes like this: If a dog bites a man, that's not news, but if a man bites a dog, that's news. The concept of news in this paradigm is that of deviating from the norm.

The routine is not news; the notable exception is. This reflects a natural extension of normal human communication. Most of our conversations are rooted in conflict or deviations. Think about this. You don't call your neighbor to tell him the sun is shining. But you might call if you saw a twister racing toward the neighborhood. This exception to the routine would be a topic for (a quick) conversation. It would be news.

Gossip is the same stuff. Typically, we don't talk about someone who does only the pedestrian. When you and your spouse return home from a cocktail party, what do you talk about? The fact that the host cleaned the house before your arrival? No, you expect that; it's normal. You probably talk about who looked fat, drunk, withdrawn, old, or sexy. It's the eccentric behavior, the deviations from the norm, that spur our conversations.

Journalists simply amplify this normal tendency to share exceptions with others by reporting anomalies that may be of interest to a town or a nation.

WHY BAD IS GOOD

Most major departures from the usual involve unpleasant things. A bridge falling down is not pleasant, but it is news. Two friends skydiving on a Sunday afternoon are not news unless one of them is strapped to a chute that fails to open. A business making a 9 percent return on investment is not usually news, but it would be if the company's profits were obtained through fraud or white slavery.

Life's unpleasantries fuel the news business. Bad news is good for the news media in the same way sickness is good for the health care industry.

The news media don't create bad news (any more than hospitals create disease); they just relay the misfortunes of the day. However, disasters, tragedies, and other events that generate bad news are interesting, even stimulating, for the journalists who report them. Hard news events—fires, earthquakes, political unrest, serious crimes, floods, corruption, and the like—feed reporters' hunger for the excitement that surrounds human tragedy. It sounds morbid, but bad news is titillating. Bad news highs can color how one defines *news*.

An example to make the point: At a news industry convention in Miami some years ago, the Associated Press was demonstrating news wires for sale to the broadcast industry. As the printers were spewing forth news of hotel fires in New York City, which had killed some 30 people and injured another 40 the night before, the news director of a network-owned New York radio station stopped at the AP booth to read the disaster reports.

He did not remark on what a tragedy had befallen his city. Instead he said, "Looks like a good news day back home, too bad I'm here. When I get back I'll probably have to talk about the prime rate."

The words are insensitive, sadistic. This journalist's criteria for "good" news paint him a vulture. But most likely, the man who made this remark—despite his apparent taste for violence—loves his family, pays his taxes, and wishes harm to no one. His attitude toward news typifies that of most mass media journalists.

Phil Donahue, the immensely popular talk show host and former local (Dayton, Ohio) newsman, addresses this in his autobiography:

The point . . . is not that journalists want to see people die, or that reporters wish pain on other people. The point is to take note of the schizophrenic personality that develops within a community of competitive professionals whose enthusiasm heightens as the story becomes more horrible and who are rewarded for being first and for providing the most detail."[3]

Hunger pangs for bad news aren't felt just in the big cities. A taste for bad news is a universal journalistic trait. A journalist working for me in Colorado complained one August day about the terrible scarcity of news. It reminded her, she lamented, of days spent as a newspaper reporter in a small, boring Idaho town. "The teachers didn't go on strike until a year after I left. When I was there," she sighed, "everyone was happy."

A news director in a well-to-do university city, with whom I was having lunch, groused, "All the people here are either writing a book or reading one. I'd like to get back to a good news town like Detroit or Pittsburgh. There, people are standing in food lines; they know what it's all about!"

What it's all about is conflict. Conflict is news (good news, the men said), and news is what reporters are paid to seek, digest, and regurgitate for public consumption.

A JADED PERSPECTIVE

Journalists deal almost constantly with negative aspects of our society—death, corruption, inequality, suffering. Their world is so different from that of an executive, whose charge is to effect positive change—growth, efficiency, better service to the customer, and so on. An executive directs tools of the corporation (money, people, resources) to implement plans for positive change. The reporter is only an observer, a powerless bystander without means to constructively attack the problems he or she must report.

The onslaught of life's problems causes most journalists to develop a cynical attitude about the world around them. They appear to be aloof, insensitive to what they encounter. This hard-boiling is similar to the metamorphosis young, wide-eyed do-gooding police officers experience as they are forced to encounter society's worst, day after day after day. The cynical attitude is a defense mechanism. It's protective armor for the survival of a journalist's sanity. Without it, a newsman quickly could become an emotional cripple, unable to cope with the wrenching realities always staring him in the face.

You cannot imagine the horrors an average eight-hour run of wire copy can bring to an editor's desk. There are reports of murders, freak accidents, robberies, sex crimes, natural disasters, auto wrecks, stabbings and shootings, political corruption, tragedies of all descriptions. The stream of copy keeps coming and coming for 24 hours of every day.

The journalists reading all this news are bombarded by the accounts of life's worst. For every editor vicariously experiencing this onslaught of despair, there are dozens of reporters in the field, on the streets, witnessing it firsthand. A street reporter in a large city can literally race from the scene of one tragedy to another. In small towns the frequency may be less, but the effect is usually the same.

Journalists maintain sanity by developing a macabre sense of humor—gallows or foxhole humor. I've heard news people joke about the saddest and vilest of human endeavors: amputations, incest, death by fire, terminal illness, and the like. It is, I guess, better to laugh than cry. Laughing releases some of the tension. Sensitivity would bring insanity or at least render one unable to do the job.

Not only tragedy hardens a journalist. Hypocrisy takes its share of the toll. Reporters have heard all the politicians promise nirvana and seen all the hopeful promises fade as quickly as the campaign posters were torn down. They've heard business leaders promise not to lay off workers or close a factory and watched as the unemployment lines grew and the plant gates were locked.

Many journalists subscribe to a tenet that holds that politicians and other institutional leaders are hiding something if they appear to be successful in office or try to impress the press with their success. Good news is presumed not to be the truth. Truth is negative gossip—or leaks—from dissidents. How cynical our press is. How unavoidable this cynicism is. How important it is for you as a business person to understand that.

WHAT ABOUT THE GOOD?

Good news occasionally gets slipped in with the doom and gloom that constitutes most of what the news media report. Once in a while, you'll see or hear a story about the selfless volunteer worker, the immigrant entrepreneur who made a fortune, the ghetto kid who rises to Harvard scholar, the rescued missing child, the injured police officer who returns to duty.

These stories are rooted in conflict, too, usually the overcoming of conflict. You know, man beats the odds. Again, it is the extraordinary that warrants coverage. And only when the good news tugs sufficiently at the heartstrings and when a break in the bad news allows enough time or space do journalists squeeze in the good.

A strike against good news is "visuality." Bad news is so graphic. Pictures of chemical dumps, huge fires, and crying widows command attention in the nation's newsrooms. TV and newspapers, the leading disseminators of information, are both highly graphic and competitive. Dramatic graphics grab viewer or reader interest, thus ratings and circulation, and finally profit. Good news stories about a bank's 100th birthday or the hiring of additional employees or the bestowing of a "good corporate citizen" award by the mayor have a tough time competing for limited editorial space with more dramatic and more visually appealing horror stories. High drama beats ho hum most every time.

The news media's preference for action-packed or contentious stories means its treatment of business will favor controversy over accomplishment. Corporate chiefs frequently find this concept irksome. As Irving S. Shapiro, former chairman of E. I. du Pont de Nemours and Company complained in *Newsweek*, "reporters come at the businessman when he's in trouble. . . . But when he has a technical success to brag about, that's not news."[4]

It probably isn't news unless that technical innovation cures cancer or creates an environmentally harmless and very inexpensive substitute for gasoline. Business people who expect the press to cover their every innovation or good deed are unrealistic. A wire service bureau chief defends the press's record on reporting business news. "The news media do a good job of covering business. We report profits and losses, corporate promotions, dividends, acquisitions, and mergers. What more do business people expect, that we run a story every day saying American business ran well again today?"

While I was with the Associated Press, we received a letter from a radio news director who was angry that an AP editor refused to run on the state news wire a good news story offered by the radio station. The good news concerned a major expansion by a local Michigan car dealer that would result in creating some additional jobs in the midst of the area's severe depression. The news director quoted the uninterested AP editor as rebuffing the story with a remark that called the report, "free publicity [that] amounts to an advertisement." He went on in his complaint to observe:

The media (including our organization) certainly jumps at the chance to print (broadcast) news of a business failure . . . of the housing industry wallowing in misery, of wage concessions, production cutbacks, and other depression related items. . . . But when a local business announces an expansion and holds a Press Conference to tout the news, our backs bristle and we call that fluff for some reason.

The mentality for conflict and strife is so ingrained in many reporters that they have difficulty (or at least little interest in) telling a good news story.

Even the president of the United States—with all the power and force of that high office—impotently laments the news media's preoccupation with bad news. Just about every modern president has demanded, with great frustration, that the news media shift their constant negative focus to things more upbeat and right with the United States. In early 1983, President Reagan challenged the television networks to report some good news along with the incessant negative news about a dreadful economy that was not yet on the road to recovery. Tom Brokaw, on "NBC Nightly News," responded by quoting NBC News President Reuven Frank, who said, "We'll report good news when it's news."[5]

And they will, when the good news is as dramatic and powerful as the bad. Such as when journalists report, with great delight, pomp, and circumstance, good news events such as the release of the U.S. diplomats who were held hostage in Iran for 444 days or a royal wedding or a successful organ transplant that saves a child's life.

As Brokaw himself says of good news versus bad, "Sure, we want people to be excited by achievement—space shots or triumphs of justice or medical breakthroughs. But shouldn't they also hear about malnutrition in America? Shouldn't they be outraged by what big money can get done in Washington?"[6]

Brokaw, like many of his journalist colleagues, defines news as events that elicit excitement or outrage. News stimulates. By this definition, "bad" and "good" are arbitrary values. Drama and conflict define what's news.

We all define news this way by what we choose to talk about between ourselves and in the kind of news we choose to consume. Intense human drama just naturally attracts us more than "snooze" reports.

Periodically, the media respond to a public outcry for more good news.

But the fact is, almost nobody cares about good news. Ted Turner's cable superstation, WTBS, tried a nightly "Good News" show in 1983. But it bombed in the ratings; only about half the people who watched reruns of "The Carol Burnette Show" preceding "Good News" stayed tuned for the program of cheerful tidings.[7] In November of 1983, WTBS replaced "Good News" with reruns of "Hogan's Heroes." A similar fate awaited Turner's weekly "Nice People" show. It endured for four years before getting the ax for poor ratings in December of 1983. "Nice People" reports were replaced by beastly stories on the syndicated program "Wild, Wild World of Animals."[8]

Sophocles contended that "none love the messenger who brings bad news." But apparently we aren't too thrilled with the conveyer of good news either.

The news we get from the press is really the news we want. To understand the nature of news, we need only look in the mirror.

WHEN BAD ISN'T NEWS

Imagine for a moment that a new computer invention has remarkable benefits for society. This creation of American ingenuity increases our efficiency manifold; it creates wonderful conveniences and provides millions of people a wealth of economic, recreational, and individual freedoms.

It seems this machine's only drawback is that every year it kills more than 50,000 people and injures another 3.5 million.

How would you guess the news media treat this wonderful/killer machine? Would you believe the news media ignore it? You would if you looked at the media's record on the automobile. About a thousand people a week are killed and another 66,000 injured in traffic accidents across the country. Yet, rarely can you find more than token mention of this in the news media.

Can you imagine the coverage such terrifying statistics would receive if they related to air travel, eating in restaurants, or drinking municipal water?

Why don't we hear more about fatal auto accidents—or, for that matter, the everyday tragedies of drug abuse, poverty, or illiteracy? They seem to meet our definition of news: they're dramatic, tragic, and graphic. But we don't hear about these terrible things because they are not news any more. Sandy Socolow, former executive producer of the "CBS Evening News with Dan Rather," suggests that people are bored with the same old sad stories. We've learned to live with recurring problems, finding them of little interest after a while because they are routine. Narcotic addiction, hunger, and ignorance are accepted as distasteful but common components of U.S. society; they're unworthy of much media attention.

So when cars slaughter as many Americans in a year, every year, as were killed in all of the Vietnam war, that's just no longer news. Truck and car carnage of 140 deaths a day is unfortunate but commonplace.[9] You'd probably slow down your car to gawk at the scene of an auto accident, but you wouldn't watch a news show or buy a newspaper if the lead stories were always about car collisions. Imagine seeing the same crash story last night, tonight, tomorrow night, every night. Who would tune in to see that? An exception: When one driver is killed on a little circular road in Indianapolis in May, that's front-page headline news. We expect collisions on the highways; at the Indy 500, an accident is an event.

A friend of mine, an amateur aviator, complains that, despite our lack of interest in car accidents, any mishap with an aircraft, no matter how minor, is newsworthy. He accurately points out that the number of deaths and injuries from airplane crashes is a minute fraction of auto deaths, but still they command a considerably disproportionate share of media attention. Stories of plane crashes that take just a few lives at one end of the country often show up in newspapers at the other end.

A plane forced to abort a takeoff or to make a landing that results in a crash, even with *no* deaths or injuries, usually makes the news. Even planes that make unscheduled landings without a crash make national news. In early 1987 an Air France Concorde jet made an emergency landing in Boston when an air conditioner malfunctioned. There were no deaths, no injuries. That made news a continent away in California.[10]

Why is this? Because while we, society—and reporters who reflect our interests—find auto travel and its hazards normal, we're still fascinated with air travel. There's something magical about defying the laws of gravity and something notably curious when that defiance poses a threat of life or limb. Traveling by air intrigues us because we know there's no heavenly shoulder of the road to pull onto when the engine quits. News reports of air travel problems touch the fear and that sense of helplessness—the flirtation with death—we all experience in an airplane. Because this emotional experience is so universal and so readily triggered by news of aviation mishaps, such incidents rate news coverage. There's no equivalent fear or fascination with terrestrial travel, not even when it is tragic (short of catastrophic multicar crashes in the foggy, rain-soaked night; we do want to hear about that!).

As for other bad-but-not-news stories, Socolow points out that there is no Mr. Drug to focus on, so it's hard to sustain people's interest in the tired narcotics story. The same might be said for absent or invisible villains in the poverty or illiteracy stories. The civil rights stories of the 1960s drew media attention because they usually centered on two clearly conflicting forces, black versus white. This visible contrast gave the news media something to focus on. When the media find a focal point for conflict, they find an agenda for coverage. No focal point, no news.

On whom should ABC or *Newsweek* or your local newspaper focus for tax loophole stories or reports on declining quality in education? It isn't easy to make news out of every human shortcoming.

The news we get—good, bad, or indifferent—is the news we find interesting. It may not be the news we deserve or all the news that's fit to print, but it's probably all the news the press can process and all that we can stomach.

Divine Right

What's special about the press is that it's the only business in
this country that has constitutional protection, and we can't keep
it if we go on behaving this way.

Richard Salant

A right to know should be related in some way to a need to
know, and an appetite is not necessarily a need.

George Will

Watch a presidential news conference, read an investigative news report
or participate in a news media interview, and you'll detect something
in the attitude of the press. Most people recognize it as arrogance.

Journalists are a distinct group of workers in that they have an absolute
right to do what they do. The Constitution's First Amendment prohibits
Congress—and by extension, any government body—from abridging
freedom of speech or of the press.

Members of the press are free to write and publish what they please,
without fear of government censorship. This absolute immunity to virtually all governmental oversight (with the exception of the courts in
the matter of libel; see chapter 21) is a unique privilege, a tremendous
responsibility, and an invitation to occasional abuse. It's a heady wine
to journalists, and it gives rise to smug feelings of omnipotent autonomy,
insensitivity, and delusions of grandeur.

THE (ALLEGED) RIGHT TO KNOW

The right to speak and publish without governmental interference has been expanded by the press to include something it calls "the right to know." This right is neither stated nor guaranteed in the First Amendment or anywhere else in the Constitution. The right to publish, guaranteed only to those who can afford a printing press, theoretically extends benefits to all Americans and thus implies a right to know.

Warren H. Phillips, chairman and CEO of Dow Jones and Company, the publisher of the *Wall Street Journal*, has this to say: "All the talk about the First Amendment rights of the press is not about special privileges for newspaper reporters and publishers, but about rights of the public—the right to be kept informed, the right of the governed to have a surrogate watching the governors. The First Amendment wasn't drafted for the publishers' benefit but for the public's."[1]

Gannett—the megamedia company—explains in an ad the so-called right to know and correctly puts it squarely in the arena of governmental affairs. "The right of all Americans to know the workings of their government and courts—local, state and national—is guaranteed by the First Amendment, which protects all our other constitutional rights."[2]

In this context, the concept of "the right to know" is a necessary and powerful check on the powers of government. The constitutionally sanctioned press has been endowed with absolute liberty so that it can ride herd over the people who control public funds and who make policy decisions with the force of law. In effect, the news media are a fourth (albeit private) branch of government, watching over the other three to preserve the integrity of the republic and to protect the citizenry from despots. Curiously, the public shows little appreciation for an untouchable press. Polls routinely show that substantial numbers of Americans favor government regulation of the news disseminated by newspapers and broadcasters!

The public's casual attitude notwithstanding, the news media's role as devil's advocate to government stands as fundamental to our democracy as an individual citizen's right to vote. As Helen Thomas, longtime UPI White House bureau chief, so eloquently stated, the news media "defend the people's right to know almost everything—for a nation ignorant and free never was and never will be a democracy."[3]

THE IMPLICATIONS FOR BUSINESS

As noted earlier, big business's influence on our society whets journalists' appetites for greater inquiry into the affairs of business. Journalists charge into the camp of business under the banner of the public's right to know.

The press blurs the distinction between "right to know," "need to know," and "want to know." The right to know, appropriate as justification for investigating bodies of government, stretches to include the affairs of important private institutions such as business. An aggressive press demands revelations of confidential information from business, suggesting that the propriety of its actions lies under the aegis of the right to know.

Business leaders should resign themselves to expect media interest in corporate affairs as a reality of life. The press will not leave business alone; it will insist on greater disclosure of matters that previously may have been considered proprietary. Even though many news media companies are members of the multi-billion-dollar corporate establishment, their journalist employees are free to investigate and question outside corporate activity as they see fit.

In addition, business people need to understand that an ironic double standard affects press coverage of business (as well as government and everything else). While expecting business to meet a standard of perfection, the press itself—with clear conscience—engages in practices fairly described as unethical, immoral, illegal, or heroic, depending on one's perspective.

Under the guise of press freedom and in valiant pursuit of truth, journalists sometimes accept confidential documents (that may have been stolen), pay informants, engage in deceptions, ignore summonses, refuse to identify sources of important information, report unsubstantiated allegations, betray confidences, trespass, and undertake other questionable behavior. If those actions are slightly illegal or unethical, well, too bad; the greater good theory prevails.

An attorney, attending a media and business seminar sponsored by the Ford Foundation, attacked the "double standard between the press and business on matters of responsibility." The lawyer, not identified in the transcript, poignantly and passionately expressed dismay at journalists' ability to whitewash practices they condemn in others.

I was, frankly, surprised to hear a TV executive say that for fear of competition he would not wait a day or two to . . . go on the air with the story about [a CIA] agent, even though it might cost the agent his life. Whereas, I don't think the press would stand for it if a drug company rushed its product out quickly for fear of competition.

I heard it said that the press will protect confidentiality at almost all cost, whereas if a business tries to, it will be considered a cover-up.

I heard it said that the press will, one way or another, buy information, while business will be castigated for questionable or sensitive payments.

And finally, I heard today that the press reserves its right to refuse to observe orders of the courts, even when none of us would tolerate the fact that the

President of the United States raised that reservation. No businessman could say, "I will reserve the right to refuse to observe an order of the court."

I think perhaps the press in looking at business could look at it from its own perspective of engaging in competitive practices, and perhaps the coverage might be a little more balanced.[4]

Yes, but don't hold your breath.

PART III

MEDIA BIAS

Men will preserve the errors of their childhood, of their country, and of their age long after having recognized all the truths needed to destroy them.

Marquis de Condorcet

Man seldom, or rather never for a length of time and deliberately, rebels against anything that does not deserve rebelling against.

Thomas Carlyle

There is no greater safeguard for the survival of our democratic institutions and our way of life than an informed and aroused public. However, when that same public is aroused but misinformed, the opportunities for mischief are endless.

John E. Swearingen

6

Objectivity and the Parallax Factor

TV cameras may never blink, but they're often selective.
Charles Colson

Everyone is a prisoner of his own experiences. No one can
eliminate prejudices—just recognize them.
Edward R. Murrow

Let's take up the subject of media bias. Rather than launching into a
tirade against left-loving media moguls, let's consider the concepts of
objectivity and fairness.

When a scientist, draped in white lab coat, pen and clipboard in hand,
undertakes an experiment, he tries to isolate all extraneous factors that
could prejudice the results of the test. With great care and effort, the
scientist attempts to control and note every variable in the test so that
the experiment stands as a complete, singular reality, capable of being
reproduced exactly time after time.

The scientist conducts tests objectively, concerned only with observ-
able, verifiable characteristics of an object's physical properties within
a controlled environment. The objective, scientific method meticulously
screens subjective factors.

In this context, the beliefs or feelings of a scientist trying to determine
the freezing point of water are without consequence. If the experimenter
believes water turns to ice at 42 degrees Fahrenheit, careful and objective

experimentation will prove the experimenter incorrect. Because the scientist's test is concerned with the objects of the experiment, the scientist's fear of water or preference for Popsicles™ over ice cubes should have no bearing on the results of an objective scientific test.

JOURNALISTIC OBJECTIVITY

The clinical standard of objectivity is often misapplied to the journalistic process. Newspeople, some suggest, should be objective in their accounts of human endeavor. This is impossible.

Journalists, unlike scientists, do not record observations under controlled conditions. They do not have the luxury of determining the variables (time, place, subject, duration) of the events they cover. They cannot replicate the conditions under which the events occurred. The events about which journalists must report are not as well defined as those observed by scientists. The freezing temperature of water is highly definable; the effects of a new foreign policy on the balance of trade, a court decision concerning abortions of teenage pregnancies, or a bitter labor strike on a community are not. Unlike the stony physical properties of objects scientists observe, journalists monitor the volatile and unpredictable human animal.

There's no meter that one can objectively observe to measure degrees of propriety in political office, correctness of social or economic policies, nobility of a war, truthfulness in corporate news releases, or a million other things.

No barometer hangs on the newsroom wall that tells a reporter whether the speech heard, the annual report read, or the crime scene observed today measures good, bad, or neutral.

No scale exists for an editor to weigh the importance of an event that comes to his attention. Literally the whole, wildly diverse world cries out for interpretation by journalists. The selection, observation, and interpretation of those millions of events is entirely subjective, as it only can be.

David Brinkley, veteran broadcast journalist, argues that a computer can objectively record information, but a reporter can't.

If you put something in [the computer] and push the button you get back precisely what you put in, with no coloring, shading, changing or anything. To put the same requirement on a news broadcaster or any human being could mean that he was not in favor of anything or opposed to anything, didn't believe in anything, did not reject anything, had no standards, no values—and therefore, I think, would probably be dangerous to society and probably should be locked up.[1]

A GAS GAUGE AND CHEESECLOTH

Whether in a laboratory, Yankee Stadium, a battlefield, or a corporate suite, a simple truth governs all human observation. It is known as the *parallax factor*. This axiom holds that the same object or event viewed from differing perspectives will appear different from each perspective.

In the physical world, this can be demonstrated when two people look at a gas gauge in a car. To the driver, sitting directly in front of the gauge, the instrument appears to register a quarter tank of fuel. To a passenger, looking at the gauge from another angle, the gauge appears to read empty. A similar process takes place in our minds, where no two of us, not even two totally "objective" reporters, share the same mental angle of view of any subject.

For journalists to bring no preconceived notions or sense of perspective to a story is impossible. Reporters, like other humans, have accumulated millions of perceptions about the world around them since they were children. Like all of us, they have a mental image of what police are like (or should be), who welfare recipients are, what business executives do all day, what constitutes an abuse of power, what right and wrong are. As a camera views a scene through its lenses and filters, so too do we view the world through our mental lenses and filters of personal experiences and beliefs.

Consider the natural differences in perspective between a 45-year-old WASP farmer and father of five, who was born, reared, and educated in Omaha, and a single Jewish woman lawyer, age 25, who grew up fatherless in the Bronx. Or contrast a Latin immigrant, 33, in Miami and a 62-year-old Boston blue blood. Might we not expect all these people (any one of whom could be working in the news media) to have quite different views of family, the proper role of government, sexual morality, appropriate size of the defense budget, religion, social justice, urbanization, regulation of industry, minimum standards of health care, fair taxation, and so on?

Which view is "normal"? Which view should pervade news coverage? Each of these people has a unique perspective on every issue we can name. None is correct. All the views might be normal—meaning a majority of Americans share the opinion—at some time in the country's history. But no one person holds the average, majority, or representative opinion on most or all the issues that confront us in the United States, now or anytime.

Every public opinion poll shows us that the United States is a pluralistic society, where the citizenry simultaneously holds many mutually exclusive views on any subject of public importance. Americans believe, all at the same time and to varying degrees, that the defense budget (or federal aid to education or cities or battered women) should be increased, decreased, and held at current levels.

Before a news story is printed or broadcast, the facts in the story have passed through many people's minds, with each mind harboring different experiences and different opinions about the issue at hand.

When covering a story, reporters can only try to push their own perceptions and prejudices to the recesses of their minds while they record their observations. A reporter isn't so much a sponge that soaks up the stream of current events as a piece of cheesecloth through which the stream flows. Inherent in the observation and interpretation of human events is some filtration, some editing.

News usually passes through another very fine filter—memory. This human device adds greater selectivity to our first impressions of an observed event (which are already colored by our beliefs and prejudices). Think of your own experience. Immediately following a business meeting, you have distinct impressions about what transpired in the conference, but in a few hours or days, your impressions will be different, altered by additional impressions and faltering recall.

Any police officer can tell you that upon arriving at the scene of an accident or crime, eyewitnesses tell varying versions (sometimes irreconcilable accounts) of the same event they all saw, but from different vantage points (physical and mental). The police officer will also tell you that those same witnesses, interviewed again only hours later, will not only differ with each other in their recollections, but they usually will contradict their own accounts of just a few hours before.

MULTIPLE MENTAL FILTERS

A reporter often gets information secondhand. That is, he or she relies not on his or her own observation (reporters can't witness everything or even most things they write about), but on the accounts of others, who themselves may not have been direct participants in or witnesses to a news event. Each person views life through a personal perspective shared by no one else, and has a highly selective memory that compounds the inexactness of any account given to a reporter.

Worse yet, the reporter will rely on his own recollection of the interviewee's recollections. The reporter's notes—if any—most likely are incomplete, jumbled, and in just about indecipherable personal shorthand. By the time the reporter sits down to compose the story, he too will be relying heavily on memory to reconstruct the details of the event he's trying to retell to the news consumer.

Fuel for the fire: The reporter may not personally write the story he's just gathered. It might be dictated to a staff writer or producer who will actually compose the final report. This happens all the time in newspaper, magazine, radio, and television reporting. It's an accepted practice rooted in efficiency and marketing. (The idea is to keep reporters reporting, while wordsmiths create a polished, salable product.) The information given to the writer then passes through that person's mental filters of experience, beliefs, and memory.

Even beyond this, the story may be edited by one or more editors who, yet again, may rearrange facts for clarity or dramatic impact. The intent is to aid understanding, but sometimes such meddling makes the story's meaning muddier. The process is reminiscent of the childhood game of Telephone, where distortion of messages verbally passed from person to person provides giggles around a campfire.

The bottom line is that by the time consumers receive the story, the facts in the report have been shaded by a multiplicity of perspectives and recollections. As news consumers, we don't view a story just through rose-colored glasses, we're seeing it through lenses of amber, green, orange, purple—a rainbow of human perception. The fact that most news reports we see or hear even approach reality is just short of miraculous, testifying to the care with which most journalists do their job.

7

They Lean Left, Right?

With a lot of crusading leftist liberals in the media, who needs
Communists?

Joseph Keeley

News people, by nature of their humanity, cannot be objective. They're
not machines devoid of feelings, prejudices, or experiences. But they
can be fair—giving us news consumers a balanced and accurate view of
the world—by seeking and reporting opposing views on issues of controversy.

Good reporters try hard to be perfectly fair. But of course, there's
never enough time to tell all there is to tell. Reporters and editors are
forced to report their stories incompletely, selectively releasing some
facts and retaining others. It's that process of necessary selection that
leaves the news media open to charges of bias.

THE SIN OF OMISSION

Despite a few famous cases of exception, most of what reporters include in a news story is true, that is to say, an accurate representation
of something that happened or what someone said. Of course, no news
story can report everything there is to tell. News stories are "an accurate
section of reality but not the whole picture," as Edwin Diamond and
Stephen Bates suggested in *TV Guide*.[1] Sociologist Herbert Gans of Co-

lumbia University says news reports are "often the highlights of high-lights."[2]

For every fact told, there are many others that necessarily go untold. When a news story appears slanted, it's probably because the reporter is guilty of the sin of omission.

Reporters deliberately shape stories, including some facts, excluding others, in a manner consistent with truth as they believe it to be. This is neither calculated censorship nor an attempt to distort. It is what journalists are required to do, in order to publish the greatest number and variety of news stories in a given day. The news media can't present the whole of reality; and if they could, we couldn't digest it. The selective paring of facts serves, on balance, to better inform readers or viewers; they're offered a wide menu of information and spared from drowning in minutiae.

Most reporters writing a story do not try to shape truth to conform to an agenda or an ideology. Rather, the facts pertinent to a story are shaped to present a picture of what a reporter believes to be real. The picture a journalist presents to us, is, ideally, as true as he or she can make it.

The usual charge of media bias concerns the favor liberal views of truth/reality seem to receive in the press at the expense of a counter-balancing (or predominant?) conservative view. (Naturally, most charges of a liberal press are not what the accuser really means. Liberal means free or unrestricted—what the American press is intended to be—not politically to the left of center).

The charge of leftist press bias was made popular and legitimate by Vice-President Spiro Agnew's 1969 campaign against the television net-works and big eastern media. The cause was taken up in the 1971 book, *The Left-Leaning Antenna* by Joseph Keeley, a former advertising and PR executive.[3] Since then, numerous conservatives have charged the na-tional news media, particularly the television networks, with a prefer-ence for the "liberal agenda," or more favorable coverage of left-of-center viewpoints.

Some academic studies based on opinion surveys of journalists claim to prove the argument that many people who work in the press hold personal beliefs that are more to the left than to the right. The studies no doubt are correct. But the argument is overstated and hollow; what-ever their personal beliefs, most journalists don't slant the news. Re-searchers at George Washington University monitored network news broadcasts for bias between 1979 and 1985. Their conclusion: "Ideological bias is one of those mistakes that the network news doesn't make. . . . On those fundamental issues that divide liberals and conservatives in the 1980s, the network news contains no consistent left-wing bias of any significance." The study's authors, writing in *Channels* magazine in 1985, found that conservative issues lagged only slightly behind traditional liberal issues in vying for attention on the evening news shows.

The researchers claimed to be watching the broadcasts with no liberal bias of their own, to avoid tainting the study. In fact, of the three researchers, two claimed to be conservatives: "Republican, or Reaganite—anything but secular humanist."[4] (While not slanted much to the left, the news broadcasts monitored by the researchers were found to be terribly negative. That preoccupation we explored in chapter 4.)

Better than half of U.S. journalists—59 percent, according to a 1983 University of Indiana survey—consider their politics, and that of their employers, to be centrist.[5]

NBC's John Chancellor speaks for the defense:

My wife says I have no politics, and I think that's true of most reporters. It is true, in my judgment, that people who spend their lives observing problems, [such as] reporters who began by covering the police beat, tend to believe in activist programs for solving problems. But all activists are not liberals, and all reporters are not Democrats. Right-wing groups have been trying for years to prove the existence of a leftist cabal in the press. It is just not there.[6]

Sociologist Gans believes that journalists espouse values that are neither leftist nor rightist but rather *reformist*. Those in the news media share values not of a Democratic or a Republican agenda, but of "good government Progressivism."[7] Journalists, he concludes, believe in "honest, fair and competent public and private institutions and leaders."

If journalists are to the left center, they surely aren't having much impact on the ideology of the "great silent majority"!

FAILED ADVOCACY?

The alleged closet-leftist journalists weakly flexed their considerable public opinion-molding muscle as far as influencing the election of liberal presidential candidates George McGovern and Walter Mondale. Obviously, after left-wing candidates racked up two of the greatest defeats, to conservative opponents, in the history of presidential politics, journalists can take no credit for any mass swaying of public opinion toward the liberal platforms. If reporters and editors were trying to subliminally influence the U.S. political agenda, they blew it. The media elite succeeded only in soundly demonstrating total ineptitude.

Put another way: For the sake of argument, let's concede that many journalists are more liberal than America's mainstream. One must ask, So what? Many teachers and many clergy also lean left of center. But this is the United States, where we all think for ourselves, thank you very much. Marxists in colleges and socialists in the media have little impact on the will or actions of the conservative majority.

This liberal bias is insignificant by every measure. Despite media coverage of the liberal agenda, the Equal Rights Amendment failed to win ratification, defense budgets swell, and college conservatism has all but replaced activism (marches, sit-ins, boycotts, and other forms of social protest are all but relics of antiquity).

In the privacy of voting booths, individual journalists' liberal leanings may make a small dent, but they're ineffective in moving the rest of us toward an ideology to which we are not inclined. As purveyors of left-wing ideology, journalists make poor advocates, mostly because they are not advocating but observing. "I've chosen the life of a spectator in this world," a radio news director confesses to me. Observers aren't participants; they aren't activists. Those who can, do; those who report, watch.

Paul Scheffler, senior producer for "60 Minutes," speaking for most of his colleagues in the press, says: "We spend our lives on the fringes of commitment. We watch others being committed."[8]

THE PARADOX: IMPOTENT AND POWERFUL

The failures of the liberal agenda that journalists are supposed to advocate seem to fly in the face of the purported power of the press. Isn't there a great paradox here?

On the one hand, any liberal bias in the nation's newsrooms has shown itself powerless to change public opinion on matters of political ideology. But, on the other hand, the news media have been effective in shaping public opinion on matters such as starvation in the Third World, the Vietnam war, and the Nixon presidency; and they can take credit for creating a national conscience for racial and sexual equality, environmentalism, drunk driving law reform, workplace safety, child and spouse abuse, and so on.

More superficially, didn't the news media spur national crazes like streaking, pet rock ownership, discos, and frivolous controversies over Bobby Riggs versus Billy Jean King and new Coke versus old Coke, and so on? Don't advertisers pay billions to the news media to promulgate brand identification and product sales through commercial messages?

Can it be that the news media are simultaneously incapable of influencing opinion and very effective at it?

The answers to these questions are all quite simple and reflect no paradox at all. Yes, the media are powerful. Yes, they've given momentum to national movements, serious and frivolous. But the extent of their power is limited to touching the national nerve. The media don't influence public opinion; they serve as an outlet for it. Pointing news cameras at Vietnam war protests did not create antiwar sentiment. It only reflected (and maybe legitimized) it for hundreds of thousands of middle Americans who quietly shared similar sentiment with those who were taking to the streets to protest.

Likewise, it was not the media poised to impeach Richard Nixon; it was the United States Congress, which had itself come to doubt the integrity of the president. The news media only served as catalyst and forum for the debate. If the American people and their elected representatives did not believe there was a credibility problem in the White House, then the "impeach Nixon" momentum would have gone the way of the "elect McGovern" movement. Race riots in the 1960s were not the product of some press convention where all the media moguls agreed that they would go home and incite minorities to riot.

The press functions simply as a window through which citizens see what's happening around them. The media can make people aware of social and political trends or fads, but if no one cares, they die of inertia. Reports of starving people in faraway lands would not yield great relief efforts unless Americans were inclined to share their charity for those distant and less fortunate.

Just as the media had no effect on promoting the left's agenda, likewise they're equally unaccountable for the swing in public sentiment toward the Reaganesque conservative camp. Rev. Jerry Falwell doesn't owe his following to the news media. They didn't make him. Falwell's message came to receptive ears via his religious programs broadcast around the country. He created a following; the media noticed. Falwell's success or failure is a result of his own credibility in the minds of those who receive his message. The media don't mold public reaction to Rev. Falwell, they only point a camera at it.

If people react to what the media show them, they're saying much more about themselves than the messenger. This holds true for media dissemination of any ideology. Sunday morning broadcasts of Catholic church services don't coerce Jews or Hindus to conversion; news reports about abortions don't encourage every pregnant woman to have one.

Advertising works in the same way. People in that business have a saying that makes a good point: "Nothing kills a bad product faster than good advertising." The reason is simple: advertising (like news reports) can only create an awareness of something. If you see an ad for the New & Improved Whizbang Cola and you are curious about the product's taste, then you might try it. But, if after trying the soft drink you decide it's distasteful, then no advertising, regardless of its powerful appeal or catchy jingle, will change your mind or taste buds.

Ads or news reports won't make socialists out of capitalists, and they won't make chocolate ice cream eaters out of people who don't like the stuff.

OUR OWN BIAS

Something else to consider is that the liberal bias one finds in the media may be the result of one's looking for it, perhaps subconsciously. A friend of mine calls this the "Purple Volkswagen Effect," after his discovering all the other purple VWs in Chicago once he bought one.

Bias is not found just in the mind of the reporter, but in the consumer of news as well. Where we sit in regard to an issue also influences the way we read (or see or hear) a story concerning the issue.

For example, in July 1985 the *Wall Street Journal* carried an opinion piece arguing that claims of liberally biased reporting were unfounded. The article, by Albert Hunt, the paper's Washington bureau chief, brought several challenging letters to the paper. One of the letters critical of Hunt's position created a stir of its own.

James P. Cain, cofounder of the conservative Fairness in Media (of "buy CBS and be Dan Rather's boss" fame) rebutted Hunt's conclusion, claiming that a *TV Guide* study showed a strong propensity for CBS to be anti-Reagan and proliberal.

The author of the study, John Weisman, the magazine's Washington bureau chief, then wrote to the *Journal* to say that Fairness in Media wasn't fair in *its* representation of the *TV Guide* article's conclusions about CBS and Reagan or about media liberal bias. Weisman said the unfairness of the Fairness organization was evidence "of a deeper and more dangerous bias."[9]

Truth, bias, and fairness, like beauty, are in the mind of the beholder. Someone who reads an article on media bias in a magazine might find implications that the author swears aren't there. Someone who believes the Democrats are, and always have been, the salvation of the nation may regard any coverage of Republican officials or candidates as evidence of media bias. Personal beliefs can color one's reading of the most objectively reported story.

Journalists love nothing better than to receive highly critical mail from all sides of a controversial issue. The thinking is that if in one story you've offended both Republican and Democrat, atheist and fundamentalist, hawk and dove, then you must have done your job well. A thorough, balanced report contains abundant food for thought and probably enough fodder for each side of the issue to suffer some intellectual indigestion.

Most of the time, in my opinion (colored by my experience and observation), most mainstream media are mindful of their obligation to be fair. Opinion surveys routinely show that the public generally believes this as well.

When there's a shortcoming in fairness, it's usually in the way of giving more exposure to some person, event, or viewpoint that challenges the status quo.

Remember, conflict is news. (William Hazlitt, 19th-century English essayist, once wrote, "When a thing ceases to be a subject of controversy, it ceases to be a subject of interest.") Dissident politicians, Democrat or Republican, are more interesting than those in total harmony with administration policy. A dissatisfied employee is more interesting than a contented one. Mutinous shareholders make for better stories than grannies depositing dividends.

Journalists aren't political activists; they aren't trying to impose a liberal agenda. The fact is, they don't like any policy, no matter whose it is! They thrive on social, political, and economic change—reporting change and conflict is their only business. News people aren't cheerleaders, they're antagonists.

As justice is blind, so is journalism. It scorns everything.

Champions of the Proletariat

> Ultimately, the press serves itself by fostering exaggerated perceptions of the world as a dangerous place, with untrustworthy people in positions of power. The press protects the public by exposing the dangers, so the more dangers there are, the more necessary the press.
>
> Mobil Corporation advertisement, 1983

> The free press is the omnipresent eye of the spirit of the people, the embodied confidence of a people in itself, the articulate bond that ties the individual to the state and the world, the incorporated culture which transfigures material struggles into intellectual struggles. It is the ruthless confession of a people to itself.
>
> Karl Marx, 1841

Allegations of leftist predispositions in reporters and editors are suspect, as we discussed in the previous chapter. But what about journalists' "antibusiness" sentiment? There's ample opinion in the business community to support this charge. Ward Smith, president of White Consolidated Industries, observed in 1985 that "let's-pick-on-the-media [is] one of the longer running top ten cocktail party topics in business circles."[1]

At cocktail parties, luncheons, and elsewhere, business people have expressed to me their frustration with business reporting. A media relations manager for a large telephone company complains, "Reporters are always looking for a villain. . . . They don't understand business is important to the country." The PR director for a large aerospace contractor laments that when covering business, "Reporters grab at straws trying to make a name for themselves." Such remarks have been echoed in recent years in more public settings by corporate chiefs who've lashed out at the press following some negative publicity about their firm or industry.

A study done for the American Management Association found that roughly one-third of public relations directors, chief executive officers, and *journalists themselves* believe the media are usually or always antagonistic toward the business community.[2]

It is cliché to note that when reporting a business story, a newscaster's raised eyebrow or indignant tone of voice, a tightly framed close-up shot of the suspect business person's face, or a bold newspaper headline implies impropriety even where there isn't evidence of any. Reports of actual impropriety seem sensational. As one public relations man complained, with some anger in his voice, "Five thousand dollars worth of impropriety is treated in bold headlines like it was five *million*." Reports about profits occasionally seem couched in an attitude of "Look at these unconscionable and obscene amounts of money!"

Geraldo Rivera, one of the new wave journalists who popularized the attack style of interviewing—occasionally encountered by business people on the defensive against the press—describes his interventionist editorial methods self-righteously. "I have no power to prosecute. I have only the power to embarrass, to humiliate, to expose."[3]

The media's critics argue that these tacit editorials cast a long and unnecessary shadow of doubt over the integrity of U.S. free enterprise. Often, the press *is* cynical and aggressive when it covers business. It's not just in reports of quarterly profits but in stories about executive salaries and perks, company responses to allegations of wrongdoing (regardless of who made the charge), the taxes paid—or not paid—by companies, and other business stories. Michael J. Davies, editor and publisher of the *Hartford Courant*, told an editors' conference in mid–1985 that media cynicism developed in "the toxicity of the '60s and '70s," when "young reporters thought the only way to get ahead was to be tougher, more cynical than the guy at the next desk."[4]

A classic care of either press cynicism or heroism occurred in early 1982, following the fatal crash of an Air Florida jet into a Washington, D.C., bridge. Reporter Robert Johnson of the *Orlando Sentinel Star* wrote a lengthy story suggesting that the disaster, which killed and injured scores of people, would financially benefit the Miami-based air carrier. The *Columbus Dispatch*, in Ohio, picked up Johnson's story and ran it as the lead item in its January 25, 1982, business section under a headline that proclaimed: "Catastrophe improves Air Florida's balance sheet."[5]

The story took great pains to show that plane crashes can make money for airlines ("Jet smashups rarely cause airlines to crash financially"). The report said this was because the insurance that airlines carry on their planes more than covers losses, because insurance premiums don't go up for the carrier (premiums are based on industry, not company, losses) and because airline ticket sales usually don't decline following a crash. Johnson also pointed out that the airlines' insurance companies would probably make money on funds earmarked for settlement that were invested in high-yield bank accounts. These allegations were contrasted with a litany of struggles that faced families of crash victims who sued the airline for damages: uncertainty of winning awards, disparity in awards' dollar value, lengthy waits for trials, large attorney fees, and so on.

The fascinating story appeared to be well researched and factual. Its tone was undeniably cynical, maybe because the ironies of reality made it that way. It smacked of classic Little Guy versus Heartless Corporate America—which always profits, and does so at the expense of defenseless victims. It was either great or inflammatory journalism.

(In July 1984, Air Florida filed for Chapter 11 protection from creditors; not because of claims from the D.C. crash but because, as *Business Week* put it, "Air Florida never made money on scheduled passenger services. . . . When fare wars and new competition began to steal its thunder, it ran into trouble."[6] Eventually the airline's assets were sold to Midway Airlines.)

Press antagonism to business seems to go in cycles. The degree of antagonism depends on the extent to which the government pursues investigation or regulation of industry and commerce (indicating presumed flaws) and the severity of national crises perpetrated by business, for example, nuclear and chemical accidents, airline disasters, severe unemployment, high inflation, and the like. After all, the media rarely create news entirely from their own initiative. But at all times, business is subject to provocative press scrutiny.

MORAL TRUTH AND THE JOE SIXPACK SYNDROME

Are journalists out to get business in a sinister, self-serving conspiracy? Do they attack business to create sensational stories to attract readers and viewers (and thus advertisers and profits)? No. Most members of the press have no interest in undermining corporate America. Journalists no more want to unfairly malign a company than corporations want to endanger public health or safety.

However, journalists like to portray themselves as fearless Davids slinging away against mean corporate Goliaths. Their role as adversaries to business (and other institutions) is spurred more by idealism than greed for ratings and dollars.

As a scientist is compelled to discover nature's truth, a journalist is driven to discover social truth. And much of society's truth lies buried under the warts of our institutions.

As capitalists are called by the lure of wealth, journalists are called by the lure of righteousness (morality is more seductive than money). John Chancellor of NBC suggests that the "essential emotion for journalists" is "outrage."[7] The executive editor of a large metropolitan daily proudly told me that he became a journalist because "I think I know the difference between good and bad. This is a profession where that means something." An editor at the AP put it this way, "Journalism is pure. Right and wrong are pretty clear-cut."

While many issues in our society are not clear-cut, many journalists believe they have insight into those that deserve public attention (and right or wrong, they have the forum). Because business often is at the heart of society's important issues, it's subject to critical news media examinations.

The press is our society's self-appointed and self-sustaining moral watchdog. Its self-determined role is to look out for the interests of its patrons, the masses—collectively known as the proverbial Joe Sixpack.

Joe Sixpack, along with his female counterpart Jane, is presumed to be an uneducated, gullible, defenseless, TV-watching, beer-guzzling slob. He toils earnestly for the better part of a day in poor, maybe harmful, working conditions for meager wages. Joe and Jane Sixpack need someone to look out for their best interests. Alone, they'd fall victim to the powerful corrupters in our society, who get ahead by stepping on the backs of the downtrodden little guys. The news media, displaying great paternal wisdom (and with the power of constitutional fiat), step up to the challenge. Paul Conrad, editorial cartoonist for the *Los Angeles Times*, describes his role in this context. "The guy on the street gets pretty angry with what's going on. He has to live with that sense of helplessness. But I get to draw what I feel and hopefully speak for those who have no outlet."[8] (When I was in college, a journalism instructor—a television news director who later became a producer at CBS News—actually said, according to my notes, "Write your news stories for 'little guys.' ")

The press, despite its growing roots in gigantic corporations, assumes a holier-than-thou attitude toward large corporations. Journalists are fond of putting their work on a pedestal above other commercial endeavors. The work of journalism is in the public interest, while that of other businesses—building and heating homes, growing and distributing food, or making automobiles, clothes, or medicines—is mere commerce. When Congress held hearings in June 1986 on proposed changes in the Freedom of Information Act that would allow businesses, in order to protect trade secrets, to classify information provided to government agencies as confidential, several news organizations protested. They said such a change in the law would make journalists' work more costly, difficult, frustrating, and fraught with delays, impairing the public interest.[9]

As representatives of the millions of Joes and Janes that make this country great, the news media aggressively seek truth and justice from society's powerful institutions. Their mission is to see that Joe and Jane are not trampled by the big feet of the Big Boys—in business, government, medicine, and so on—who control their little lives. Business critics—self-appointed consumer advocates—are portrayed as heroes. As media critic Edith Efron observed, "The anti-business side of any controversy must be the good, the true and the noble."[10] Reporters taking investigative swipes at huge corporations—or the people who run those companies ("the new aristocracy," as one AP manager called them)—view the contest as roughly equivalent to kids throwing spitballs at armored cars.

The big boys of the media are surrogate little guys, defenders of the defenseless. Even the million-plus-dollar-a-year television anchor (making about 50 times more annually than the average Joe Sixpack) sees himself as champion of the common man.

Harmony between business and the press is said to be dangerous. As the prestigious *Columbia Journalism Review* once put it: "With business and the media both on the home team . . . how's a mere citizen going to know the score?"[11]

ONE OF THE GUYS

As a group, journalists are mostly little guys themselves. In 1983, a University of Indiana study showed the typical U.S. journalist to be 32 years old and earning $19,000 a year.[12] A 1986 study by the American Society of Newspaper Editors found that the starting salaries for newspaper reporters were typically $1,500 to $4,600 below entry level wages for new teachers, with annual compensation averaging about $11,000 to $15,000.[13]

In broadcasting, the story is much the same as in the newspaper newsrooms; despite the network anchors' huge salaries, most radio and TV journalists toil for much less. A 1985 survey by the Radio-Television News Directors Association found the median salary for radio reporters was under $17,000, in *major* markets. The median pay for television anchors was a hefty $26K.[14]

Like other people, rank-and-file journalists may find it difficult to understand or appreciate the wealth or culture of aristocratic capitalists. Reporters, like most people, don't have staff meetings or company-paid working vacations in Vail, Hilton Head, Palm Springs, or other such places. They, like most workers, don't have "golden parachute" severance protection and usually don't have many occasions to conduct their business on golf courses or in country clubs or on their company's private plane. Reporters are mostly everyday middle-class people in their wages, politics, and attitudes.

While the individuals in newsrooms are young and relatively impoverished, their employers are increasingly large and wealthy corporations themselves. Concentration of media ownership intensified with changes in FCC regulations (which increased the number of broadcast outlets a company can own), the demise of several major newspapers, and the 1980s penchant for corporate mergers. Control of more and more media outlets now rests in the hands of multi-billion-dollar conglomerates. The media business is a healthy one. Average pretax profits of large and small newspaper publishers in North American weighed in at just under 18 percent in 1985. Many broadcasting companies are accustomed to 20 percent or better returns.[15]

With the media business's riches and power, business is being watched and second-guessed by a formidable and remarkably similar profit-driven adversary that claims to represent the "real people" of America.

IGNORANCE IS BLISS

When business people complain about the way the press covers business, it's usually not because of vendettas by reporters. Those are rarer than they once were. Rather, the news media often perturb business people because when it comes to business and economics, reporters—like many Joe Sixpacks—just don't know what they're talking about.

Business news is often vacuous, void of perspective. We're told sales are down 5 percent or profits are up 23 percent, without a benchmark. Up from last quarter, last year? Is that good? Why? What's the industry average? How much capital was at risk to extract those profits? Often, we don't get answers to those kinds of questions because they're never asked.

It's quite possible for a person majoring in a college journalism program to graduate with honors without having taken one course in business or economics. (Just as one can start or run a business with the same academic deficiency.) Journalists, like most Americans, don't understand much about business, and there's little incentive to find out. Most journalists will live on a guaranteed (albeit modest) salary for all their working lives. Not only are things like Dow Jones averages, return on investment, cash flow, depreciation, and FIFO/LIFO strange notions, the very concept of risk is foreign.

Reporters and editors are not so much biased against business as ignorant of it. Jack Hogan, past president of the national Radio-Television News Directors Association, suggested to me that such ignorance is rampant throughout our whole society. Teachers, according to Hogan, don't understand the role of business and profit in our society, so Americans are not taught about the values of business and profit in school. "Most teachers can't tell you what a millage rate is, and their salaries depend on millages!" The same lack of understanding extends into the newsrooms of America, Hogan contends. "The people in the newsroom don't have any business experience; they don't even understand the budget of the news department."

Hogan is in good company regarding his theory. George Gallup, the pollster, says, "Many people are graduated from college as economic illiterates. They just are not exposed to the basic facts of business: at the elementary school level, or high school level, or even college."[16]

The sentiment was echoed by Frank Bennack, Jr., president and CEO of the large media company, Hearst Corporation. "A large segment of the American public is sadly deficient in its knowledge of basic business and economic facts of life. The media, which many people say are their primary sources of their business and economic information, do not appear to be making any significant impact on this ignorance."[17]

The media aren't educating the U.S. public about basic business and economics because they can't; they don't understand them, either. William A. Henry III, journalist and press critic, researched the relationship between the media and major U.S. institutions in 1985 for the Gannett Center for Media Studies. He suggests, "The consequences of lay reporters' ignorance [about business] cannot be overstated. . . . [I]t is hard to find any reporting so consistently wrongheaded as even big league reporting about business."[18]

Even those in the big leagues concede their own lack of understanding. Van Gordon Sauter, when he was president of CBS News, admitted to me, "We, like the other two networks, do a generally inadequate job [covering business and the economy]. It probably represents the most obvious editorial fault of network television."

Jane Bryant Quinn, a pioneering financial journalist who has reported on personal finance for CBS and written for several publications, hints that education of journalists in business and economic issues will come, but, oddly enough, from an interest in perpetuating the Joe Sixpack Syndrome. After noting that "the system of capitalism tends to produce tremendous wealth, better wealth than any other system, but it tends to produce it inequitably," she predicted that business and economic reporting won't "really come into its own until you get the next generation of newspaper people—who grew up in a period where economics was the thing that scared people more than politics scared them."[19]

The fact that journalists lack an understanding of even the U.S. economy's fundamentals is made worse by the increasingly complex business issues that reporters are called upon to bring into the public spotlight. Advances in science and technology make covering business more and more difficult. Reporters, not having the background, time, or resources to fully grasp the nuances of the stories they're chasing, often reach flawed (some say biased) conclusions as they rush a business or economics story to meet the impending deadline.

Reporters take shortcuts. Library research represents either a bother or a time-consuming luxury in which few reporters can indulge. Sources who can yield quick, snappy quotes are preferred over experts who speak in jargon or terms that would require translation for Joe Sixpack to understand. T. K. Smith, vice-president of government and public affairs at Dow Chemical, contends that reporters are "inclined to personalize or attempt to dramatize a story by finding a vivid living example, and sometimes that example is not representative or leaves the [wrong] impression."[20]

The Media Institute, in 1982, chastised the three commercial television networks for their awful performance while covering the energy crises of the 1970s. After studying 1,462 network stories, it said the networks did little to educate the public on the possible causes of the problem. Instead, they focused on the visible effects of the situation, like pictures of gas lines and interviews with angry consumers.[21]

As is typical, the news media tried to script the energy problems in the usual "good guy versus bad guy" scenario, casting big oil as the dastardly villain. This approach was familiar, dramatic, and a lot easier than looking for the origin of the problem in market causes. The networks didn't conspire to poorly cover the energy situation, they all just fell into the trap of succumbing to their own deadlines, relying—without question—on the usual government bureaucrats as their main information source and treating important issues superficially.

Three Mile Island is another example. The misinformation that resulted from misunderstanding on the part of many who were involved in the nuclear power plant crisis has become a textbook case. Peter Sandman, a Rutgers University communications professor and consultant to a presidential commission that investigated the incident, concluded that "news coverage problems at TMI were far more the fault of sources than they were of reporters." The public relations people were uninformed ("they knew next to nothing") and weren't always completely honest with reporters, Sandman argues. Making matters worse, not all experts agreed on the severity or the implications of the nuclear accident. The general press had a difficult time getting, understanding, and disseminating accurate information.[22]

Journalists are by their nature generalists, not experts. Their sympathies tend to lie with the powerless, not the powerful; their professional training dwells more on mechanics of telling stories than on insights for understanding them. But the public looks to the press to interpret economic, technical, and scientific developments. Many in the media like this aggrandized role of telling Joe Sixpack what it all means. Ken Goldstein, professor at Columbia University School of Journalism, says, "Science writers must go beyond merely recording events. They must be critics, able to judge. Otherwise they're not doing their jobs."[23]

Faced with the time pressures they work under every day and their general lack of specialized education, it's amazing that reporters do as good a job as they do, deficient as it may be. However, if the news media are to cover business in a meaningful way, business must do much to help reporters and editors—who may well sit as critics and judges—to understand and communicate the important issues. The next parts of this book recommend appropriate action.

PART IV

HALF-TRUTHS, SMOKE SCREENS, AND OTHER CORPORATE POLICIES

For unlike the occupant of the White House, who has certain forbidden zones when it comes to public scrutiny, business people are fair game—for the press, the IRS, other government agencies and private groups. As a result, some of the seemingly astute business executives in recent times have become invisible men, almost escaping historic notice.

Thomas V. DiBacco

If the thing believed is incredible it is also incredible that the incredible should have been so believed.

St. Augustine

What *Is* Public Relations?

An ounce of image is worth a pound of performance.
                                        Laurence J. Peter

It's not possible to have a better image than you are.
                                        Joe Tennessen

As the nuclear power plant quakes in the midst of a disaster, alarms sound, lights flash, sirens wail, and reporters are descending on the company like vultures on carrion. The CEO summons his nervous public relations man and frantically—pathetically—barks orders to get the media people out of the facility. This scene, from the move *China Syndrome*, portrays a view of modern public relations, that of the palace guard impotently defending the holy corporate image against marauding crusader-reporters.

The classic public relations function is that of publicity-seeking press agentry. In this role, the PR person plays the cheerleader, hawking mundane merchandise or events as if they're the Second Coming. (A spokeswoman for a new shopping mall, opening in Toledo, said in a radio interview, "This center is 'superer' than anything Toledo has ever seen before!")[1]

Public relations people, who call themselves counselors, profess to have expertise in many areas: company publications, customer/employee/investor relations, lobbying, opinion research, speech writing, image shaping, product promotion, protocol, corporate goodwill, training, publicity, news media relations, advertising, trade show hospitality events, and anything else for which a client might be willing to pay. Public relations seems to be a bunch of things. Defining PR is like defining true love or intelligence—everybody thinks they know what it is but can't precisely say.

I'd offer this as a definition: *Public relations represents plans and programs for public understanding and acceptance of an organization.* This broad, "define the universe" explanation encompasses all those functions listed above and more.

THE "WHY" OF PUBLIC RELATIONS

Whether a company is a consumer products manufacturer or an office park developer, a restaurant supplier, or a farm implement maker—publicly held or privately owned—its success depends on favorable relations with its constituents. These include customers, employees, suppliers, government officials, investors, community neighbors, even competitors. Those relationships become the focus of the company's public relations effort.

Public relations is aimed at favorably shaping the constituents' perceptions of the firm. A successful PR campaign is one where the intended audience believes what the company wants it to believe. A company may want people to think that it respects the environment, makes only quality products, supports civic projects, has fair hiring practices, or embodies any of many ideals.

Some examples:

- Dow Chemical, long tormented over its image as an evil chemical company—from its history of producing napalm, dioxin, and Agent Orange—took to the TV airwaves in late 1985 to launch a multi-million-dollar five-year campaign. Its ads show young college graduates proud and eager to begin working at a concerned company like Dow that "lets you do great things."[2]

- Apple Computer, 7-Eleven stores, American Express, Upjohn, General Foods, Chrysler, Mobil, Pepsico, Coca-Cola, IBM, local banks, retailers, consultants, and companies of all sizes generate goodwill (and sales) by donating to such causes as disease research, restoration of the Statue of Liberty, public broadcasting, higher education, the arts, and other social concerns.[3]

- Anheuser-Busch, brewer of Budweiser, Michelob, and other beers, shows its civic-mindedness by buying advertising to remind people to drink responsibly. "Know when to say when," the ads admonish.

- The National Rifle Association wanted to change its image as an organization that exists solely to defeat gun control legislation. It created ads for consumer magazines featuring women, a little boy, and an astronaut under the caption,

"I'm the NRA." The idea was to show the organization as a group of regular people who happen to like guns.[4]

• McDonald's Corporation, king of the fast food (some say junk food) emporia, wants to show its concern for health and fitness and has used a variety of methods to communicate its message. The company sponsors temporary residence facilities for families who've traveled in order to provide medical care to their seriously ill children. It enlisted Olympians Bruce Jenner and Mary Lou Retton to explain nutrition and fitness to grade schoolers via video tape. And, after decades of silence on the issue, McDonald's did the 1980s kind of thing and even released a list of ingredients for Big Macs, McNuggets, McCookies, and other McFood. The landmark disclosure drew considerable media attention. "McDonald's Food: The Facts . . . " includes calorie counts for various ingredients, because "at McDonald's we believe you deserve straight answers. . . . " The purveyor of more than 55 billion hamburgers followed its ingredients' grand unveiling with a print ad campaign launched in 1987 featuring a photo of a milk carton stacked on top of a burger resting on an order of french fries, next to the word "Balance." The ad's copy advised consumers to "make sure your McDonald's meal balances with other meals you eat."[5]

More than ever, impressions about a company are molded with the help of public relations rather than relying strictly on straight product advertising. This is because there's a glut of products and services in our economy, and many products tend to be alike. Brand loyalty depends to some degree on how people feel about the *company* that makes or sells goods and services.

Messages about brands, companies, and all kinds of things compete for attention in individuals' minds. People in our society are bombarded by thousands upon thousands of persuasive messages a day, in advertising, at work, in the news media. There is limited time and capacity for people to consider this constant onslaught of information. To create effectively a lasting impression among all the mental clutter, a company must carve a *position* in the minds of its target audience.

This position is filled with an *image*, a mental picture or impression created by the accumulation of messages concerning the company and its products. The messages are derived from numerous sources: personal experience, testimony of a friend, news reports, advertising, hearsay. Public relations experts are charged with determining the desired image and then generating messages to create and reinforce the perception. In other words, public relations markets the intended mental perception of the company to the various groups the company affects.

In this framing, PR is a marketing function; but it's not one strictly allied to the classic marketing function: to sell products. The broader aim of the PR program is to sell *the company*, or rather its prescribed image.

TO RELATE OR NOT TO RELATE

Whether a firm wants to see its name in the news or not, it cannot ignore the broad mission of public relations in our complex society. A communications axiom holds that "one cannot not communicate" to the surrounding world; that holds true for corporate persons as well as individuals. So every corporate action and policy, and even failure to act, communicates something to somebody. In this context, public relations is almost everything the corporation does or *doesn't* do.

To affect its significant publics, a corporation must compete with all other messages aimed at the targets. To do this effectively, an organization must make a commitment to communicate, to communicate in a manner that establishes credibility, and to communicate with consistent, memorable messages. These messages help form the company's position in the minds of the intended receivers.

Many firms already believe this and employ a scad of experts dedicated to addressing corporate communications. Other companies, many privately held, resist. To them, out of sight and out of mind is the kind of PR they like; public image building is frivolous and a waste of money. Such companies are not necessarily doomed to disaster in the information age, but they are vulnerable.

Good public relations doesn't mean that a company's name is a household word. It means that a company effectively communicates to the publics (government officials, customers, community neighbors, trade press) it wishes to influence and prepares to communicate to audiences it normally doesn't address (e.g., the general news media in the event of a disaster).

A public relations program simply formalizes the corporation's attitude toward issues of importance and prepares the firm to deal with circumstances arising from its attitudes and actions. Without such a formal program, a company leaves itself exposed to harm in the public affairs arena. A company doesn't have to know the politicians who represent it. But when a bill—with negative repercussions for the corporation—is about to be made law, it's too late to introduce the corporation to its elected representatives. A company doesn't need to establish rapport with the news media. But if a disgruntled employee files a suit, if a competitor starts a vicious rumor, or if a serious accident, strike, or some other disaster suddenly propels the firm into the public spotlight, then it's too late to ask for a knowledgeable and sympathetic ear. A company need not be active in civic affairs, but when the city council proposes a significant property tax hike on commercial property, it's too late to start generating community goodwill.

Corporations aren't required to have any public relations program, but it sure helps to have friends before you need them. There's no such thing as retroactive goodwill.

It's difficult to ascertain the value of a program for public relations. Even to many believers it still sounds like so much mumbo jumbo. On a balance sheet, PR is assigned an arbitrary value under the heading of "goodwill." But what is the appropriate level of resources that should be dedicated to the task of creating goodwill or preserving it? The answer is nebulous; it's another question: How much would you lose if you lost your corporate goodwill?

Take some arbitrary percentage of what the company stands to lose from lost credibility, and that becomes the PR budget. It's a risk management expense, like any other insurance.

MEDIA RELATIONS

In every major city in the United States, you can find a journalist dating a PR counselor. But that's not what companies have in mind when setting up media relations divisions.

Even without grand plans for sophisticated image crafting and expensive publicity campaigns, many companies pay employees or consultants to deal with the press. Their mission usually is to anticipate, prepare for, and intercept media inquiries and to generate a little positive publicity about the company.

A press-oriented public relations function is virtually a necessity for public companies. As noted earlier, private as well as public companies are subject to media scrutiny. The proliferation of business coverage in the mass media generates more press interest in companies. Employees trained in the ways of the news media can help a company successfully negotiate routine inquiries and assist the corporation in times of crisis when rumors or unsubstantiated and conflicting information threaten stability.

Media-savvy employees often act as liaison when the press needs information from company officials who are uncomfortable talking to the media. A media relations specialist for a pharmaceutical maker points out, "Someone who has his nose to a microscope all day is not versed in the media." The same might be said for someone who spends the day poring over P & Ls or marketing data or overseeing manufacturing operations.

The appropriate role of media relations personnel is basically twofold. First, they should function as coaches and assistants to company officials to help them be effective in media interviews. Second, they should work to protect corporate interests by accommodating reasonable press inquiries for information and interviews. Effective media relations doesn't mean always running to the press to detail every corporate fault to comply with a self-imposed obligation to full public disclosure. The proper function of media relations is to serve the corporation's interests by dealing with the news media in a forthright manner that keeps corporate integrity intact.

Unfortunately, many companies, even some spending a fortune on PR, do a terrible job with the investment they've made in public relations. We'll look at that in chapter 10.

Kamikaze Public Relations

To be persuasive, we must be believable. To be believable, we must be credible. To be credible, we must be truthful.

Edward R. Murrow

Hypocrisy never persuades anybody.

Muriel Fox

There's a lot of sham in corporate public relations.

Scott M. Cutlip

In this chapter, we'll explore how some corporate practices cause well-intentioned public relations programs to backfire. We'll see that companies many times choose the wrong people to carry the corporate banner, insult the intelligence of press people, frustrate rather than aid journalists, and generally defeat the whole PR objective of creating credibility.

CREDIT CREDIBILITY

U.S. corporations devote hundreds of millions of dollars annually to public relations in order to create goodwill for themselves. A major public relations goal is to make people believe that an organization exerts a positive and desirable force in society. This process is called image building; ideally, it creates credibility.

Businesses should not take lightly this matter of credibility. Any company can find itself entangled in a sensitive situation where a little cooperation from a compassionate reporter (or press corps) can go a long way toward preserving the firm's public image and fiscal security. Credibility is especially critical when the company's reputation stands on ice as thin as the shadow of a doubt.

Sometimes public relations image building works marvelously. When Tylenol was threatened with being withdrawn from the market (twice, in 1982 and in 1986) following the deaths of people who'd taken tainted doses of the pain reliever, Johnson and Johnson capitalized on years of positive press relations. The consumer products company marshaled an unprecedented public relations effort to counter the negative publicity and restore the brand's credibility. The slick, aggressive campaign worked. Public confidence in the brand returned, and so did Tylenol sales (twice).

Another example: Ford Motor Company was under fire from consumer groups and the U.S. government stemming from charges that transmissions on millions of its cars were defective and could slip from park to reverse. Critics charged that the alleged defect resulted in hundreds of deaths and demanded that the government order a recall of the purportedly dangerous cars. While Ford's advertising campaign ironically cautioned, "Look Out World, Here Comes Ford," the company reached an agreement with the Carter administration to mail warning stickers to owners of vehicles with the potentially fatal tendency.

While critics of the agreement between the auto maker and the government were outraged—claiming millions of lives might still be endangered by the engineering flaw—Ford decided to convince Americans that its cars were the product of superior engineering and quality manufacturing. New advertising heralded, "At Ford Quality Is Job 1."

The positioning strategy worked. Not only did Ford enjoy healthy car sales, but even as critics still tried to push Ford into greater accountability for the suspected transmission problems of older model cars, Ford was winning the public perception war. In September of 1985, a prime-time CBS News program again brought into the public spotlight the charges concerning what CBS called Ford's "killer cars." About a week later, the Center for Auto Safety filed a lawsuit trying to force the U.S. government to reopen its investigation of the transmission problem. However, the following month, Consumers Digest magazine applauded Ford for the design and engineering of its cars. Readers of the magazine, with more than a million circulation, voted Ford into a Hall of Fame for consumer needs responsiveness! A year later, Ford was still on a roll: 1986 profits surpassed those of larger rival General Motors for the first time since 1924.[1]

Whether or not Ford ever built a transmission that harbored a dangerous design flaw, the company successfully created a perception in the public mind that it builds cars that are superior in design and engineering. This, regardless of how you feel about Fords, must be regarded as a great public relations success story.

The Ford and Tylenol examples are testimony to the tremendous power of public relations to influence public opinion even in the face of great adverse publicity. Naturally, most public relations efforts take place in an atmosphere far more mundane. Paradoxically, it is in this context that PR is often far less effective.

While the goal of most day-to-day PR is to generate corporate goodwill—credibility—for an organization through the news media, many times the PR effort has the opposite effect. It may surprise you, but many corporate public relations departments, which use the news media as important instruments of communication, command little respect from the journalists with whom they work. Corporate PR representatives—the image makers, the ambassadors of goodwill—often fail to endear themselves and their organizations to the news media. Rather than spreading goodwill, they generate animosity or disrespect.

THE FLACK ATTACK

For people who claim media relations as a prime area of expertise, PR practitioners often fail miserably. Journalists generally detest public relations people. One big city radio news director declared to me, "PR stands for Philosophically Repugnant." References made in newsrooms to "PR types" usually include characterizations such as whores, scum, dirtball, and numerous obscene pejoratives, along with descriptors such as greasy, slimy, unctuous. An Associated Press Managing Editors' publication described, in 1969, an attitude toward PR that still prevails among journalists today. It called public relations people "flacks," a term of disdain.

Flack is popularly believed to derive from the German *flak*—antiaircraft guns that forced servicemen to wear protective flack jackets. The connection to press agentry may be drawn if one considers that many PR practitioners assault journalists with worthless news releases and press conferences and frequently evasive, misleading, or patently false answers to press inquiries. (One PR veteran suggested to me that flacks may be the ones who need the protection—from "press bullets of inquiries they can't answer or respond to.")

Those AP guidelines for newspaper editors typified PR agents, flacks, unkindly. "A flack is a person who makes all or part of his income by obtaining space in newspapers without cost to himself or his client. . . . The flack is the modern equivalent of the cavalier highwayman of old who looted the king's coach. The elegant manners of the earlier gallants obscured the basic fact, they got the gold.

"Today it is the courtly P.R. gent who waylays your male or female editor. . . . You (the newspaper) are the one who has been robbed, and the (public relations) gallant is the one who has got the gold." News editors were advised to "perform bravely your role as s.o.b. and tough it out" against the flack attack.[2]

Today, it's as it was in the 1960s. Journalists still try to avoid manipulation by self-serving press agents looking for free gold. The *Wall Street Journal* began an article in 1985 by pointing out, "To the usual who-what-where questions that reporters ask their news sources, the financial journalist often adds another: Why are you telling me this?"[3] Likewise, Don Hewitt, executive producer of "60 Minutes," complains, "Business wants reported only what fits the carefully tailored profile that Madison Avenue and public relations people have put together."[4]

PR people often are viewed by their colleagues in the news media as hired guns, sophists, or washed up journalists. Journalists who've crossed over to PR are said to have sold out. Leaving the priesthood of the press for greater monetary gain in secular corporate America is viewed as something between sad and tragic.

The image of the image makers is low, low, low. How can this be? Why do the image experts fail so terribly with their own constituents? Much of the blame lays with the corporations that PR people serve.

BAD CASTING

When the press seems combative or antagonistic toward business, sometimes it's retaliating for what journalists perceive as abusive behavior from public relations representatives.

The first media relations mistake many companies make is hiring the wrong kind of people for public relations. There is no magic set of job qualifications for people who work in media relations. But there are certain personalities companies should avoid putting on the front lines.

Reporters despise "high-pressure salesman types" who push too hard in their role as corporate advocate. The forceful personality may be highly valued within the organization's management, but in the role of media liaison, it really can be self-defeating. A helpful, facilitating attitude is much more endearing to the press than a pushy or combative one. The pushy PR person is perceived as having an ax to grind or as one whose aggressiveness is a front for hiding skeletons in the corporate closet.

Journalists afford little respect for "I'm-totally-into-image" public relations staff. This segment of the PR universe seems more concerned with fashionable hair styles and trendy clothes than matters of substance. Business managers who hire such people to represent them either have no appreciation for the public relations function (and the expertise required of one to properly execute it) or must truly view journalists as saps. Cut from a cloth similar to that of the image-consumed PR rep is the perky, cheerleading, "life-is-so-wonderful!" public relations personality. This kind of person rarely inflicts serious harm on her (it sounds sexist, but a high preponderance of this category are women) employer. But they tend to drive their more earthy journalistic counterparts crazy with incessant Pollyanna.

Also scoring few points with reporters are the "couldn't-cut-it-in-journalism" flacks who left reporting or editing because they weren't very good at their first trade of choice. Frequently, these ex-journalists turn into "hey-look-at-my-big-bucks-now" characters who garishly flaunt their newfound financial success to their poorer press brethren.

Common wisdom holds that former media people are naturals for public relations (about 60 percent of PR people are former journalists).[5] Sometimes they *are* naturals for the job. Good ex-journalists understand the editorial needs of the press and can be of tremendous value to reporters (and thus their corporate employer). These former press practitioners are also likely to know the tricks of the trade, which they can ply skillfully to their company's advantage.

Talented journalists who leave a field they adore to work the other side of the street may do so not because they're psychically called to public relations but because the lure of a corporate salary is often greater than their poorer paying journalistic labor of love. After a time of transition, many of them become effective advocates for their new employers. (The road between journalism and public relations is virtually a one-way street. It's common to see journalists migrating to public relations, but the opposite is rare.)

Unfortunately, some media dropouts widely miss the mark. Former newspaper people are often oblivious to the needs of broadcasters. You'd be amazed at how many press releases sent to radio stations contain a useless 8 X 10 glossy and no pronunciation guide for difficult names! Broadcast alumni, accustomed to writing news that's read aloud, may pay too little attention to correct spelling, punctuation, and other stylistic matters that concern print publications.

Good journalists, with the skills and credibility that a corporation should want on its staff, are difficult to attract. They may not be making the money or have the fringe benefits a corporate employer could offer, but the very independence that often contributes to the journalistic success of these candidates makes them uncomfortable in the role of company spokesperson. So sometimes, rather than attracting solid players, companies end up hiring the media benchwarmers. These second-stringers may harbor a grudge against the fraternity whose good graces they never achieved; they can't wait to get in a power play position of sharing or withholding information from the media club to which they once marginally belonged. Such an attitude deeply provokes media people.

The point of media relations is not to win a popularity contest with journalists, but neither is it to antagonize them. Hiring (or retaining on a consulting basis) the wrong kinds of people for media relations—those whose inappropriate personalities weaken rather than strengthen corporate credibility—amounts to wasting money that could better serve the interests of an organization. Miscast PR people can encourage press animosity. It may be a rare breed that can and wants to speak fluently the languages of both business and media, but companies would do well to find those people and pay them to come aboard.

Even when competent professionals are attracted to corporate public relations, they can't guarantee flawless media relations. These ideological foot soldiers often find the execution of their responsibilities difficult because their own employers undermine their credibility by engaging in defeatist PR practices. Companies often impale themselves on their own public relations sword, as we are about to see.

INTIMIDATION AND CONDESCENSION

A perverse notion of "condescension equals good media relations" has crept into the culture of some organizations, which seem to believe that journalists possess simple minds and are suckers for a little candy-coated arm twisting. The theory is that if you feed or entertain reporters, or provide them with gifts or a junket, you'll have them eating propaganda out of the corporate hand. Often this strategy comes back to haunt its architects.

News reporters (some sports writers feel differently) hate to be patronized with flattery or payola. "I find it demeaning to attend a 'press appreciation night' or to be invited to a junket on the company plane," explains a news executive.

"It's insulting to my intelligence the way some flacks think they can buy my objectivity for a bottle of booze or a meal," protests another. "I'm not a whore who's for sale at any price; I deeply resent any attempt to compromise my integrity."

Respectable companies usually don't overtly try to purchase the influence of journalists, but sometimes well-meaning attempts at positive press relations are as effective as four flat tires.

An example: An influential business reporter was invited to discuss an upcoming labor contract between one of the Big Three auto makers and the United Auto Workers "by a company flack who said, 'let's have lunch.' When we met for lunch, I was escorted to the executive dining room where we were served filet mignon. Around the table there were

2 reporters in sport coats, including myself, and 11 gray-suited executives. I wasn't expecting that kind of display and found it very intimidating."

A similar experience is related by a reporter who was doing a story on a major utility. "I offered to visit their executive offices but was told that for my convenience, some executives would visit the newsroom to answer my questions. These guys came in in their $400 top coats and I'm sitting there in my Tie City tie feeling very uncomfortable."

The Disney organization, one of the grandest press romancers, found itself the target of a *New York Times* editorial in October 1986 following a big media bash commemorating Disney World's 15th anniversary. The Disney World birthday party boasted such luminaries as former Chief Justice Warren Burger; Nicholas Daniloff, the reporter who was held by the Soviets on a spy charge; and singer Michael Jackson in a 3-D film. Despite these newsworthy appearances, the *Times* claimed that "the biggest story from Florida was the way the press debased itself." The newspaper objected to the fact that many of the 5,000 attending members of the news media partied as house guests of Mickey Mouse and his commercial friends in Orlando (transportation, meals, hotel, and funsies all at no charge). "It appeared . . . that the entire Fourth Estate was on the take," the editorial charged. Disney's chairman, Michael Eisner, described the relationship between the press and his company as "a marriage." But the *Times* saw it in other terms, saying, "The event smacked of a different, paid relationship, the kind that once was disgracefully commonplace."[6]

Like junkets, little cutesy PR gimmicks intended for the amusement of journalists also can amount to shooting one's organization in both feet. Many years ago, when I was a radio news director, retail coffee prices were rising frequently and dramatically. Apparently as a gesture of goodwill, a coffee industry promotion organization sent to me, via U.S. mail, a little silver spoon. The rather cryptic letter accompanying the spoon invited me to participate in a contest, the objective of which wasn't revealed.

While I'm sure the promotion was well intended, it struck me as terribly frivolous and as an insulting intrusion on my time. I didn't want or need a little silver spoon. Receiving one was not amusing to me. Why the hard-pressed coffee industry would spend the money to send me this goofy item without telling me what it wanted from me is a mystery that only can be solved by the flack who conceived this sophomoric idea. Rather than being amused, I was insulted and angry. My instinct was to retaliate. Color me vindictive, but I couldn't wait for the next story about rising coffee prices, which I played prominently. As a goodwill PR campaign, the concept failed.

When an auto club sponsored a tennis tournament, it tried to garner lots of free publicity. It offered reporters the usual free admissions to the tournament. But the campaign didn't stop there. Journalists who were invited but didn't attend received a hand-delivered press packet called "A Highway Survival Kit." Along with the customary self-serving news releases, the survival kit included liquor. While the gift probably was sent as a cordial gesture, the implied promotion of drinking by an auto club struck an editor friend of mine as being terribly incongruous and irresponsible. The editor's esteem for the organization unquestionably fell. The poor judgment cost the firm the respect of at least one important newsman.

Companies need to be more sensitive to the way they approach the men and women of the news media. Journalists are intelligent and sometimes cynical people who are not impressed by corporate airs or gimmicks. What they want from companies are facts and a little cooperation. A friendly lunch now and then can be a nice gesture, but corporate favors shouldn't be dispensed as bribes, payoffs, or tools of influence. Ever.

THE PALACE GUARD AND CREDIBILITY

Contrary to the gains that apparently would be made by fostering an atmosphere of corporate approachability, many companies employ media relations personnel as tight-lipped palace guards rather than as information facilitators.

For these businesses, good PR is not measured in the column inches or minutes of air time devoted to covering the company or its products, but rather in the lack of same. A good week is one where the company name was successfully kept *out* of the news. Press curiosity be damned; no news is good news.

For some companies, especially privately held ones, this protective stance comes from a belief that what the corporation does is "nobody's damn business." For others, it represents what one might describe as "organocentric" behavior—a philosophical myopia which can be expressed as "nobody but us really understands us." I believe this intense, nearly paranoid, attitude stems in part from the physical structures in which most business is conducted—modern office buildings, where windows can't be opened. Business managers are forced to live in a sealed environment. Fresh air, literally and figuratively, is hard to come by. Insulated from all but internal currents, business people recycle ideas along with their stale air. The alienation breeds defensiveness. Like the isolated Soviets, heads of an insulated institution seek to protect the misunderstood mother land.

This approach gives rise to the "Mother Hen" theory of public relations. In a company guided by Mother Hen PR, public relations managers are very protective of the corporate image and the company's personnel.

"We try to function more as a screen than an open window for access to corporate executives," says a spokesperson for a large manufacturer. "We're afraid," she continues, "the chairman will intimidate the reporter. That could result in an unfavorable story. We try to shield some of our executives because they may appear either brazen or corny. We've been stalling on interviews from *Business Week*, the *Wall Street Journal*, and [a major state newspaper]."

Mother Hen PR proponents profess that company public relations personnel are professional mouthpieces, savvy to the ways of the media and, therefore, adept at gaining the upper hand in press relations. These experts are presumed to have the experience and skills to inhibit unfavorable news coverage and when unsolicited publicity is inevitable, to present the company in the best possible light. News interviews with such professional representatives are expected to occur without the embarrassing gaffes that might be made by other company executives who are inexperienced at media relations.

Companies subscribing to the Mother Hen method instruct their employees to have all press inquiries directed to the public relations staff. In addition to having professional communicators speak to the media, this approach, in theory, assures the firm that it will have control over its public image by presenting a consistent, unified message to the press and, by extension, to the public.

This sounds reasonable, but reporters see it differently. Instead of finding this approach helpful, they ascribe sinister meaning to it. Journalists interpret a PR department's running interference on behalf of company executives as a stall or veiling technique. They want to know, What's the company trying to hide; why won't someone with line authority talk? *Fortune* quoted an unnamed reporter expressing frustration at companies that try to manipulate the press by touting good news but shielding the corporation from journalists pursuing less favorable information. "When it's all take and no give, that prejudices a reporter. I'm fair-minded, but sometimes I go away mad. If an opportunity comes along to use a company like that as a bad example, I will."[7] (They do try to get even!)

Reporters' intolerant attitude toward the professional corporate spokesperson is not as indefensible as it appears. Even companies that go to great lengths to attract qualified and effective public relations people often thwart their effectiveness by other self-defeating and contradictory corporate policies.

Companies hide behind their PR departments. Some corporate policies prohibit company mouthpieces from identifying themselves when speaking to the press—which is a great way of having no one on the record and holding no one accountable. A company that doesn't like what its spokesperson said simply denies that the statement was authorized or correct. When the public opinion trial balloon bombs, executives simply countermand the "obviously mistaken" PR statement. This old trick buys the company time or lets it test the waters of public opinion without exposing so much as the big toe of any ranking individual.

Another common practice is to keep a company's own PR people in the dark regarding corporate activities. This might be done for two reasons. First, if the PR people don't know what the company is doing, they can't inadvertently spill the beans to their brother journalists. Second, the company simply may not regard the public affairs department enough to keep it abreast of developments. This isn't so much distrust as neglect.

Needless to say, PR people in the dark about their own firm's activities do little to brighten corporate credibility. Don Webster, CBS News correspondent, told me an uninformed PR department makes its company appear "erratic and unpredictable, much to the disadvantage of the company." It's horribly difficult for a PR department to gain the media's respect when, apparently, it doesn't even have the respect of its own company.

The worst sin is when an organization undermines the credibility of its PR people by lying to them. A study done for the American Management Association revealed that 61 percent of journalists believe business people are not honest with their own public relations department.[8] Sending out PR people to carry false, misleading, or incomplete information may seem to be a smart strategic move on occasion, but this short-sighted practice puts a spokesperson in the regrettable role of fool. It permanently impairs the corporation's credibility.

Business people may not really care whether the media love their companies or PR representatives. But to bear the expense of maintaining a public relations effort only to internally assassinate it by lying to the company's own public relations department is not only incongruous, it may be suicidal.

When a business taunts the press by intentionally misleading or lying to a reporter—by an executive directly or through a PR representative—it's inviting retribution. The business may command money, assets, a political power base, legions of lawyers, and other resources, but the lowly reporter carries with him the power of the press. It can be a mighty formidable opponent in a contest of words and wills.

As one TV news director confided to me, "If a PR guy burns us by lying, I may not get him on the story we're working on, but we'll get him. It'll take time, but we'll cream him. We'll cream him!"

Suggestions for improving corporate public relations follow in the next chapters.

Taking Responsibility for PR: Whose Job Is It, Anyway?

> Unfortunately, the sense of personal responsibility for doing
> a job right seems to be declining, particularly in large organi-
> zations where responsibility is broadly distributed.
>
> **Adm. Hyman G. Rickover**

Because every company functions in the public arena, a firm cannot hide forever from public perception or opinion. A company does, however, have choices as to how it wishes to deal with the issues that relate to its public reputation. In this chapter, we'll look at some options for implementing the PR function, whether a company has an in-house PR department, keeps outside consultants on retainer, or doesn't budget a penny for public relations activities.

One of the fundamental questions a business must ask itself is whether it should formalize public relations as a corporate function. If your firm doesn't have much of a public relations department, you're in good company. Many companies, even 20 percent of *Fortune* 1000 firms, don't have a formal public relations department.[1] These companies may believe that public relations is a function that is everyone's responsibility, from the CEO to the receptionist, or that PR is an occasional need best served by outside consultants, or that PR is nothing but an invented need that wastes corporate resources.

Even in companies with PR departments, there's often an unappreciative or ambiguous attitude toward the function, and few people are

dedicated to it. Basically, many executives don't know what PR is supposed to do. Unlike the accounting, manufacturing, personnel, marketing, legal, or administrative functions, which are crisply defined,
public relations is amorphous, mystic. Because corporate officers don't
know what to expect from it, they don't know how to value it. When
times are lean, public relations budgets are usually among the first cas-
ualties in austerity moves.

Many PR departments exist because company executives fear the media. Whereas corporate management normally exerts control over most
everything in the corporate environment, it has no influence over the
media (which offer little recourse after inflicting pain). A PR department
can put a buffer between the organization and the press.

PR people play on executives' natural fear of the media. As a vice-
president for a PR firm admits, public relations staffs tell their corporate
chiefs, "You don't want to talk to the media! Let us handle them; that's
what you pay us for." Naturally, this advice reinforces the fear and sets
up PR people as media gurus. This role may not be advantageous to
the corporation. The helpfulness of the gurus may depend on to what
extent they function as a fence to protect, or a gate through which to
give access to, company officers.

Companies employing PR departments solely to shield their executives from the news media would be better off training their managers
to deal effectively with the media rather than paying a staff to hide them.
Journalists appreciate the direct-from-the-source approach, and it's often
to the company's advantage for responsible managers to respond to the
media directly; it saves time, money, and is just plain simpler.

The ideal corporate PR situation, PR executives say, sees the public
relations department reporting directly to the CEO's office. This relationship makes PR independently accountable and accessible to the organization's highest level. In this scenario, the public relations
department functions not just as a line of defense against the media but
works to shape the company's total public image. The PR department
may be responsible for lobbying, charitable activities, employee communications, and advising the CEO on the possible impact on the company image for most every important decision. In this role, the PR
department is not a "media go-fer" but the corporate conscience. It is
an intimate confidant of and adviser to top level corporate authorities.

This description, PR people lament, fits far too few PR departments.
In most companies PR just isn't elevated to such a top-echelon role. Not
only are the PR people not respected by the media people they deal
with, but they command little respect within their own organizations
(precious few PR people rise to CEO). It's a stressful spot to be in, and
it takes a toll. One study, reported in the *Wall Street Journal*, showed
that PR and advertising executives were dying of stress-related causes

at a rate of 14.2 percent above that of other business executives.[2] One of the reasons for that stress is the constant strain of being torn between raising the voice of corporate responsibility—the conscience role—and acting like a team player. Nobody likes a nag. In corporate America, he who rocks the boat not only doesn't ascend to the captain's chair, he may very well be thrown off the ship.

A good PR chief should nag, whine, and buck the tide at least occasionally. When the public relations department can't play the role of corporate conscience, it exists in a vacuum. The public relations function cannot simply be that of organizational speaker or breaker against the waves of media inquiries; it must embrace a meaningful role in policy formation and prompt senior management's public accountability.

As Joseph Awad of Reynolds Metals, former president of the Public Relations Society of America, assessed it: "Unless top management really believes in the value and principles of public relations and ensures that this belief is inculcated down the line, the public relations function is doomed, no matter how abundant the resources of money and labor dedicated to the task."[3]

The CEO of an organization bears ultimate responsibility for public relations. Strong, competent assistance is advised.

IN-HOUSE VERSUS OUT-HOUSE PR

Some companies believe an in-house PR staff is unnecessary because all senior executives carry a responsibility to be aware of the PR implications of company policies and decisions. Public relations constitutes a regular part of the company's business conduct. When extraordinary circumstances arise, outside PR experts are consulted (such as when there is sudden media interest in an otherwise quiet company or when the company decides it wants some free media publicity). For this reason, there are about 2,000 public relations consulting firms in this country (many of them one- or two-person shops) that perform PR functions on a contract basis (sometimes supplementing a company's own PR staff).

Companies that don't have their own PR department also hesitate to secure regular public relations counsel from external consultants. "Some firms still think that retaining a public-relations firm is slightly less acceptable than herpes," claims David M. Grant, president of his own consulting firm.[4] "People usually call us to bail out their ass," says a blunt Denver public relations consultant.

Many times outside PR firms are employed to handle information crises. They are the fire fighters who extinguish the flames of controversy, the SWAT teams that defuse potentially explosive situations.

Using outside PR consultants is most effective when those consultants are a regular part of the corporate team (perhaps augmenting, with special expertise, internal staff). When called in strictly on an emergency basis, too little time is available to educate the hired guns about the business as well as the problem at hand. Like lawyers, accountants, and other business consultants, the public relations counselor needs to know the company's players, products, business structure, competitors, and other important matters unique to the company. An emergency crash course on a corporation forms a poor foundation on which to build a cogent response to a serious situation. To derive the greatest value from outside PR counselors, a corporation should allow them to make a sustaining contribution.

By regularly using outside PR counsel to supplement an in-house staff, a company gains the benefit of independent judgment. As noted above, PR people may need to cut against the company grain in the course of doing their jobs. They're the ones who sometimes must tell the corporate emperor it wears no clothes. There's a natural, subtle pressure for one not to disagree with his employer. An outside agency should bring with it the greater objectivity of a detached outsider. While outside counsel also has a financial interest in pleasing its client, the stake is not so complete and overwhelming as it is for someone whose entire livelihood depends on the company payroll. If the client company doesn't like what it hears from its PR consultants, it's welcome to go elsewhere; but the credibility of the outside agency must remain intact if the agency is to maintain professional worth.

PUBLIC RELATIONS IS NOT SPELLED L-A-W-Y-E-R

Ideally, a company would have some professional PR personnel on its own staff and use outside counsel as warranted. Sometimes, especially in times of adversity, companies confuse legal advisers with public relations advisers. This isn't good.

It may be something in their genes, but lawyers and public relations counselors differ in their natural inclinations. While the PR adviser wants to portray the client who's under fire as an open, approachable, and respectable company, a lawyer instinctively wants to prevent the company from publicly exposing any failings or weaknesses by shutting off public communication. The attorney who's advising silence in the face of an emergency is acting consistently with his or her training, which required thorough research and thought before advancing a public position on an important issue. The lawyer also is seeking to protect the client corporation from opening itself up to expensive liability suits based on its public statements.

To illustrate this tug-of-war, let's look at a hypothetical example. Fictitious RealCool Fan Company manufactures portable electric fans for household use. It's been in business for ten years and never had one of its fans involved in a consumer accident with injuries until one hot summer day, a man lost a finger while moving a partly disassembled but plugged in and turned on RealCool fan from a high closet shelf. Within hours after the man was admitted to the hospital, his attorney announced to the press that the man intended to sue RealCool for $5 million in damages.

A newspaper reporter dutifully contacted RealCool Fan Company seeking a reaction. The puzzled receptionist transferred the call to the president's office. He took the call and was horrified to learn of the accident—no prior word had reached the company, which sits a few time zones across the country from the site of the accident. Caught unaware and off guard, the president correctly told the reporter that this was the first he'd heard of the incident, and could he please call the reporter back. The reporter said that he was on deadline and needed to hear from the company very soon in order to include its comments in the story.

Confused and anxious, the president summoned his attorney and his chief public relations counsel, both of whom were not on the staff of this relatively small company but were outside consultants on retainer. (Fortunately, the president had the experts he needed on retainer so he wasn't scrambling madly just to find a place to start.) Both outside experts were busy with other matters when the president called, but he informed their staffs of the urgency of the matter. Both counselors returned the call in short order.

The attorney advised the president to minimize any damage to RealCool's reputation by saying nothing. "The suit that the injured man claims he's bringing against us hasn't been filed yet. We don't know what he'll claim, so our best course is to clam up. We can't answer charges that haven't been brought!"

"But," said the president, "I feel just terrible about this thing. I'd like the company to publicly extend its sympathies for the unfortunate accident along with our best wishes for a speedy recovery. We have a moral obligation to do that."

"No, no, no!" cried the attorney. "We want to say nothing that could prejudice our position in court. If you send your regrets, that might be interpreted as an admission of responsibility. The resulting liability judgment could be astronomical! From what you've told me, it sounds as though the man suffered injuries because of his own negligence."

The president was frustrated. It was not his nature to hide from problems; he preferred tackling them head on. "Wouldn't it make sense for me to just tell the press that RealCool stands behind its products, and we wish the injured man well?"

The attorney was steadfast. "The worst thing we can do is legitimize the complaint. If we say nothing to the press, there's less for them to say about the incident. You want as little publicity as possible. If you talk to the press they'll begin asking questions you don't want to answer, and you never know if they'll quote you fairly. Just say 'No comment.' That's the way to avoid blowing this unfortunate thing all out of proportion."

The president hung up the phone, disappointed. He didn't want to see the name of RealCool slandered in the press without some response from the company. Just then, the public relations firm returned the president's call. They had already checked on the reporter from the *Sunnytown Gazette* who had called the president.

"It's a good paper and the reporter, according to our affiliate agency in town, is a fair journalist. We should get a decent opportunity to have our side represented in the news coverage," the PR counselor reported with optimism.

"My attorney is convinced our best bet is to say nothing so as not to draw any more attention to the matter or to imply any acceptance of responsibility," explained the president.

"It's the correct position to say that we shouldn't accept any responsibility. But at the same time, there's no reason we should allow RealCool to suffer negative publicity without offering some positive information about the company. You don't want to see a one-sided, damning news story, do you?"

"No, of course not. But I don't want to prejudice any legal action either. Besides, Sunnytown is just a little burg and maybe no one will hear about it," said the president hopefully.

"We can hope for that," the PR adviser said, "but there's a good chance one of the wires will pick up the story, or the injured man's lawyer will get in touch with the local broadcasters. The story may get big play in Sunnytown if it's a slow news day. In fact, it may get heavy coverage statewide."

"You're kidding!" exclaimed the RealCool president.

"No, but I wish I were. Product liability," continued the public relations consultant, "is a hot item in that state, which, our research shows, is close to enacting a new, very tough tort law. The media are hot for liability stories now. For you to say nothing about the incident might imply an unspoken admission of responsibility."

"What could we say that wouldn't incriminate ourselves?"

Because the PR consultant was familiar with the company and its operations, she was immediately able to recommend a course of action. "I'd suggest that we make a statement to paint RealCool in an overall positive light. We could point out that RealCool has sold more than, what, 60,000 units without an incident of injury."

"We've just topped sales of 65,000 units, and we're damn proud of our products," declared the president.

"And that's the story readers in Sunnytown should get," advised the PR counselor.

The president was quite perplexed. His two expert advisers were making radically different recommendations, each logical, reasonable, and defensible. The tough choice in front of this president is roughly the same one that every CEO faces in times of adverse publicity. A company can give the press the silent treatment, hoping the bad news will be reported and forgotten; at worst that approach makes the company look unconcerned, unaccountable, and guilty. Or the company can talk to the press, hoping for fair treatment that could minimize the bad news with some positive information to offset the negative; at worst it could give greater importance to the story by drawing more attention to it, or the press could twist the words of the company and make it look even worse. Decisions, decisions! It's a little like facing the choice of whether to fight for your life in a pit of alligators or, if you prefer, crocodiles.

There's nothing inherently mutually exclusive about the PR and legal functions, and the dichotomy of choosing either your legal or PR counsel's advice in a legal matter of public interest may be narrowing somewhat. More lawyers are becoming attuned to the advantages of an aggressive posture toward public opinion, such as in criminal trials where attorneys take their position statements to the public via press briefings and news releases.[5] Employing the media also is a strategy for public interest groups or others portraying themselves as Davids versus governmental or corporate Goliaths. Obviously, they recognize that the court of public opinion can be an effective mechanism to gather public support for their cause.

There's no reason that corporations shouldn't also use the news media as a tool of communication even where legal issues are involved, so long as such tactics don't endanger a fair trial. Such an aggressive approach is perfectly defensible in our society, which presumes corporations aren't innocent until they're vindicated and where "no comment" is presumed to mean "guilty as charged."

Making a positive prepared statement to the press not only gives an organization a chance to mitigate negative publicity from some pending legal action, it also can relieve some of the frustration silence brings to the staff of embattled companies. Some companies make such statements through their lawyers, but for reasons similar to those cited in the last chapter regarding PR people as corporate representatives, a well-briefed and coached senior executive is likely to have the greatest effect in most cases.

Using the press successfully to influence court or government proceedings is something easily evidenced in the takeover arena. When Mobil Corporation tried to take over Marathon Oil in 1982, Marathon fought the unfriendly takeover in the courts and in the press. The *Wall Street Journal* credited the public relations effort, spearheaded by the large PR firm Hill and Knowlton, with having "strongly influenced the court proceedings."[6] In 1986, Goodyear bitterly and successfully fought a takeover attempt from Sir James Goldsmith in the press and in Congress.

Chapter 13 details specific recommendations on press interviews, but it's appropriate to note here that speaking to the media about a pending legal action or any matter doesn't mean a company must tell everything. The company shouldn't hide information, but it shouldn't risk prejudicing a legal action. A spokesperson is perfectly within his rights to politely defer from directly answering questions that may incriminate or work against the goals of the company.

I strongly urge you to retain competent legal counsel to consult on public relations strategies that concern legal matters. Encourage your firm's legal and PR advisers to work *together* to devise plans acceptable to both. The goal is to highlight some positive information about the company, not to try legal actions in the news media. Discretion, careful planning, and effective execution should prevent disastrous faux pas from marring this communications strategy.

A final note to this section on lawyers and PR. It's interesting to note that some legal departments even are hiring their own public relations counselors. CBS attorneys did this when news media inquiries about the General William Westmoreland libel suit against the network and other pending legal matters generated more press traffic than the law staff could handle. The legal department referred media questions to the PR firm for background information and status updating.[7] This saved the corporate attorneys from resorting to the dreaded "no comment" and freed the legal experts to attend to the matters for which they are paid.

PART V
MEETING THE MEDIA

O Printing! how hath thou disturbed the peace of mankind! That lead, when moulded into bullets, is not so mortal as when founded into letters.

Andrew Marvell

The Media Are Coming, the Media Are Coming!

For in this mass communications society, if you don't exist in the media, for all practical purposes, you don't exist.

Daniel Schorr

With the public's voracious appetite for information, the pervasiveness of OmniMedia, and the press's growing interest in business activities, most any business in the United States faces the prospect of media attention on its affairs. Organizations must anticipate interactions with the news media and prepare for them. This chapter addresses issues that concern an organization's response to routine press inquiries. (Advice regarding principles and techniques an individual should use during media interviews appears in chapter 13.)

OPEN DOOR VERSUS BRICK WALL

Whether a company has a legion of public relations people available to it or none, each request for information from the news media represents a set of decisions the organization must make. Foremost, someone in the company must choose whether or not to cooperate with the inquiring reporter. While some companies have written policies governing press inquiries, most do not.

For some companies, there is little need for a detailed policy. They just don't talk to the press, period. This is the brick wall approach to public relations. An editor for the Los Angeles Times declares that "90 percent of businessmen will not pick up the phone" to talk to reporters.[1] The editor speaks in hyperbole but not pure fiction. Some companies actually have written policies forbidding their employees to speak with the press. Others, while not prohibiting interviews, discourage them and are very selective about the news outlets with which they'll speak.

Ignoring press interest in one's corporate affairs is seen by many business people as prudent. Say no evil, incur no evil. "A whale is harpooned only when it spouts," cautions Henry Hillman, president of the low-profile 1-billion-dollar-plus Hillman conglomerate.[2]

Journalists generally attribute suspicious motives to people who refuse to talk to them, concluding: If you had nothing to hide, you'd gladly talk to us. Conversely, many business people reason that talking to the news media—with their negative preoccupations—can mean only trouble. When reporters shine their news lights on a company, they always seem to cast the darkest shadows. Self-preservation instincts guide many companies' protectionist media policies.

The news media may be nosy, arrogant, and presumptuous, but generally they're not evil. More often than not, a press request for information or an interview is not rooted in an attempt to nail one's enterprise. The mainstream mass media devote much more time and space to business than ever before. Business-oriented newspapers, magazines, TV shows, and trade publications have proliferated in great numbers in recent years. So there are hordes of reporters contacting thousands of companies every day to ask harmless questions.

Like: What's your firm's general expectation for growth in the industry next year? What's your company doing to control rising health care and T & E costs? Is attracting qualified minority managers a problem for your firm? How will proposed tax legislation affect your business? What's your company doing to protect itself from activist shareholders? Are MBAs still prime recruitment prospects? And on and on. These questions are quite benign and pose no threat to the organization. Many times, press interest actually is positively motivated. Journalists call because they want to profile your company's new product or to discuss the "tough but fair" management style to which analysts attribute your organization's long-time success, or to feature your new employee recreation facilities.

On most occasions when the press calls, the business executive has nothing to fear but fear itself. Media attention offers a company an *opportunity* to show itself in a good light. In the rare event that a company is asked to respond to some negative publicity or is questioned about potentially damaging or sensitive information, it usually gains little by outright refusal to speak to the news media. Every media request, even the ambush interview, as we shall see later, is an opportunity for the company to hold its head high in public.

Throwing obstacles in the path of a curious press, in an attempt to hide company problems from the public, is akin to the theory of management that states, "If you sweep your problems under the rug where they can't be seen, they will go away." As with sweeping problems under the rug, not talking to the media won't make public relations problems go away. It may, in fact, make them worse.

When a railroad was suffering financial problems, raising questions of worker and employee safety, the situation piqued the interest of some state lawmakers. An Associated Press business reporter, preparing to write what was turning into a fairly damning story, tried earnestly to reach an official of the railroad. She made several phone calls that got no further than a well-coached secretary who said the executive was unavailable. The official in question never returned the phone call and apparently gave no instructions that the reporter be referred to someone else. When the deadline for the story finally came, the frustrated reporter turned in her lopsided story.

"All I was trying to do was give the guy a chance to defend himself before I ran the story one-sided," she said, exasperated. The story ran, with a decidedly antirailroad slant, no doubt infuriating the railroad people (who probably grumbled to themselves about the "biased, leftist, antibusiness media"). The reporter did her job, correctly reporting that powerful people were concerned about the railroad as a potential threat to safety. She tried to balance the story by giving rail officials a chance to air their side of the story. The company's refusal to extend to the reporter the courtesy of a response left the journalist little choice but to run an incomplete, "biased" view of the situation over a news wire available to state and national media. The company has no one to blame but itself.

Responding to reporters' queries, even in adverse circumstances, can usually salvage something fruitful out of a rotten situation. If the railroad official had spoken to the reporter, he might have said something to this effect: "It is no secret that the railroad has seen healthier balance sheets, but we are making progress on our financial situation. We want to assure residents of this state, our employees, and our customers that we share the legislators' regard for safety issues. Safety is, and always has been, our top priority. We plan to work with the legislators and intend to address their concerns with great urgency."

Now this statement probably doesn't negate the incriminating, anecdotal indictment of the railroad in the reporter's story. But it does give the company a chance to say to the world, "Okay, we're human, we've got problems, and with your help we'll solve them." A responsible reporter hearing the railroad's official statement would include at least some of the comments, even if just to say, "In response, the company says it is concerned about safety and plans to work with lawmakers to solve its problems." Anyone reading or hearing a news report that included such a line would have little reason to flat out condemn the company. At least the company appears concerned and willing to do something about its troubles.

Consider news reports that carry lines like, "The company refused to comment on the allegations." The company's dodge encourages many people to believe that the firm was so clearly caught red-handed that it had nothing to say—except maybe, "Have mercy on us."

Saying "no comment" easily equates with pleading "no contest."

The one occasion when "no comment" *may* be justified is in the event of a pending merger or acquisition involving a public company. The Securities and Exchange Commission (SEC) has both encouraged *and* discouraged disclosure of discussions concerning such transactions. In 1985 the SEC signaled a desire for candor in company statements but added that "no comment" was okay, too! The two-pronged response came after the SEC ruled that Carnation Company violated federal disclosure regulations when an *uninformed* spokesman said the company wasn't exploring a merger when in fact it was. Section 10(b) of the Securities Act of 1934 requires companies to present truthful and accurate information in public disclosures or statements.

Disgruntled shareholders have brought lawsuits against companies for not disclosing merger talks. The courts have sent mixed signals as to whether firms should reveal all in their public comments about deals in the works. False or deceptive statements are often at the heart of these matters; not saying yes and not saying no isn't the same thing as saying no when the truth is maybe. If your company says anything, *don't* lie.

But even no comment, from a normally responsive company, may signal to some observers that a deal is brewing. This is an evolving and tricky area. If you're involved in such merger discussions or are contemplating them, do two things. First, consult the SEC and your own legal counsel for advice on the government's current thinking on the matter. Second, talk to your public relations staff or consultants to keep them fully abreast of developments. Don't mislead your own representatives. If they inadvertently lie to the public about the status of talks because they don't know what's happening, their ignorance will stand as a weak defense when the company is accused of intentionally misleading shareholders on a material matter.[3]

Many news organizations now have policies requiring reporters to say why there was no comment. The Associated Press instructs its reporters to indicate why there "was no immediate comment" from an interested party to a story, because "an issue of credibility might be raised." The guidelines for AP reporters include this example: "If you left messages with the chairman, the president and the production vice president but got only a response from the chairman's secretary, who said he was in conference, say so."[4]

Some news organizations go to great lengths to elicit comments from principals of a news story, and when they continue to hit the brick-wall public relations machine, the results can be rather amusing or embarrassing , depending on whether you're one of the elusive principals. In early 1987, *USA Today*, in a report about the large consumer electronics retailer, Crazy Eddie Inc., noted the company's reluctance to reveal the whereabouts of Eddie Antar, chairman of the company. The paper pointedly said, "Crazy Eddie Inc. is stonewalling."[5]

When Philip H. Dougherty, advertising industry columnist for the *New York Times*, tried to dig into a story about reported improprieties at a unit of mega-agency J. Walter Thompson in 1982, he wrote: "Thompson would not go beyond its brief statement and would not give out [an executive's] unlisted Manhattan telephone number so that an attempt could be made to reach her for comment. None of a half-dozen business acquaintances had the number. Finally reached on the house phone of her East Side apartment, [the executive] suggested getting in touch with her lawyer."[6]

A television station in Albuquerque, KNAT, was forced to go off the air in 1985 after suffering severe financial problems. Because the station was owned by Johnny Carson and several other national media personalities, it drew quite a bit of media attention. *Electronic Media*, an industry trade paper, tried hard to balance a negative story about the station's predicament.

Efforts to contact . . . owners and representatives of station management also failed. In response to a mailgram sent to his office, a secretary for Mr. Carson, who is chairman of the broadcasting company, said the "Tonight Show" host was on vacation and currently unavailable for comment.

Neil Simon, president of the company, was in Europe and couldn't be reached for comment, according to his secretary.

Attempts by phone and mailgram to reach owners with smaller shares of stock, including Paul Anka, David Letterman, Art Ulene, Joan Rivers, Fred Nigro, John Powers, Michael Karlin and Mark Segal, also were unsuccessful.

Similarly, numerous attempts to contact Henry Bushkin, Mr. Carson's attorney and a director on KNAT's board, were unsuccessful. . . .

A series of written questions was sent to Beth Gelin, an attorney on Mr. Bushkin's staff in Los Angeles, who was also involved with KNAT, by *Electronic Media*, but she didn't respond to these. Nor did she return repeated telephone calls to her office.

By comparison, former KNAT staffers are more than willing to share their thoughts about what went wrong at the station.[7]

The last paragraph of that account (a gallant attempt at press fairness), is the most telling and instructive for our purposes. It reveals a truth that business people must recognize: Someone always willingly talks to the press.

Whether the story is associated with a small Albuquerque TV station or a manufacturing plant, a railroad, or a bank in Anytown, USA, the media invariably find people who'll talk to them. Sometimes the people who do talk are uninformed, vindictive, or malicious. But the press is not concerned much with motives. If someone levels a charge, the news media report it. If the person or organization against whom the charge is directed chooses not to respond to the allegations, so be it. With rare exception, the news media go with a "good" (read dramatic) news story whether or not the subject of the story consents or cooperates.

It's difficult for reporters to be fair in a vacuum, without the help of people who might be harmed by a story. According to the ethics of their industry, reporters need only *attempt* to represent a balancing point of view in an unfavorable story.

Some business managers don't talk to the press about bad news because they believe their silence keeps the negative news reports from being dignified by a company response. Poppycock. "No comment" is no answer.

Contrast the response of two airline PR people asked by Times-Mirror's *Denver Post* to comment, in early 1986, on disturbing charges of safety problems in the deregulated airline industry. American Airlines' Joe Stroop, manager of corporate communications, responded, "We have nothing else to say on the question of safety and maintenance. We've said all we have to say."

Western Airlines' Glenn Bozarth, director of press relations, said, "There hasn't been any common thread to the recent accidents but every one has led to action that's made flying today safer than ever.... We really believe deregulation is irrelevant to safety, particularly as it applies to major established carriers. All the established carriers are doing all they've ever done, and more, to promote safety."[8]

Now, which of the approaches better served the industry, the spokesperson's company? Based on these remarks, which airline would you expect a reader of the article to be more inclined to fly?

If your company believes allegations concerning it are undignified, malicious, or without foundation, then say so! (A news executive friend of mine calls this the "Jello™ approach" to public relations: no matter how hard somebody hits us, we'll slop back.) In August of 1985, when Aetna Life and Casualty sued oil baron Marvin Davis and his Davis Oil

Company, Davis didn't take the allegations of fraud lying down. The *Wall Street Journal* quoted a Davis spokesperson as calling the lawsuit "frivolous and absurd." The spokesperson continued, "To think we would engage in the conduct they allege is absolutely preposterous. We will vigorously fight the suit in the appropriate arena and fully expect to prevail."[9]

Touché! Davis didn't *dignify* the suit or the media coverage of the accusations against the company by publicly responding. To the contrary, the company aggressively attacked the attacker. It sought to mitigate any damage to its reputation by questioning the propriety of its nemesis.

ABC's "20/20" aired a story in early 1987 concerning an artificial heart valve that sometimes malfunctions without warning. The officials of the Irvine, California, company that makes the valve didn't want to face the interviewer, but they provided the program with a videotaped statement. The president of the company appeared in the tape and explained the company's position on the issue. The network aired some 120 words of the statement. TV news producers won't always concede to including a prepared statement, but providing a statement is an option preferable to saying nothing.[10]

Sometimes, reporters call companies asking for a comment on the actions of a competitor. Many firms, reluctant to contribute to the publicity of a competitor, decline to participate in the story. Such "no comment" responses deny a firm an opportunity to mitigate the report's possibly positive effect on a competing company.

McDonald's passed up an opportunity to publicly call the bluff of rival Burger King. The second largest fast food chain threw out a challenge in early 1987 to Ronald McDonald and company. Burger King was encouraging a taste test between its Chicken Tenders and McDonald's Chicken McNuggets by offering rebates to consumers in southern California who bought chicken at *either* restaurant. "That's Burger King confidence," the ad campaign boasted. A newspaper's prominent account of the marketing battle noted that "McDonald's officials did not return phone calls placed to its headquarters in Oakbrook, Ill."[11]

One wonders why not; were they too chicken to respond? McDonald's could have balanced and deflated the free publicity dished up for Burger King by returning the reporter's call to say, "If Burger King wants to pay customers to eat at our restaurants, we think that's great. We want them to compare because we know they'll be back after tasting our wholesome and delicious Chicken McNuggets and other fine food. Ask Burger King if it'll pay people to try our world famous french fries too!" (I promise you, any reporter would have included that last line.)

This was exactly the approach Walt Disney Studios took when a competing studio trespassed on Disney's animated entertainment turf in late

1986. The movie *An American Tail* for which Steven Spielberg acted as executive producer, earned the critical acclaim and box office success that eluded several of Disney's recent family-oriented productions. Disney executives answered press inquiries bravely.

"We're delighted [with the film's success]," claimed the chairman of Disney Studios, Jeffrey Katzenberg. "The entry of other producers into the family motion-picture business is a positive move and will have positive effects on the Disney company as long as the [competitors'] product is the same quality."

"The more the merrier," echoed Roy Disney, vice-chairman of the Walt Disney Company. He said that competition in the family movie market "draws attention to what is better. We think we do it better than anyone else."[12]

Adept media relations skills of these Disney executives gave them positive press coverage related to the success of a competitor.

A closed door or a stone-faced response to a reporter's questions never furthers a company's cause. View every expression of interest from the news media as an opportunity for gain.

THE SNEAK ATTACK

Admittedly, not all news media interviews are polite exchanges of information. On rare occasion, a reporter is antagonistic, dishonest, blatantly unfair, or out to get a company. "It's difficult," says a PR director for a defense contractor, "for us to get fair coverage when a reporter is 'chasing an angle' and already has the story before hearing our views."

Unfortunately, some reporters do shape the collection of facts they've gathered about an issue to conform to the story they set out to write. Sometimes this is the fault of an editor or producer to whom the reporter answers. I've seen many instances where a news chief says to a reporter something like, "Bring me a story about how budget cuts have forced otherwise normal families to go live under bridges." Or, "Go talk to some truckers and get some quotes about how industry deregulation and rising fuel costs are making their lives miserable."

This "pre-fab" news gathering really happens. I've done it myself. Usually, an editor sees a story covered by some other news outlet and then attempts to replicate it or give it a local angle. Manufacturing news shortcuts fulfilling the demand for news, especially on slow news days when finding news in routine life is a lot of work, or on heavy news days when there just isn't time to start every story from scratch. It's much easier for reporters to get information to complete a story they've already mostly written than it is for them to start a new story.

If you knew in advance that an interview with a reporter would center on fulfilling preconceived notions, no doubt you'd flirt with temptation to cancel the interview. Of course, you usually don't receive such warning, and the first hint of trouble may not come until you're deep into the interview. There are techniques one can employ successfully to change the course of such an errant exchange, and these are detailed in chapter 13. Fear of slanted news stories or unfair interviews should not keep your organization from talking to reporters. It bears repeating that an organization faced with an invitation to speak to the media should view the exchange as an opportunity to generate public goodwill.

Beyond chasing an angle, journalists commit other ethical sins that provoke protectionist press policies in organizations. To gain access to an elusive news source, unscrupulous journalists employ false premises. These come in a couple of varieties. The first is that of a reporter who lies about his or her identity or the publication he or she represents. The other is the false reason the reporter gives for the interview.

After a company has been burned by a particular reporter or news outlet through phony quotations, having its views misrepresented by quoting out of context, or otherwise receiving unfair treatment, some organizations will bar any further contact with the offending reporter or publication. This won't stop a determined reporter. PR people tell stories of reporters who contact companies and lie about their names and the publications they represent.

Certain supermarket tabloids and extremist ideological publications have gained a reputation for using such tactics, and not surprisingly, many people refuse to speak to them. It's easy for renegade journalists to call a company and ask for information while falsely identifying themselves as reporters from the Podunk Star or Radio Station WLIE, Falsehood, North Dakota, or even claiming to represent real and better-known news outlets.

There's no surefire way to prevent being tricked, but an adept media relations staff, familiar with the journalists and media outlets with which the company has had prior contact, should help unmask the impostors. A handy way to discover phonies is to insist on returning calls from unfamiliar journalists. Then, check with directory assistance for the main telephone number of the press outlet. If nobody's every heard of the publication and it isn't in the phone book, watch out!

Free-lance journalists, who may not have found a home yet for the piece they're working on, shouldn't be shunned, but they should be approached with appropriate caution. Likewise with student journalists. Budding student reporters sometimes sell their journalism schoolwork to major publications, so don't let your guard down with young journalists just because they're enrolled in a learning institution.

Even with your guard up, there's no way to be sure that a reporter who says, "I'd like to do a feature story on your successful program to cut absenteeism" isn't really planning to lambaste you with questions about sexual harassment charges recently brought by an expatriated employee. Throwing the reporter onto the curb, after discovering the ruse, will neither endear the company to the news medium who sent the inquisitor nor prevent the publication from proceeding with a recounting of the disgruntled former employee's charges against the firm. There are ways to turn such situations to the company's advantage; these are discussed in chapter 13. For our purposes here, the point should be made that there are no guarantees when it comes to media relations, but shutting out the press usually does a company no good.

The Adolph Coors company, a privately and closely held brewer, shunned media contact for years. But in 1982, the company found itself the subject of a boycott movement resulting from serious allegations made by union organizers. The charges against Coors included physical searches of employees, confiscation of workers' personal property, misusing lie detector tests of potential employees, and racial prejudice in hiring. This attracted the attention of CBS's "60 Minutes."

Coors consented to cooperate with a request for an interview because it was confident that a full examination of the company and the charges against it would vindicate the brewer completely. After intense internal preparation, the firm gave the "60 Minutes" team carte blanche access to the company's employees. Mike Wallace, the quintessential TV interrogator, queried employees and executives alike. The resulting story was very pro-Coors, full of glowing testimony from real working people as to what a wonderful employer the company was. Had Coors not consented to (and not prepared for) the "60 Minutes" interview, Wallace and company may have run a Coors story anyway, but painted a radically different picture.[13] (The once reclusive Golden, Colorado, company ran ads in journalism magazines inviting queries from reporters under headlines like "Silence is no longer Golden" and "We used to say no comment. Now we're asking for your questions." More recently, it's run corporate image ads in journalism magazines. The April 1987 *Washington Journalism Review* included a Coors ad that bragged that the company employs ex-convicts, under the headline: "The jury gave me ten to fifteen. Coors gives me 9 to 5.")

When a company is mulling whether to submit to an interview with a reputedly tough journalist, it faces a dilemma. To accede to the interview request may be like consenting to enter the arena and wrestle the lions bare-handed. To refuse the request is to risk having a trench-coat-clad reporter stand outside the company offices and say to an an audience, "We offered these people an opportunity to answer the charges, but the lowlifes inside there [pointing a thumb over his shoulder] refused to talk to us, obviously afraid we'd uncover whatever it is they're trying to hide."

Granting an interview with a responsible journalist, even in times of adversity, at least gives an organization a chance to minimize otherwise damaging publicity, save face, and maybe score a few points on the public credibility meter.

AMBUSH!

It's not as common as it was, but an executive who refuses to talk with the broadcast news media may still be ambushed. You know the scene. A reporter and camera crew, with lights blazing and camera rolling, corners some poor devil in an elevator or parking lot, shouting questions and accusations, demanding an explanation.

This "confrontation journalism" was popularized by "60 Minutes." Star confronter Mike Wallace explains: "We will walk into an office and ask to see the boss. If the boss comes out and says, 'Well, I'm not sure I want to talk to you,' but then decides he is going to talk ... we sit down with him and we can put in front of him a piece of information he didn't know was coming, then we have some drama."[14]

A CBS crew got some drama when it followed Supreme Court Chief Justice Warren E. Burger, no fan of broadcast journalism, into an elevator in Lincoln, Nebraska, with camera rolling. Justice Burger gave the TV crew more drama than it bargained for. The jurist knocked the camera out of the photographer's hand, saying, "Don't stick that think in my nose."[15] The Chief Justice, while embarrassed on the national news by a replay of the 1981 incident, can get away with such action. For other, mere mortals, a violent reaction to invasion of privacy by a media ambush probably would be self-defeating.

The appropriate response is to look the accusing reporter in the eye and say something like, "I do not wish to speak to you under these conditions. Please show me the courtesy of calling me so that we can arrange to discuss—in a more civil manner—my opinion about whatever it is you're trying so hard to get me to talk about. Here's my card. I'm usually available between 9 and 5." Making such a statement won't guarantee that the reporter and crew will stop harassing their victim. But anyone seeing such a composed request for decency and civility surely would feel some empathy and compassion for the hunted and some disdain for the hunters.

Fortunately, the ambush interview has been widely condemned in journalistic circles. Even the executive producer of "60 Minutes," Don Hewitt, admits the combative interview tactic "has been abused," likening it to getting "a man to testify against himself."[16] Which of course, no one should be forced to do, at least according to the Bill of Rights in our Constitution.

Short of an ambush, journalists sometimes become quite pushy and insistent that their professional curiosity about some aspect of a company's business be satisfied. A cable TV executive relays an incident in which a reporter demanded an interview with him when he was the manager of a large cable system in Texas. "She demanded I speak with her. 'You *have* to talk to me; the public has a right to know,' she insisted. I told her I didn't have to talk to anybody. We shouted at each other; I asked her to leave. She wouldn't, and I told her to call her boss. She did, and left in a huff."

The "public's right to know" is a moral force that drives some reporters to demand responsiveness from those they pursue. But as pointed out earlier, the press really invents this right when applying the concept outside government matters. A business should always reserve its right to determine its affairs. A company is under no legal obligation to speak to the press, although almost always it's in the organization's best interest to do so.

In chapter 13, we'll examine some very specific principles and techniques for you to use while meeting the media.

"Sir, a Mr. Mike Wallace Is Here to See You," or, How to Remain Cool While on the Hot Seat

The only problem I've had [with the press] is when I've said something dumb and they quoted me accurately.
                    Harold McCormick, Colorado state senator

Never talk to a strange man on the street if he is holding a microphone.
                                        Robert L. Kimmel

The voice at the other end of the phone says, "Mr. Executive, I've got 5 minutes to deadline and I want to hear your company's side of this story I've been working on the past couple of months." Or maybe you pick up the phone to hear, "Hi there, this is Kathy Callthemasiseeum, from WZING Radio, we're live on the air and I'd like you to respond to some listener complaints about your shoddy products."

This is no time to start thinking about developing media relations strategies. Whether you have a month to prepare to meet the media or no time at all, when the actual moment comes you're likely to feel a gripping sense of fear overwhelm your normally confident self. Remain calm. Remember, this is an *opportunity*. While the inquisitor(s) will try to get as much information out of you as possible, it's unlikely you'll be subjected to heinous torture.

When Business meets Media, it shouldn't be a collision but a meeting (albeit a carefully planned and executed meeting). The real key to making the meeting successful is to know what you want out of it and to put in the time and effort to be adequately prepared. Even if you only speak to the press once every 17 years or so, it pays to know what to do when the fated moment does arrive (probably without warning).

PREPARING FOR SUCCESS

A media interview isn't a battle, but it is a contest; it's not you against the journalist, but you against the possibility of embarrassing yourself or your organization. As in any contest, the interviewee/contestant betters the odds by the degree to which he or she is ready for the sparring match.

There are several areas in which one should prepare before an interview.

Materials. You cannot reasonably expect that the reporter will have read your annual report or that he'll even know anything about your company when he requests an interview. The journalist interviewing you may have no experience reporting business issues. He may never have heard of your company. The reporter's superior may have sent him to obtain the information without telling him the context in which it will appear. Or worse, he may hold misconceptions about your firm. While the reporter may not know anything about your company, be prepared in case he or she knows a great deal about it!

To adequately prepare for an interview, you must answer the following questions satisfactorily. Can we provide articulate and responsible answers to the questions we're likely to encounter? Do we have handy current vital statistics? Do we have visual materials (e.g., maps, diagrams, charts, etc.) to aid the reporter's understanding? Can we give the reporter position briefs, biographies, a company history, photos, and the like to aid recall and to fill in the interview's gaps? Who else should we make available to help the reporter get information? The more a company can help a reporter do his job, the more likely the reporter will write a complete and balanced report.

Without question, the services of a professional media relations staff or consultant help immensely to keep the necessary information up-to-date and easy to use. But even operations with a small PR budget can help themselves by assembling key company information into a press kit (and reviewing it at least every six months). The key to making this information useful to the journalist is to keep it simple and easy to use. A 200-page document will be thrown away rather than read. A reporter working feverishly under deadline will cherish a few typewritten pages with essential information clearly offset (such as in outline form). Even better is an information kit that addresses the exact topic the reporter is reporting.

Interview Training. Harold Carr, vice-president of public relations and advertising for Boeing Company, declared in December 1986, "Few corporate managers are trained to deal with the media, to understand their needs or to cope with their demands."[1] Yes, most managers wing it when it comes to meeting the media. But many organizations—from big companies to labor organizations to federal agencies to police departments—are trying to close the knowledge gap by providing press interview training to their people who are likely to face the news media.

Public relations firms and consultants specializing in media training administer "self-defense" courses. Some may find such training expensive (costs are usually in the thousands of dollars) and demeaning. But if you aren't a natural communicator, such preparation probably is a worthwhile investment. Even if you're blessed with the gift of eloquence, such training may pay by honing your skills and increasing your sensitivity to the rules of the media game. Even Mike Wallace himself endorses the idea: "It makes perfect sense to me because people should have every opportunity to make the best case they can for themselves."[2]

The Press. Understand with whom you'll be dealing in your interview. Most media interview requests come on short notice. It's to your advantage to have someone in the organization (or on retainer) who's familiar with the media you may encounter.

You'll want to have the answers to the following important questions. Who is the reporter? Is he or she familiar with the company? What is the reporter's, and the publication's, reputation for fairness? What audience is reached by the publication? Should we expect a cordial or combative session? If the interview will be broadcast, ask: Is it a live broadcast? Will the interview take place before a live audience? Who else will be there? Are they assumed to represent an opposing viewpoint? Know thy potential adversary.

Interview Questions. A vitally important question to have answered is, About what information can we reasonably expect the reporter to ask? One of the best ways to answer that question is to simply ask the reporter, "What topics of information should I prepare to discuss?" Do *not* ask for a list of questions! Reporters consider this an imposition and a trespass on their right to ask whatever questions they please. (It constitutes a form of censorship, they claim.)

Generally, requesting some idea of the interview topics is not considered intrusive by a reporter. Most reporters gladly comply with such a request because they realize that if the company is prepared to answer questions, the interview will yield more substance. A reporter who refuses even to indicate the areas of discussion ahead of the interview is probably up to no good. (A sneak attack's only value is to destroy the enemy. If you're the intended victim, decline the invitation to dance.)

Beware! Because a reporter cordially outlines his areas of interest prior to an interview doesn't restrict him to those subjects, and it doesn't indicate what he plans to do with the information you provide. One shouldn't be lulled into complacency by the cooperative or friendly approach of a reporter; it may be a guise.

Witness the case of William Westmoreland, the retired army general and subject of the CBS documentary, "The Uncounted Enemy: A Vietnam Deception." The program accused him of conspiring to suppress information about enemy troop strength in the Vietnam war. General Westmoreland claims CBS misled him about what it planned to ask him in an interview. The network provided General Westmoreland with a list of possible questions. However, the general says he was ambushed by CBS because he received the questions with too little time to prepare adequately for the interview and didn't expect the emphasis on one of the casually worded questions appearing way down on the list. The general said the placement and wording of the question "gave me the impression" that the question relating to enemy strength estimates "would be almost a minor detail that [CBS] wanted to cover."[3]

That "minor" question became the focus of the program. The other questions on the preinterview list, in the general's opinion, served as "camouflage" to mask the issue the broadcasters really wanted to focus on. Westmoreland, who was not prepared to adequately answer the questions relating to statistics of some 14 years earlier, made, by his own admission, "some unfortunate slips" in the interview.

The general was caught in a trap he allowed to be set around him. He carelessly "trusted" the list of questions provided him by CBS. In effect, they were a Trojan Horse gladly accepted by General Westmoreland.

Bait and switch is not the way reporters usually conduct their business. But it can happen. Never assume that because a reporter says he plans to cover certain topics in an interview that the topics are in any particular order of importance or that they are the only issues that will be raised in the discussion.

Preparing for interviews won't guarantee success or fair treatment, but it will greatly improve the odds.

WINNING STRATEGIES

No one should be made a fool of by the media. Toward that end, here are some strategic rules of thumb to guide you in preparing for media interviews. These will be followed by tactics for successfully handling interviews.

Understand the Game. You arrived at a position of power and responsibility in your organization because you are competent. The media may be unfamiliar, but that shouldn't intimidate you. Win at the media game as you won in the game of business: Learn the rules and play smart. If you've read the preceding chapters in this book, you've a good working knowledge of how journalists think and work and in what they're interested. The rest of this book focuses on what *you* can do to meet the media effectively.

Accept Media Interest. Believing that the news media should ignore your company's troubles in favor of investigating more important stories is like telling a police officer not to give you a speeding ticket because he or she should be out chasing real criminals. Reporting the bad news of business (even yours) is part of a journalist's job, just as traffic citations are part of the police officer's.

Don't Shun TV Because It's TV. Yes, television is frightening with its hot lights and reputation for drama. But it can also be a marvelous tool for communication. "One of the values of television . . . is that you can always spot a phony," opines Senator Howard Baker.[4] The extension of his claim is that sincerity also shines through TV. Use that to your advantage. A television interview is a wonderful vehicle for conveying your deep-felt concern, your integrity and moral character. It's not a medium to be feared but one to employ to fullest advantage. TV, as Walter Cronkite suggests, can tell it "the way it is."

Additionally, unlike print or radio interviews, where journalists have great leeway with your quotes, the logistics of television make it somewhat more difficult for an interviewee's statements to be taken out of context, especially if you answer using the techniques I suggest below.

A word about makeup. Men understandably recoil at the thought of wearing "a painted face." Some women resent the suggestion that their personally applied makeup needs touching up. Ignore your emotions. Be pragmatic. Stage makeup only enhances your appearance on television (even if you entered the studio wearing regular cosmetics). If you wear it, no one will say, "Boy, did you look made up." But if you don't, you may hear, "You didn't look so hot; are you feeling okay?"

Let the TV people put makeup on your face, and if they suggest it, remove distracting jewelry from your hands and neck.

Prepare for the Interview. Anticipate what you'll be asked. List every question that might come up. Write down at least three questions you're afraid to be asked. Rehearse some answers to them. Don't allow yourself to be caught unaware! If Murphy had a law for press interviews, it would be, "The questions you dread are the ones that you'll have to answer." When you're ready for the tough questions, the easy ones are that much easier to handle.

Plan Your OWN Agenda. You don't have to restrict yourself to just answering questions. Use questions as an entrée to effectively communicate your side of the story. Give reporters the facts you want them to report. Before the interview, write down from one to five positive message points you wish to interject into the conversation. Rank them for priority. Create a few quotable remarks, using illustrations, analogies, and witticisms to convey that information. You don't just want to talk in an interview—you want to impress your ideas upon your audience. Try to come up with ideas and phrases that people will remember, that they'll repeat to a friend.

Practice relaying your agenda information in a natural and appropriate manner—frequently referring to notes on television can make you look unsure of yourself (though it is acceptable to double-check a figure, date, or other detail). Be familiar with your material, but not so rehearsed that you sound like a robot.

Plan to Be Honest and Straightforward in Your Remarks and in Accepting Criticism. A broadcast news director suggests that it's *business people* who make media interviews unpleasant experiences because they "always turn [the interview] into an adversary relationship. They see everything as win/lose." A wire service reporter says it's the coy, less than honest business person who "creates the 'us versus them' " attitudes between business and the press.

Journalists are resourceful, intelligent, and persistent. They work hard to get their stories. Assume that if you try to hide something in an interview, the reporter already knows what you're hiding or will find out from someone else. A cover-up approach to media relations hurts your company. It fails to prevent negative information from being published, and it indelibly scars the company's credibility.

Speaking with candor, on the other hand, is more like making a blood donation: it stings briefly but provides long-term benefits. A company that is "fully open when it's in trouble makes it more credible when it's not," is the way one journalist put it. "Openness is the biggest secret for successfully dealing with news people. There is nothing as refreshing as candor," suggest the Foundation for American Communications.[5]

Only Address Problems That Are of Real Concern. Candid remarks win respect, but talking to a reporter is not a confession, psychoanalysis, or a time for mea culpa. Answer frankly those questions that are put to you, but don't create trouble by dragging every skeleton out of the corporate closet. Honesty is the best policy, but you need not tell all you know. Proprietary information is secret. Competitive information is confidential. Personnel matters are private.

One of the great PR blunders in recent memory was made in the spirit of misplaced candor that, while not expressed in a news interview, quickly drew lots of media attention. This was when William Agee, chief executive of Bendix, gathered 600 employees together to deny company rumors that he and his newly promoted top aide, Mary Cunningham, were having an affair. Agee was taking the offensive against the rumor mill. But what he did was dumb. It would be like introducing a new diet soft drink with an advertising blitz that proclaimed that the new product "Tastes Good and Doesn't Cause Cancer!" (*Time* reported that the "Mary and Bill story had rated coverage in practically every major newspaper and magazine, several sober editorials, a *Fortune* cover and, the crowning touch, a gossipy, five-part series" sold to major newspapers.)[6]

When speaking to the news media or when saying things to others (employees, analysts, etc.) who may repeat your remarks to the media, confine your remarks only to those issues that are of real concern. Don't conjure boogiemen for the media to chase.

TACTICS FOR SUCCESSFUL MEDIA INTERVIEWS

When it's you and the reporter, one on one, it's easy to feel your heart race and palms sweat, hear your voice crack, and watch both feet fly into your mouth. Can this be avoided? Yes. To some extent. What follows are some specific techniques to use during the interview.

Show Respect for Your Interviewer. You might no more want to meet with the press than you would a police SWAT team. You wouldn't invite either group to your office Christmas party, but if either shows up, you'd do well to extend to them all due respect.

If your visit from the media comes in the wake of intensely adverse circumstances, as it often does, you may vehemently resent the intrusion of the news media into your turbulent affairs. You'll have tremendous pressure on you to fix whatever catastrophe thrust you into the media spotlight. You might've had little sleep and not eaten well. You're tense, tired, physically and mentally drained. You're operating mostly on the adrenalin triggered by your body's survival instinct; you've little psychic reserve. Not exactly the ideal circumstances from which great public appearances are made.

The situation is worsened because your interviewer is harsh, inconsiderate, dispassionate. You feel threatened by what seem to be unfair and hostile questions. Discipline your reflex to strike back. Summon your self-control.

The very presence of a reporter seated across from your desk or on the other end of the telephone may remind you of your troubles, but don't shoot the messenger. The reporter is doing his job. Help him do it well (and to your favor) by fostering as much as you can an attitude of cooperation and helpfulness. If there is any leeway in how the reporter treats your story (and every story is shaped to some degree by the reporter's frame of mind), a favorable impression from your contact with the journalist can help. A negative impression certainly will hurt.

The media truth squad that's invaded your privacy may not be your friend, but it probably isn't your enemy either. Be courteous, professional, businesslike.

Resist Temptations to Be Overly Familiar with Your Interviewers; Don't Patronize Them. You may have seen their by-lines, pictures, or televised images in your home a million times before, but that doesn't make them your acquaintance. Rather than addressing your questioner as Dan, Dianne, Tom, Barbara, or Peter, respectfully refer to him or her as Mr. or Ms. Jones. This will help you keep the proper professional frame of mind for the interview (even if, or maybe especially if, you do know your interviewer personally).

Your job in the interview is to communicate information to benefit your company. Like you, journalists meet many people every day and know sincerity when it crosses their path. They'll appreciate the genuine respect you show them and the professional attitude with which you conduct the interview. The journalist is there to obtain information from you, not to begin a friendship.

Don't Insult the Reporter By Questioning His Professionalism. Do not demand to know all the questions the reporter plans to ask before the start of the interview. Do not ask the journalist to read your quotes back to you. Do not stipulate that you must see the story before it is printed or aired. Do not try to intimidate the reporter by hinting that you'll ask your good friend the publisher to review the story before it's run.

Never Remind the Reporter That Your Company Spends Big Advertising Money with His Publication. First, the reporter doesn't care; the argument means nothing to him. Second, he probably doesn't like the advertising department guys anyway. And third, you've just implied a threat. When threatened, one's instinct is to retaliate.

Any attempt to gain control over the reporter's story implies that you fear something you'd rather hide has slipped out. Telegraph "secret" to a journalist and his interest is really piqued. The intrigued reporter will look for that hidden bad news until he finds it.

When you agree to an interview, you're acknowledging the professionalism of your interrogator. You must trust in the capabilities and ethics of the media people with whom you're dealing. Trying to get control over the reporter's story is like expectorating into the wind; all you get is spit in your eye. Why bother?

Record the Interview. Your well-placed trust in the reporter need not be blind faith. It is acceptable for you to record the interview for your reference. This quietly signals your concern for fairness and accuracy to a reporter without being offensive. Later, if you believe you were unfairly or inaccurately quoted, you possess an objective record to remove all doubt or suspicion from your protests.

Allow the Reporter to Record the Interview. It's not a sneaky device for the reporter to trap you. To the contrary, the recording should aid the reporter in quoting you accurately, and that of course, serves your best interest. If the reporter records the conversation, but you don't, be careful in your claims about being misquoted. Audio- or videotape, unlike human memory, isn't influenced by what you meant to say or what you thought you said. It's an impartial and nearly infallible arbiter of the truth about what was or wasn't said in an interview. (Vice-President George Bush once claimed he never called candidate Reagan's campaign promises "voodoo economics." NBC produced a videotape showing Bush uttering the damning words during a 1980 primary speech. Mr. Bush conceded with a letter to NBC, "Well done on your research, darn it.")[7]

Listen Carefully to What You Are Being Asked and Answer with What You Want to Communicate. Interviews come in many flavors. Among them:

1. General to specific. ("Tell us about your company" to "Exactly how did the comptroller embezzle the hundred grand?")

2. Specific to general. Reverse of above.

3. Random. ("What were last year's sales?" followed by "Are you planning another public offering?" followed by "What is the name of your marketing chief?" etc.)

4. The no-question interview. Everything said by the reporter is a statement to which you are expected to respond. ("Your market share is slipping, the company must be headed for doom." Or, "The suit against you suggests the company intentionally kept important safety information from regulators.")

5. The 50-questions-at-once interview. ("Isn't your market share slip-, I mean sales of the whole widget industry are . . . uh, aren't consumers losing interest in the, your advertising really is off the mark isn't, but I mean, if you adjusted for seasonal factors you still would see a significant decline, you know what I'm trying to, you know what I mean?")

6. The lots-of-silence interview. (A few harmless questions, followed by long, agonizing periods of quiet that beg for you to fill them by nervously prattling. The reporter hopes you'll let your guard down and say things you otherwise wouldn't.)

7. The "I'll-tell-you" interview. This is antagonism calculated to elicit a response. (Phil Donahue frequently resorts to this grandstanding technique. It goes something like this, "You guys knew your product could kill people, but in the name of the almighty dollar, you greedily put it on the market to victimize innocent consumers so you could reap the profits of death!") A variation on this is the pretend-to-have-all-the-facts interview. The reporter bluffs, makes you believe he knows what he couldn't possibly know, hoping you'll confirm his suspicions.

8. The lay-a-trap interview. ("Earlier, you said you tested the Rackafrack Widget for two years. But this company memo, obtained from a former employee, says the testing really was conducted for less than six months and under

subpar procedures. Your company broke the law, conspired to defraud the government and the American people, and today you lied to us!")

With few variations on the themes, this sums up the most common interview styles. Most interviewers mix at least a few of these approaches. For the most part, you won't need to consciously worry about the interview style your questioner employs. However, there are some specific techniques you should be familiar with and ready to employ.

Keep Your Mind Focused on What Is Actually Being Asked. Answer what you are asked, not what you expected or assumed you'd be asked. Don't just hear one or two key words and plug in response #37a. There may be a false premise in the question you'll need to debunk. Listen to the whole question, really think about it as though you've never heard it before, and *then* answer. A pregnant pause before answering won't make you look unprepared if you answer thoughtfully. Most people ascribe more credibility to one who thinks before speaking than one who glibly gibbers.

If you don't understand the question, or if you have the slightest doubt as to what the interviewer was really driving at, ask for clarification. There's no shame in saying, "I'm sorry, would you repeat or rephrase the question."

The interviewer who asks 50 questions at once needs your patience, understanding, and help. Without offending the reporter, ask for clarification. "George, those are some good questions. Where would you like me to start?" Or, "I'll try to answer each of those questions; if I forget one remind me. I'll start by addressing the issue of . . . "

For the journalist who enlists silence as his most compelling question, be patient. We Americans have a quirky cultural hang-up about silence. It makes us uncomfortable, so we rush to fill the void. Don't do this. Give the answer to the question that was asked of you and shut up. (Mike Wallace: "I find that if you'll just let the answers sit there for a while, the interviewee sometimes will become uncomfortable with the silence and add something that perhaps he hadn't expected to add to an answer.")[8]

Wait for the journalist, who will either continue to stare at you or pretend to be endlessly checking his notes. If an unbearable amount of time passes before you're asked to entertain the next query, go ahead and ask the reporter, "Is there anything else I can tell you?" Or look at your watch and ask, "Have you any other questions?" The reporter sensing your apparent need to get on to other things will probably hurry things along. If not, you might suggest you have another appointment coming up shortly and that you would happily schedule another time for you to finish the interview at a time convenient for the reporter.

If the Interviewer Makes a Mistake in the Premise of His Question, Let Him

Finish the Question, and Then Immediately Correct the Error. Obviously, if you are not paying attention to what the interviewer is asking, you'll miss the erroneous premise and will fall into a trap of defending something you never should. By the time you belatedly discover the error, it will be too late to emerge from the pit you've sunken into. Listen for the implication of the interviewer's remarks. If he offers you an incorrect statement—"You must be discouraged by fourth-quarter sales"—clearly and firmly disagree. "No, not at all. We're quite pleased." Or, "Fourth-quarter sales are close to projection, and we are satisfied that the slight lag is a temporary response to the sluggish economy."

If you can't discuss a subject, explain why—cite litigation, SEC rules, trade secrets, whatever the real reason—and then segue to some message point from your agenda.

Schedule an Interview to Last No More Than a Half Hour. You can only stay fresh and alert for so long. Beyond the 30-minute mark, you're hanging by thin mental threads. If the reporter needs more time, offer to schedule an additional session for another day, or even later that day, but take a break. Don't allow yourself to be worn down; that's when you make mistakes.

Keep Your Cool. Even if you're facing the firing squad using the "I'll-tell-you" and lay-a-trap interview styles, stay calm and alert. Keep listening and thinking. Think your way out of this; don't shout, argue, name call, or punch your way out.

Don't engage in sarcasm and try not to look defensive, even when a reporter comes on strong, especially in a radio or TV broadcast situation. For goodness' sake, don't start off on the defensive! No one wants to embrace someone who says hello with a shove. (Cal Thomas, himself a former journalist, appeared before a meeting of broadcast reporters while he was communications vice-president for the Moral Majority. Thomas obviously expected a hostile reception. His strategy appeared to be that of "beat ' em at their own game before we start to play." In his opening remarks he was sarcastic, cutting, flip. His demeanor probably did more to inspire hostile questions than if he had just stood at the lectern and said something humbling like, "I know some of you consider me and my organization fanatical, but I'd like to entertain your questions in the interest of understanding.")[9]

If you face an antagonistic atmosphere, respond in a nonthreatening way. Rather than making you appear weak, it makes you appear in control. Don't play into the aggressive interrogator's trap. The harder he pushes, the more you assume a tone of reason and cooperation. This scores points on the empathy meter, and regardless of what the reporter accuses you of, it makes him or her look like the heavy and you the victim.

People generally don't remember the specific arguments in an interview; they're not flowcharting the discussion. People form an impression and give nearly as much emphasis (if not more) to how you say something as to what you say. You want people to see or hear your interview and think, "Boy, he handled himself well under pressure; I believe him."

Because of the subtleties that go into an audience's impressions, watch your nonverbals in any TV appearance. Try to be comfortable. Sit still. Don't swivel or rock in your chair, don't nervously play with your watch, mustache, or hair. Beware of nodding during your interviewer's questions—you do it to show you're listening, but others may read it as agreeing.

If your interviewer persists in making allegations that you know are unfounded and unfair, just say, "I'd like to set the record straight. What you continue to suggest is untrue and unfair. It's not correct to characterize the situation as . . ."

If you are dealing with someone bent on backing you into a corner and goading you to say things you'll regret, terminate the situation before it gets to that point. Say: "I'm speaking with you in good faith. I'm trying very hard to be forthright in our discussion, but I am finding it difficult to continue because I believe you are not playing fair with me." Or, "I'm interested in addressing the issues you want to raise, Mr. Jones, but in an atmosphere of cooperation and mutual respect. If you'd like to continue this conversation, I suggest we do it after we each have had a chance to consider the ground we covered today. Shall we reschedule?"

Keep Your Wits during a Sneak Attack. When a reporter lies to you about the real reason for the interview or presents you with purported, damning evidence (as in the example of the Rackafrack Widget maker above), start asking questions yourself rather than giving knee-jerk answers. What is it exactly that the reporter is insinuating? What, generally (you don't want to ask for names, that'll smack of retribution), are the sources of the accusations? Might there be some phony documentation involved? Could you have a copy of whatever it is you are being asked to validate or deny, in the interest of fairness and completeness?

Do not respond to blind accusations; ask your interviewer, "Suppose you were on my side of the desk, and I was interviewing you for the paper or on TV. In the middle of the interview, I say, 'I have it on good authority that you are a plagiarizer; you intentionally slant stories you report; you accept payoffs from subjects of stories you cover.' How would you feel? Wouldn't you want to confront your accusers, to deny specific charges? I'm asking the same of you."

When allegations surprise you, admit your shock. Appeal to the reporter's sense of fair play. "I'm taken aback by what you are suggesting. I'd like to look into this matter. I know you are trying to get at the truth, and I trust you'll afford me the opportunity to do some fact-finding. Can we schedule a meeting for Thursday to revisit this issue?"

The reporter may be on deadline, ready to go with the story, but any time that you can buy to investigate the issue and formulate a reasoned response will be to your advantage. Even a couple of hours are better than sitting there like an idiot saying things you'll regret or be forced to eat later.

Redefine the Issues When Your Interviewer Strays into an Area You'd Like to Avoid. Don't be evasive but redirect the conversation by shifting to the material you'd like to discuss with phrases like, "The real issue is ..." or "The thing to keep in mind is..." or "That's not the issue we should be focusing on. In my opinion, what's important is..." Then proceed to introduce items on your agenda. Most likely, the reporter will change gears with you, and the conversation will now respond to the ideas you've introduced. If the reporter persists on trying to pin you down, answer the question or explain why you can't.

You can insert your own agenda broadly as well as in response to a specific question. When Tylenol capsules were poisoned the second time, in 1986, James E. Burke, Johnson and Johnson's chairman, tried to shift interviews from discussing a Tylenol problem to discussing a problem of capsule medicines. When the American Medical Association suggested that all tobacco product advertising be banned, spokesmen for the Tobacco Institute tried to shift the discussion away from the health effects of smoking to a civil rights (free speech) issue posed by the proposed ad ban.

Think Before You Speak. It may be trite, but there is no better advice to heed in a media interview situation: Engage brain before moving mouth.

An interview isn't court testimony, but it is less a conversation than an oral exam. You want to keep a collected, open attitude about you and the tone conversational, but the mind must be sharp at all times. Remember the One-Bullet Axiom: Every reporter is an unloaded gun. Give a reporter one bullet by misspeaking, and he'll blow you away. Don't make his day.

Take a deep breath before speaking (gets oxygen to the brain and helps you relax) but don't clear your throat nervously. Collect your thoughts before saying a word. This will help you avoid a bunch of "ers" and "ums" and "ya knows," which make you appear uncertain and disorganized, especially in broadcast interviews. Have the complete thought before you begin to articulate it; you'll appear decisive. You don't want to grasp for what you're trying to say midway through a sentence. If you need to buy thinking time, take a drink of water to wet your whistle—your mouth may be dry from tension anyway.

Speak with conviction. This will help you convey an aura of authority.

You'll say what you mean and at least sound like you mean what you say.

Speak Concisely. Practice being cogent in succinct sentences. The better you get at this, the better your chances for direct and correct quotes. Let your words convey your thoughts so the reporter won't be forced to interpret through paraphrasing what you were struggling to communicate.

Put the bottom line up front in your answer. State the conclusion, then give the supporting evidence. This helps reporters, especially broadcast ones, edit your remarks to represent your position correctly.

Short, salient answers are easier for the reporter to understand and easier to enter correctly in his notebook and the final story. It's immature and mistaken to believe that if you talk long enough about something that people will start to believe you. The reporter is talking with you to hear your comments, not to be converted. Don't repeat yourself by saying, "Like I said before . . . " If offered an opportunity to cover familiar ground again, state your position using another example.

Use Simple Sentences and Simple Language. Avoid jargon and lots of big numbers. Before the interview, practice expressing complex concepts in simple terms. Use analogies, anecdotes, and stories to illustrate your points. Abstractions don't "listen" well; they're as hard to visualize as 38 right angles intersecting 13 half circles on a one-dimensional plane. Stories, on the other hand, humanize facts, figures, relationships, and the story teller. "Stories amplify," says theologian Harvey Cox, and they "often tell us more about the narrator than about the plot."[10]

Compare numbers to things people can understand. For example: affects more people than the entire population of Minnesota; a dangerous level of consumption would require someone to eat 53 pounds of the product every day for 67 years; costs less than what the federal government spends on paper clips in a year; "reminds me of the story about the little boy who went ice fishing for the first time . . . ," and so on. If you need help creating appropriate analogies or stories, enlist the aid of your PR consultants or perhaps teachers, who boil down the complex into the understandable for a living.

Keep Your Tone Conversational. Don't preach, sell, argue, refute, rebut, retort, dispute, deny, or defend. Just talk.

Beware of Phrases That Are Common in Vernacular Speech But Appear Profane in Print. Avoid saying things like: whole hell of a lot, what the hell they're doing, give a damn, screw 'em, bull shit, and the like. News organizations at one time sanitized such remarks. But today, there is an emphasis on reality reporting that will leave you quoted more accurately than you might like, to your detriment. Speak no evil, read no evil.

Be Yourself, above All. A media interview is not so much a performance as it is an opportunity to express yourself. Think, choose your words carefully, but be yourself. If you've a good sense of spontaneous humor, use it when appropriate. Be candid. Let your warts show. Journalists appreciate an honest, unpretentious display of humanity; it's so unusual.

OFF THE RECORD IS OFF LIMITS

Politicians get in trouble occasionally because of misunderstandings about a journalistic tradition known as "off the record." Information provided a reporter on an off-the-record basis is considered to be not for publication. The practice is used to satisfy a hungry and persistent reporter's need to know something while keeping him or her from telling the rest of the world. Newsmakers use "off the record" to give reporters the "inside skinny"; it makes reporters feel privileged and in the know.

"Off the record" is used as a tool to delay the release of information. "If you won't publish what I'm about to tell you until the official release date, I'll give you all the information about our new widget now. You'll break the most complete story ahead of the other press."

Sounds good, but beware. Invoking the reporter's trust to tell him something off the record can be a manipulative and potentially explosive situation. Many people who are not accustomed to dealing with the press tend to treat reporters as confidants, confessors, or cathartic sounding boards because journalists tend to be good listeners. Beware of this. The reporter is talking to you to get a story, not because of personal interest in your problems. People who are accustomed to press interviews sometimes try to hand out off-the-record information as some kind of reward or perk to reporters. Being bright and naturally suspicious people, reporters recognize when "off the record" really means "eat out of my hand." If journalists feel used, they'll get even.

Commenting off-the-record always is a dangerous tactic for a business person to employ. Some reporters aren't careful in noting what was told to them for publication and what was not to be published. Others sometimes violate their pledge not to publish information because the value of the story is deemed more important than the friendship or confidence of the news source.

Any number of politicians can tell you about the hazards of off-the-record remarks. Ask David Stockman, former budget director. His comments critical of Reaganomics, made off the record to a journalistic confidant, wound up as page-one news across the country. It cost him a trip to the presidential woodshed for a good tongue-lashing and a considerable loss of credibility on Capitol Hill.[11] Ask Jesse Jackson. During his 1984 presidential campaign, an anti-Semitic remark, uttered in what he thought was an off-the-record environment, brought him negative publicity and cost him credibility.[12]

Off-the-record gaffes do not just result from information preceded by a caveat to the reporter that "what I'm about to tell you is strictly off the record." Sometimes comments the speaker didn't intend for a reporter to hear find their way onto the record, such as when a microphone is on when one believes it to be off. Ask Louie Welch, who ran for Houston mayor in 1985. When he was on live TV, a microphone thought to be off was not, and it picked up the candidate's tasteless remark about AIDS. Welch weakly explained, "It was a moment of levity before we went on camera. It was an unfortunate choice of humor."[13]

Ask President Reagan, the "great communicator." His "humorous" off-the-record remark about signing legislation to "outlaw Russia forever," followed by, "We begin bombing in five minutes," sent chills around the world. Reagan, a former broadcaster, uttered the words during a radio address when a microphone the president thought was off was on.[14]

He, too, should know better, but ask CBS's Mike Wallace. He reportedly made a racist reference to watermelons and tacos while interviewing a California bank executive. (The remark was taped by the bank's film crew who recorded the CBS crew at work.) Wallace's ethnic humor made news from the *Los Angeles Times* to the *New York Times*. Wallace said the utterance was made off the record. The others present during the interview didn't see it that way.[15]

There are a couple of lessons to be learned from these unfortunate experiences. First, bad jokes made around microphones are like those made near airport security stations—they're no laughing matter, and they can get you into some real trouble. Second, not-intended-for-publication remarks can become premature or embarrassing news.

When in the company of journalists, even in social settings (some PR experts advise especially in social settings), don't say anything you're not prepared to see as a newspaper headline or as the lead item on the evening news. Never assume; never let your guard down. Period.

Kahlil Gibran said it most eloquently. "If you reveal your secrets to the wind, you should not blame the wind for revealing them to the trees."

Practicing What's Been Preached

Is there anyone so wise as to learn by the experience of others?
Voltaire

To illustrate some of the principles outlined in the previous chapter in a real-life setting, here's an example of how to handle media interviews.

A REALCOOL TALE

Our case study takes us back to the offices of the fabled RealCool Fan Company, a privately held consumer products maker.

It was a hot, muggy August day. The president of RealCool was apprehensive, but his PR counselors thought he should respond to some reporters' questions about a rash of unrelated and unfortunate mishaps involving the company's fans. Within about a month's time, at least 20 people across the Midwest, RealCool's market area, had been involved in injury accidents with RealCool fans. This attracted the attention of an alert wire service reporter, who noted various newspaper stories concerning liability suits filed against the firm. After a story about the suits appeared on the news wire, RealCool received numerous other requests for news media interviews.

When the flood of calls came pouring in, the media relations specialist—who spent most of her time creating product publicity materials—answered a few of the reporters' questions and promised them that the company president would speak with them personally. She told the inquiring journalists that the president wanted very much to talk to them and to give them a reasonable chunk of time without interruption. Because of a heavy schedule and a need to gather relevant information, the president couldn't take their calls right now, but gladly would return their calls at a mutually agreeable time tomorrow. This strategy allowed RealCool to appear responsive (which it was), to prepare for the interviews (check on reporters, gather pertinent information, brief the president, etc.), and to exert some sense of control over the interviews, all without a sense of panic.

Some news reporters were miffed that the president wouldn't take their call immediately—as was his normal policy. RealCool's PR people spoke at greater length with those journalists, but politely stalled the others because the nature of the story was such that it was "enterprise" and not "spot" news. In other words, the news organizations were following up news stories of injuries to create original stories about the company and its perceived problems. They weren't reporting breaking news that had to make today's paper.

It may be ideal for a company to grant every press request for information, but that doesn't mean the CEO should drop everything every time a reporter dials the company phone number. The short delay in responding to the queries likely would not damage RealCool's credibility. The company's chief spokesperson still was going to answer the reporters' questions fully and in a timely fashion.

The company's public relations consultants, called soon after the media inquiries began to pile up, directed the president to clear his schedule for two days in order to prepare for and conduct several media interviews. Rather than call a press conference, which might indicate a sense of urgency or suggest a magnitude to the problem that really wasn't there, the PR people arranged one-on-one interviews between the company president and reporters. The PR advisers scheduled phone interviews with out-of-town newspapers, radio stations, and trade press, as well as some in-person interviews with local media, including one with the I-Team reporter from a local television station. Scheduling the TV interview for later in the day allowed the president to practice in less stressful interviews.

When the PR department set up the interviews for the next day, it asked each reporter if he or she would give RealCool some idea of the general topics they'd like to discuss so that the president would be adequately prepared and not waste the reporter's time searching for information. (Note: The PR people did not ask for a list of questions the reporter would ask. Reporters hate this.) The reporters were mainly interested in the company's explanation for the recent rash of accidents involving the company's fans, whether the company was taking short-cuts on safety, and other matters one could anticipate.

The company was in litigation relating to some of the incidents, so the PR people told the reporters that the president could not discuss the particulars of any specific case. He would, however, the reporters were told, discuss the company and its products as finitely as he could.

After the interview appointments were set, the advisers sent, by overnight courier, a press packet containing vital information about the company to each of the scheduled interviewers. The packet contained general information about the company, a bio on key officers, an important summary sheet on the company's outstanding safety record, copies of industry design awards, diagrams of safety devices found on RealCool fans, some actual warning stickers, and most important, a sheet briefly summarizing the company's position on the recent incidents. The summary sheet included some quotable quotes attributed to company officials. (The company assembled most of these materials some time ago for use in just such a situation.)

The president and his staff of employees and consultants then began reviewing expected areas of interest to the reporters. They agreed on five key message points that the president would try to insert into all interviews.

1. RealCool assigns top priority to safety in both the design and manufacture of all its products.
2. All fans made by RealCool meet and exceed government safety standards.
3. The incidents involved various fan models, spanning a five-year production period. The only common thread is apparent customer mishandling. The timing of the unrelated occurrences is strictly coincidental.
4. No government agency has cited or investigated RealCool for any impropriety.
5. RealCool retained an independent engineering firm to investigate each reported incident to ascertain its cause.

After drafting the president's communication agenda, the team drew up the following questions and answers in anticipation of the press queries.

Q. How does the company explain the numerous injuries caused by its fans recently?
A. The company conducted its own exhaustive preliminary investigation. That investigation shows that in most cases the fans were handled improperly, in violation of the safety warnings clearly labeled on the fans.
Q.. What kind of improper handling of the fans caused the accidents?
A. In several cases the fans were operated with their protective grills removed. In one instance, a man placed an open fan on a high and unstable shelf from

which it fell. In another instance, someone tossed paper clips at the fan; the clips were then turned into dangerous projectiles. One woman operated the fan in the bathroom near a sink. The fan was knocked into the sink, which resulted, as it would with any electrical appliance, in a short-circuiting of the motor and a burn to the woman. And so on. The company has contracted with an independent engineering firm to investigate thoroughly each incident.

Q. Does RealCool plan a recall of fans?

A. No. There's no need, and no one has suggested that RealCool should even consider a recall.

Q. Had the fans made by the company met government safety standards?

A. Yes! RealCool has *always* surpassed government safety standards. (If a reporter didn't ask this question, the point was to be made by the president.)

Q. Doesn't it seem awfully odd that RealCool fans would be involved in so many mishaps in such a short period of time just by coincidence?

A. The recent injuries stand in stark contrast to an outstanding safety record for RealCool fans. For years, the company's products have led the industry in safety and have earned the company a deserved reputation as a quality manufacturer of safe and reliable products. The fans involved in the injurious accidents were of several different model types built over a period of five years. RealCool wants to assure consumers that its fans are safe when handled with reasonable care. Only an unfortunate coincidence can explain the recent mishaps.

Q. Has any RealCool product ever been recalled?

A. No, not by any government agency. RealCool did interrupt the first shipment of a new model fan about five years ago because the company discovered that a screw assembly holding together the molded plastic body of the fan was not fastened properly. The shipment was returned to the factory before the fans ever reached store shelves. The company replaced the screw assembly.

Q. Were any of those model fans involved in the recent incidents?

A. No, not to the knowledge of RealCool.

Q. Has RealCool seen any impact on its sales since the injurious accidents came to light?

A. No. When the incidents were reported, RealCool already had shipped most of its seasonal inventory to wholesalers. RealCool is not aware of any effect on retail sales following the recent news items.

Q. Had RealCool reached any settlements with injured parties?

A. All incidents remain under investigation at this time. RealCool expects its quality products to prevail in any court action.

Q. Was RealCool planning to make any changes to its fans' safety features?

A. RealCool continually reviews its products to make sure they're safe. No changes related to any recent incident are planned.

After the potential questions were reviewed, the president rehearsed some mock interviews with the PR staff. The public relations people, impersonating reporters (which some of them had been), tried to intimidate, confuse, and anger the president. His business savvy and prior interview training served him well. After a few dry runs, recorded on videotape and carefully reviewed, everyone felt confident that Real-Cool's CEO could effectively make the company's case before the press and public.

The next day, the phone interviews went remarkably well. Most questions closely paralleled those anticipated by RealCool's consultants. There were few surprises. Most reporters gave the president ample opportunity to present the points he wanted to make.

After each interview, the president conferred with someone on the PR team who listened to the phone conversations on a muted phone. Because the president was prepared and competent, the reviews consisted mostly of compliments for a job well done, with a little fine tuning of minor points, such as the turning of a phrase and ordering of message points in an answer. By morning's end, many phone interviews were complete. It was time for a face-to-face interview. For the convenience of the reporter, RealCool's president had scheduled lunch with a journalist from the home town *Truth and Beacon Daily News*. That interview also concentrated on many of the same questions, but in addition, the reporter asked what seemed to be sympathetic questions about the strain the negative press coverage placed on the company and its employees. The reporter bought lunch, in accordance with the paper's policy, without objection from RealCool's president. The executive gave an information kit to the journalist and asked her to call him or his PR representatives with any other questions.

The president went back to his office, returned a few business calls and indulged in a scheduled hour of relaxation, insisted upon by the PR counselors. "Rest so you'll be fresh for the TV interview this afternoon," they warned. The president took the advice, leafed through a magazine, called his wife, and took a walk around the factory chatting with employees.

By the time the secretary announced that the television crew had arrived, the president was refreshed and ready to face the hot seat. Before asking the crew to come into his office, the RealCool president conferred with his chief media interview adviser, who was from an outside agency on retainer to RealCool. "The other interviews went well, but I'm scared to death of this TV stuff," he confided.

The PR whiz, Barbara Truespeak, reassured her nervous trainee as she applied a little makeup to his face. "The hot lights, microphones, and all that gear can be a little intimidating, but try to ignore them. Just look past all that paraphernalia. Listen to the reporter's questions, and answer them simply and honestly. One good thing about TV is that you probably won't be misquoted, and for 20 seconds or so, they'll let you speak uninterrupted. Just answer the question in a normal voice and manner. You'll do fine. If you like, I'll quietly sit over here in the corner."

"Please. Will you be recording the conversation?"

"Yes. We thought about videotaping the interview, but decided it wasn't necessary. We don't want to spook the news crew or give them the impression that we're apprehensive about anything. I'll record the conversation with this small audio recorder, and we'll tape the newscast tonight on our VCR."

"Sounds, good. Let's get it over with!" With that, the president asked his secretary to show in the TV reporter and crew. He smoothed his hair and straightened his tie. Yesterday, Barbara told him he should dress normally and comfortably, to wear neutral colored clothing (no checks or wild patterns). The president wore a modest blue suit and club tie. He felt as comfortable as one can before entering the lions' den.

When the TV crew came into his office, the RealCool president was a little surprised at what he saw. The I-Team reporter, Brad Breakem-down, was impeccably dressed. A wolf in executive's clothing, thought the president. Brad's hair was perfectly coifed, his nails manicured, his suit beautifully tailored—all compliments of the station's advertisers, Barbara later pointed out.

The camera and sound crew was almost the antithesis of Brad's polished, stylish look. No custom shirts, no salon, blow-dry hair styles. One of them wore dirty blue jeans, a casual shirt, and cowboy boots, was unshaven, and let his cigarette ashes fall on the nice carpeting of the president's office. The president observed the careless act but ignored it. The other crew member, a young and better-dressed woman, also smoked but with decorum.

Brad's attitude was bold, brash, theatrical. "Okay folks, let's do our thing and let this captain of industry get back to work!" he ordered.

"The window's no good," the camera man said to Brad.

"Excuse me sir," Brad said to the president, "could we move you from behind your desk to another chair? The light from the window behind your chair is going to give us trouble."

"No problem," said the president, who moved across the room to a chair next to a plant and some bookshelves.

Then the intensely bright TV lights came on. They made the president squint. "Just allow yourself to get used to them," advised Barbara in a whisper.

The sound technician was pinning a microphone on the president's suit. "Can you give me a level?" she asked.

"What?" said the president.

"Say something so I can set the sound level of your microphone," she instructed.

"Oh. Okay. Uh, let's see, how about, I like Channel 5, the news leader."

"Yeah, that's fine."

Brad heard the president's remark. "Do you really watch our news?"

"Yes," said the president, a little embarrassed.

"Hey, didja see my exposé on the nursing home last week?"

"No, I'm afraid I missed it."

"It was a real hummer. The guy who ran the place was real pond scum. Okay, I think we're about to get started!"

The president adjusted his tie nervously and took a sip of water. He wondered about his decision to wear makeup. Barbara told him that it gave his face good color, took the shine off his high forehead, and masked his dark beard which can be seen through his translucent skin.

The TV reporter ran his fingers through his hair and sat down. He spoke to the president in a helpful tone. "Allright, what we're going to do here is have a little chat. I know the lights are in your eyes, and you're worried about how you'll look on TV, but try to forget about that stuff. Just talk to me like we're having a conversation. Don't worry about looking into the camera. Just look at me and everything will be fine."

Brad turned to his cameraman, "Are we rolling?"

"Ready when you are, Slick."

"Let's begin," Brad said, dramatically lowering his voice a little. He cleared his throat, looked straight into the president's eyes and drove home his first question.

"Tell me, how does it feel to be the president of a company whose fans have mercilessly injured at least 20 people in the last month?"

The president of RealCool Fan Company didn't have to die in front of his whole community while struggling to answer the loaded opening question of TV reporter Brad Breakemdown.

The president took a breath, gathered his thoughts, and calmly responded.

"Customers' safety has always been our top concern at RealCool. Consumers trust our products because we have one of the best product safety records in the industry—we've won awards for it. In the past month or so there have been some unfortunate accidents involving fans made by my company. We've investigated those incidents. As far as we can determine, they were the result *not* of any defect in our products but rather of improper handling. An electric fan requires care in handling, and our fans are labeled to remind people to use them correctly. RealCool fans are safe—they've *always* exceeded government safety standards."

The president effectively deflected the stinging remarks in the reporter's question and ignored the implication that he was a worthless slug because his products were involved in some injurious accidents. The TV reporter's next questions were less inflammatory. He asked how RealCool could explain the number of injuries in such a short time. The president gave an answer consistent with his preparation: "Because the fans involved represent different models manufactured over five years, it would appear that the only fair answer is unfortunate coincidence. All the information we have points to people doing things with our fans that they just shouldn't. Let me give you some examples . . . "

The remaining questions concentrated on what the company was doing in light of the safety issues raised by the accidents. The president explained how the company had hired an independent engineering firm to investigate the reported incidents carefully and to assess each case. "We want to establish beyond any doubt that these incidents were unrelated to anything that our company has any control over. We put safety stickers on all our appliances, and we encourage consumers to read them and heed them." He also pointed out again that the company exceeds government safety standards, and in response to a question he pointed out that RealCool was not under investigation by any government agency.

That night, the president watched the TV station's coverage of RealCool. He was pleased. While the news reporter had edited the president's initial response to exclude the point about exceeding government safety standards, the president appeared concerned about the accidents but not worried. His appearance on the show inspired confidence in his company and its products. Brad Breakemdown had a little fun mocking the stupid things people did with their fans. RealCool came out looking good.

The next morning, Barbara Truespeak and her staff collected copies of the newspaper stories resulting from the previous day's interviews with the president. The stories, while peppered with sensational quotes from the attorneys who were bringing product liability suits against RealCool, were balanced and quoted the president liberally and correctly. One employee stopped by the president's office to say she'd seen the interview on the nationally televised All News Network on cable. "OmniMedia meets Our Town," the president thought.

The president and his advisers sent thank-you notes to each reporter who interviewed the president. In the notes, the president expressed his appreciation for the reporter's interest and the fairness with which RealCool was treated in the resulting news story. The note invited the reporter to call again with additional questions on this or any other matter. The president also distributed a summary of his interview remarks to his senior staff so that if they were interviewed—the president was going to refer all further news media requests downward to marketing, manufacturing, or public relations staff—they'd know the company line. The president directed the PR department to draft a special newsletter to update all employees.

In the months following, the company slightly increased its normal advertising budget to offset any possible lingering doubts about the firm's products. A modicum more than usual (imperceptible to anyone but the closest observer) emphasis was given in the ads to RealCool fans' safety features.

RealCool's insurance company, quietly and for little money, settled out of court with most of the people who brought suits against the company. In two cases that did go to trial, RealCool successfully defended the design of its quality products and was not required to pay either compensatory or punitive damages. These legal vindications were modestly noted in simple news releases distributed to the trade press and those news outlets that had interviewed the president about the cases earlier. Even though the company emerged the victor in the litigation, it did not wish to call undue attention to the allegations that gave rise to the trials.

Periodic polls of retailer and consumer attitudes toward RealCool, conducted by its PR firm, showed that the company retained its reputation for safe, reliable products. Wholesale orders for the rest of the year showed no appreciable drop. The following year, sales were up, consistent with projections made prior to the adverse publicity.

And so ends another public relations success story attributed to preparation, quick response, and effective execution of a considered communications plan.

Part VI

CRISIS!

All too often, you learn of a crisis when a reporter calls for verification.

Joan Capelin

Planning for the Unthinkable

Many managers have difficulty in dealing with the unexpected.
Colin J. Coulson-Thomas

An acute event with the potential for devastating consequences is generally called a *crisis*.

The word *crisis* derives from the Greek word *krinein*, meaning to separate, to decide. In the midst of a crisis, if we don't clearly separate between the important and unimportant and quickly make good decisions, the crisis may become a *catastrophe*—from the Greek *katastrephein*, to overturn, to overthrow—a prospect frightening to any organization.

Entire volumes have been written on the fine art of avoiding and managing crises and catastrophes; most center on handling crisis *events*. This chapter reviews crisis planning basics with an emphasis on *communications*—a function critical to avoiding catastrophic consequences.

Even if you do everything that management books advise to prevent a crisis, your corporation—without warning—can be hurled into a disaster, a violent controversy, or other emergency that qualifies as a crisis. Enlightened managers anticipate trouble's inevitable arrival and prepare to greet it firmly.

Many, many companies tiptoe on the razor's edge without a formal crisis plan. Executives of such firms suffer shortsightedness or delude themselves by denying their vulnerability to crises. Of course, having an emergency plan in your company doesn't mean that you're prone to disasters.

Denying your susceptibility to a crisis—by not preparing to deal with it—won't keep it at bay (any more than not preparing a will prevents death). Readying for the remote, unthinkable event is consistent with the strong management that usually prevents such occurrences. A well-conceived crisis plan helps to head off crises by forcing leaders to anticipate (and think through responses to) potentially devastating events. When properly executed, such a plan precludes small incidents from growing to crisis proportions and contains true emergencies within manageable confines.

IDENTIFY POTENTIAL CRISES

When framing your crisis plan bear in mind that *crisis* is a relative term. Management must decide what constitutes a crisis. In doing that, it's helpful to appreciate the potential crisis value in every mundane aspect of your business. Understanding the hidden emergency potential for almost everything in your business will help you spot clouds of potential crises before they converge into a major storm.

If you employ people as workers, recognize that someday they may strike or cause a work slowdown. One of them may sue the company for unfair dismissal, for sexual harassment, or for discrimination in promotion. One of them may assault a coworker or supervisor, or start a vicious rumor, or sabotage your plant, or carelessly handle materials that endanger or injure fellow workers or members of the community. If you make a product, admit that your company is vulnerable to accusations that your product caused injuries or that it was contaminated, of inferior quality, falsely advertised, or that it otherwise failed.

The most effective way to expect the unexpected is to perform a crisis audit within your company. This procedure not only identifies all possible crises but also tries to determine the probability of each event and anticipates the potential impact of each.

As you consider each possibility and form a response to each, your crisis plans should recognize the difference between a firecracker and a ton of dynamite. Assign a gradation to the possible emergencies your firm faces and designate them Level 1, 2, or 3. There are two measures of importance to which you should assign potential crises. One concerns its importance internally, that is, how it affects your normal operation as a business. The other measure relates to its external significance, that is, the importance to your firm's reputation. After assessing the possible crises, detail effective procedures to respond to them.

THE PLANNING PROCESS

Resist delegating crisis planning solely to an outsider. Many management consultants—such as attorneys, public relations firms, marketing consultants, or accounting firms—are offering crisis planning services. *Time* magazine declared in 1986 that "crisis management has become a growth industry."[1] Consultants offer an outsider's perspective and, one hopes, insight and experience. But like any business planning, your emergency plans won't benefit from a cookie cutter approach. Crisis plans must reflect your firm's particular structure, nuances, and "culture."

People charged with executing the crisis plan need to play a strong role in shaping it. They need to understand and support it. The consultant won't be there when the gas main explodes!

Management consultant Robert F. Littlejohn recommends a team approach to crisis planning. He suggests identifying three teams within an organization to plan for and manage crises. These are the policy, management, and liaison teams.[2] The teams may share many of the same members but each represents different tasks and responsibilities in the crisis planning process.

Top-level executives comprise the *policy team*; they establish broad policy guidelines for crisis planning. The *management team* takes those broad policies and applies them to the specifics of crisis planning. Management team members identify the issues within the organization that hold crisis potential, and then they create a plan, in Littlejohn's words, "to mitigate, manage, and recover from any crisis." When a crisis strikes, the management team actually handles the crisis.

The *liaison team* supports the management team by offering specific expertise in planning and execution and by helping to communicate crisis plans to different constituents within the organization. Members of this group are selected for their expertise in specific areas (i.e., manufacturing, labor relations, product management of a particular brand, etc.).

The liaison members have a dual function. First, they lend their knowledge to the management team in both planning for and managing specific crises related to each liaison team member's area of expertise. And second, they promote and explain the crisis management program to others in their area of the company. For example, the manufacturing chief might advise the management team regarding the impact a workers' strike might have on inventory, machine maintenance, or the like. In addition, the manufacturing chief would communicate to his subordinates the plans related to manufacturing that the crisis management team devised to deal with a labor strike.

Some tips for creating your plan follow.

Involve People from throughout the Organization. The CEO, PR chief, and corporate counsel are vital members of the planning team but they can't be *the* team. Get the expertise you need for an effective plan from every corner of the organization. Include your security, insurance, legal, securities, and other specialist advisers in the planning process. Consider all the far-flung ramifications that a crisis poses and give your plan the benefit of expert advice from every affected area.

Secure Senior and Middle Management's Blessing. Everyone must believe in and feel comfortable with the plan if it is to work effectively on the firing line. Second-guessing the plan in the heat of the moment could defeat all the time and effort spent on creating the plan.

Keep a Solid Grounding in Reality. Don't expect that the CEO always will be available to direct the response to every problem. Don't expect that "someone" will type press releases, call all the shift supervisors, or magically tie up all the loose ends. The plan shouldn't call for a satellite-delivered press conference if your firm could never afford that. Poring over the details (and related costs) today prevents explaining the screwups tomorrow.

Be As Specific and Thorough As Possible. Generalities (e.g., "contact someone in senior management upon learning of the emergency") are meaningless in the face of a crisis. People need to open up that *Emergency Handbook* and find specific instructions on exactly what they're to do.

Clearly Indicate Responsibility by Name or Title. Leave no doubt as to whose job it is to do all that has to be done. The critical nature of a crisis affords no leeway for wasteful duplication or inattention to vital tasks.

Specify a Crisis Manager. Someone must be in charge and have the final word. When the dam is bursting, there's no time for rival colleagues to debate the best approach to the problem. The CEO may or may not be the best selection for crisis manager, but in any case leave no doubt as to where the decision-making authority rests (outline a contingent line of succession).

Indicate the Official Spokesperson. Concentrate the communications flow by appointing one person or team as the official spokesperson. Discourage other members of your organization from speaking to the media. Multiple, disharmonious information sources spawn confusion and make it difficult for the press to know what's accurate or most current. This was a major problem during the Three Mile Island nuclear crisis.

Clearly Define Priorities,. Make sure people know to call the fire department before "Eyewitness News." Emphasize that in all cases safety comes first!

Be Mindful of Logistics. The vice-president of public affairs may not secure a flight to the remote plant site for several agonizing hours. What then? How will central management and field management communicate? Will managers confirm telephone communications via telegram or facsimile, and are there adequate provisions to do this? Where will out-of-town managers stay during the crisis?

Where will press briefings be held: at the site, in a nearby hotel, or in another facility? Will your company encourage the press to call for updates? Who will take those calls? Over what telephone lines will the press calls be taken? Will the news media need to compete for telephone access over the same lines serving calls from employees and members of the general public? When the information demand exceeds management's physical ability to supply immediate answers, who will take the messages? How will they get to the right people? Who will see to it that all requests are answered in a timely manner?

Keep in mind that the crisis will generate greater phone volume into the company switchboard. Many interested constituencies will bombard your receptionists with information requests. You'll need more than 9-to-5 phone coverage. Your staff will be overworked and tired. Plan to provide reinforcements. (During the 1982 Tylenol crisis, Johnson and Johnson set up special phone lines and enlisted volunteers and a large answering service to take questions from the public. Over 136,000 calls were received in just 11 days.)

If the news media descend on a facility in person, how will they be accommodated with outbound phones, copy machines, typewriters, electric current for their portable computers, camera, and recording gear? How about food for their sustenance? (Some believe the way to a reporter's heart is through his or her stomach. At the very least, it stands to reason that a hungry, tired, and frustrated reporter is less likely to show empathy to an organization embroiled in a crisis than one who's been fed and accommodated with adequate support facilities, as well as provided with truthful and helpful information.)

While you're comfortably in the planning stage, identify the vendors you'll need to call on for food, beverages, office supplies, temporary office help (to supplement your overworked staff), phone facilities, and so on. When considering telecommunications, keep in mind that deregulation of the telephone business eliminated one-stop-shopping for phone services. Discuss emergency communications with your local dial tone service provider, your long-distance carrier, and phone equipment vendor. Find out how you could quickly establish additional phone services to aid press, government, and safety personnel. Talk to your phone services suppliers now.

Remember that disasters don't always happen during convenient business hours. How will your plan work if trouble strikes at 3:00 a.m. on a Sunday? Anticipate the worst that could happen in off hours and when no one of authority is minding the office.

Always List an Alternative. Cover contingencies. What if Ms. Brown is sick, away on vacation, or not answering her page? Have at least an A & B list for everything.

Keep the Plan Current. Names, addressess, telephone numbers and relationships change periodically. An out-of-date plan may be as harmful as no plan at all if it wastes precious time in a true emergency. Review and revise it frequently.

Rehearse Implementing the Plan. Go through some drills. Discover the plan's shortcomings in the comfort of a simulation. Make sure everyone understands—and is prepared to handle—their responsibilities. (Test press readiness by allowing an outsider to interview the appointed, as well as the nonofficial, spokespersons. Analyze their statements.)

Unless everyone in the organization understands the importance of the emergency plan, it's worthless. A disaster specialist with AT & T in Los Angeles told me that many businesses both comfort and delude themselves by saying they have a crisis plan—there's a "minuscule plan somewhere so the management believes there's a plan in place, but many of these companies have never tested their plans. . . . If there really is a disaster, their business is going down the tubes, literally."

Union Carbide suffered negative publicity and embarrassment when it apparently failed to follow its own disaster plan at its plant in Institute, West Virginia, when a toxic gas leak sent more than 130 people to hospitals. The *Wall Street Journal*, citing a local emergency services official, reported in August 1985 that "under an emergency plan developed in response to the Bhopal disaster, a Union Carbide official should have reported to a command post near the plant, but one never came."[3] Another *Journal* article reported allegations that officials at the chemical plant waited too long to warn local authorities that the toxic gas had escaped into the air.[4]

Your emergency plan must adequately anticipate emergency situations and provide realistic response mechanisms. *Everyone* must take the plan seriously. After all, as consultant Littlejohn suggests, the goal of going through this whole planning exercise is nothing less than "organizational survival."

Communicating Control amid Chaos

The media and the corporation are each dealing with the crisis for the first time.

James E. Lukaszewski

There is no time during an emergency to read the disaster plan.

Nate McClure

When the long-dreaded emergency erupts, how well you manage communications may determine whether the emergency becomes the organizational equivalent of a cold or of terminal cancer.

As pointed out in chapter 1, it's about impossible in this age of OmniMedia to hide emergent bad news from the press. The news media (which constantly monitor the radio traffic of emergency agencies and inspect court and government records) show an uncanny ability to learn—and disseminate—details of crises nearly the instant they happen. As management consultant Steven Fink points out, "If the media can communicate the news the instant it happens . . . a company *must* be prepared to respond almost as fast."[1]

This chapter examines strategies and tactics for your critical crisis communications.

React Proportionately. Before calling out to the major media to expose some corporate crisis, you need to assess realistically how interested the general public might be in the information. You'll disclose information that you're revealing only to comply with Securities and Exchange Commission regulations very differently from information that affects the immediate safety of your surrounding community.

Manage external communication in a manner appropriate to the crisis. Determining what in fact constitutes a crisis is key to a proportionate response. Harold Carr, Boeing Company's vice-president of public relations and advertising, suggests an interesting approach. He recommends that an organization facing what may be defined as a crisis should delineate between a crucial time when the company is truly threatened and "the temporary discomfort of unwanted media attention."[2]

In other words, adverse publicity doesn't necessarily constitute a crisis. Sometimes excessive news coverage of an event spurred more by media competition than newsworthiness, Carr argues, can lead to a perceived crisis for executives. Sound crisis communications management requires the company to keep a cool head and not overreact to a media-inspired crisis.

Gerber Products, the baby goods company, took dramatic crisis action in 1984 after a glass fragment was reportedly found in a jar of its baby food and after an isolated shipping accident caused some glass to find its way into eight jars of juice. At the cost of millions, Gerber recalled more than 700,000 jars of juice and baby food. The company's sales and stock price both dropped (sales by 6 percent, the per share price by over 18 percent). Company executives later conceded that they had overreacted to the incident.

Gerber reacted differently in 1986, when it received a wave of consumer complaints alleging to have found glass fragments in its baby food. While supermarkets in several states pulled Gerber baby foods off shelves, the company stood squarely behind its products and refused to recall them. *Advertising Age* described the company's posture as "tossing out the 'Tylenol textbook'" in its response to the widespread allegations.

After the Food and Drug Administration (FDA) found no harmful glass particles in a sample of 40,000 jars (and Gerber found no pattern to the complaints indicative of a systemic problem), the company went on the offensive. This time, rather than a crisis recall, Gerber—doubting the veracity of many complaints made against it—asserted that there was "no reason for all the hoopla." It filed a $150-million suit against a Maryland ban on one of its products and threatened lawsuits against other states considering a ban.[3]

One way to help keep a potentially damaging incident from mushrooming into a crisis is to balance the news coverage of it with a sense of perspective in the company's remarks. Merrill Lynch demonstrated this when the Securities and Exchange Commission censored the brokerage firm for failing to supervise one of its sales people. The salesman was accused of defrauding several investors. A censure by the SEC clearly holds significant potential for damage to a securities company. But Merrill Lynch issued a statement putting the 1985 censure into perspective. It described the incident prompting the censure as "a matter in which some of the events occurred nearly five years ago, and . . . involves an account executive who was fired 2 ½ years ago." The statement also pointed out that the company cooperated with the government, acknowledged that it made mistakes, and said "we have agreed to settle the SEC's charges, if only as an effort to put these events involving a single individual to rest."[4]

Merrill Lynch took its lumps in public, but by helping to frame the bad publicity in a context, it managed to emerge from the incident with its image mostly unscathed.

Make Decisions. One way to view a crisis is to think of it as a series of decisions that haven't been made yet. Certainly, in the time of crisis one doesn't want to make hasty and therefore bad decisions. But delay in admitting a crisis situation exists or in mobilizing to respond wastes time and tends to exacerbate the damage. While no one wants to cry wolf, it's better to err on the side of false alarms than to miss an early response to a brewing disaster. (Warren M. Anderson, CEO of Union Carbide, announced in August 1985 a new policy requiring plant personnel to notify local officials immediately in the event of a toxic chemical accident. His advice is sound. "You pull the cord first and then apologize later [if] it was unnecessary."[5])

The difference between a minor incident and a disaster may well be a few minutes' warning and immediate action. This is why you can't afford to think an impending problem ad infinitum. Gather the best available information, consider the alternatives, make the best decisions you can at the time. Waiting for the ultimate best decisions paralyzes the organization and makes it appear indecisive.

When a banker in a small Wisconsin town read his newspaper one Sunday he knew he had trouble. The paper erroneously listed the bank as having lost money, according to a federal report. The bank president took action fast. He had to; everyone he met that day wanted to know what went wrong. The banker called the paper that made the error and also enlisted the support of others to help set the record straight. Not content to wait for his customers to find the correction in Monday's papers, the president and some aides personally visited area coffee shops to deliver copies of the reassuring news.[6]

On a much grander scale, Johnson and Johnson swallowed hard in 1982 and destroyed 31 million bottles of Tylenol capsules after it quickly determined that it couldn't assure consumers that the bottles were not tainted. The cost of recalling the capsules and introducing substitutes was about $300 million.

The company swallowed hard again in 1986 when it announced that it would stop producing over-the-counter medication in capsules. That announcement came nine days after a woman's death was linked to cyanide-tainted Tylenol capsules that were taken from a tamper-resistant bottle. Stores in 25 states removed the capsules from their shelves, and the governor of New York ordered a statewide ban on selling Tylenol capsules. In making the announcement that Johnson and Johnson would no longer make over-the-counter medicine in capsules, James E. Burke, the company's chairman, admitted that "the company can no longer guarantee the safety of these capsules."

J & J pulled its capsules off the market and scrapped their production. Estimated cost: $150 million in 1986. (Capsule sales represented about $158 million of Tylenol's total 1985 sales of approximately $525 million. The brand as a whole contributed about $123 million to J & J's 1985 profits of $614 million.)

President Reagan praised the decision by Burke to recall the capsules, saying it represented "the very highest ideals of corporate responsibility and grace under pressure." Nonetheless, Chairman Burke revealed to *U.S. News & World Report* a less idealistic rationale for the drastic action. Johnson and Johnson executives "could see public confidence [in Tylenol] beginning to erode again . . . We didn't see how the reputation of, first, Tylenol and, more important perhaps, Johnson and Johnson could survive." Decisive marketing, not altruism, guided the decision.

Making decisions and taking action solves crisis problems. Overanalyzing creates doubt. Doubt creates fear and a greater need for thinking and analyzing. Mental grid lock and inaction ensue. Precious time and credibility are lost.

H. J. Heinz, the food giant, silently sat on its corporate hands in the face of allegations in 1985 that its Star-Kist subsidiary had shipped a million cans of rotten tuna in Canada. While management sat mum—refusing for weeks to respond to the press or public—revenues from tuna sales dived 90 percent. Star-Kist president Richard L. Beattie said the company was "massacred in the press." In retrospect, Thomas McIntosh, a Heinz spokesman, said the delay in responding to the press "was ignorance" and "truly embarrassing." Heinz learned from its painful experience, and since the incident, it's prepared for other crises.[7]

When an organization is pressured by a crisis, swift and decisive action instills confidence, beats the rumor mill to the punch, and can keep a situation from mushrooming into a crisis.

Use an Appropriate Mouthpiece. The rank of the official spokesperson should reflect the severity of the crisis. The chief executive officer of a firm need not push himself out front on every urgent matter. In fact, the CEO's involvement signals a severity that may not represent the relative importance of the matter. Sometimes a division head, plant manager, or other junior but authoritative figure might be preferable to a more senior executive in the role as spokesperson.

If the appropriate authority is not well suited to standing in the heat of the public spotlight, a skilled communicator (e.g., someone on the PR staff) can relay a statement attributed to the authority. This melds the force of corporate authority with professional presentation. A possible drawback to this approach is the inevitable time lag in communications between the "pinch presenter" and the official authority. This factor becomes especially acute as developments change rapidly or as the press insists on answers to questions not anticipated in the presenter's prepared statement.

When deciding whom to push out front, a corporation needs to assess quickly the trade-off between appearing responsive, appearing to react at the appropriate level, and communicating skillfully.

If you select a team approach to disseminating information (with two or more officials out front dispensing information), make sure the team members communicate effectively among themselves. Be absolutely sure the choir is singing not only from the same song book but that they're in tune and on the same beat of the same hymn every measure of the way.

Regardless of who's appointed the official spokesperson, make sure to identify that person or team for the press. Promise that the official channel will keep them informed, and journalists will focus their attention on that outlet for as long as he/she/they speak truthfully and in a timely manner.

If your statements seem to draw or lend themselves to suspicion, establish credibility by enlisting a disinterested third party to validate your statements. Seek someone such as a government agency official, respected politician, clergyman, university professor, independent expert, or trade group representative to rally support for your position.

Direct the Information Flow. Follow your crisis plan's priority for disseminating information to internal senior management, government officials, employees, customers, and the press. It sounds trite, but make sure that the left and right hands of the organization each know the movements of the other. Real problems ought not be compounded by deficient internal communications. Marathon Oil suffered criticism in the *Wall Street Journal* for its "lack of preparation" and "uncoordinated reaction" to Mobil's hostile takeover attempt in late 1981. Citing stock market analysts, the *Journal* reported that "the company's New York investor relations office first learned from outsiders—reporters—that Marathon had hastily called a news conference in Findlay [Ohio] to respond to the Mobil offer."[8] (Later, of course, Marathon regrouped and launched an effective public relations assault on Mobil.)

Notify the media just as soon as you're ready to speak intelligently about the situation. Being the first to release bad news gives you momentum and control over the information. By being the first voice the media hear, you frame the discussion. If the news comes from some other party—prosecutor, government agency, plaintiff's attorney— you'll be on the defensive, always responding to someone else's agenda and terms.

When it is time to talk to the press, rank priority for press contacts. Depending on the situation, you need to balance the sometimes competing needs of network and wire service journalists (the widest reach), live radio and television broadcasts (immediate need and reach—could be key to calming or instructing concerned local citizens), general print media, and others such as trade, foreign, and specialized press. Your crisis plan should assign the priorities appropriate to the type of emergency to which your firm is responding.

Employ the correct means of communicating the crisis details. Should you disseminate information only in written press releases, in a full press conference environment, or in one-on-one interviews? The answer to this question, of course, is: It depends.

In almost every situation affecting public health or safety, written communications are unacceptably slow and unresponsive. In other matters, such as complicated financial dealings that may affect stock performance, written communication probably is preferable to other forms.

The press conference, for situations of major import, has certain advantages: you can reach a great many journalists and their respective publics quickly, and you maintain control of the situation to some degree. But you risk finding 10, 50, or 100 or more antagonists swinging at you all at one time in something that resembles a cruel caricature of a circus. Consider as well that press conferences are typically cold, clinical, and short on interpersonal subtleties that can affect such critical coverage.

One-on-one interviews consume the valuable time of executives who may need to concentrate on dealing with the immediate challenges of the crisis. But interviews offer the advantage of intimacy between a reporter and the manager-as-human, a quality that can help shape the tone of news coverage. A happy medium may be found in having several ranking company officials holding small group interviews with key journalists. This may be done in person or via a conference call. Some reporters may balk at sharing an interview, but their egos likely won't get in the way of their news sense for long, and if the interview goes well, the fact that it wasn't exclusive really won't matter.

In any crisis situation you'll probably enlist several media communication techniques. There are many possibilities and no magic formula. Considering all the possibilities before the heat of the moment, however, saves precious time and positions the organization to meet public communication challenges forthrightly.

Something else to keep in mind about crisis information flow: Remember to keep internal information flowing. This gives confidence to your staff and allows them to continue concentrating on their regular responsibilities. The more accurate information that's flowing in an organization during a crisis, the less likely that rumors and idle speculation will debilitate your work force.

The more you contain the crisis through timely revelations of truth, the less likely it is to cripple normal activity. Allow the crisis to direct the entire organization's focus only if it's beneficial to do so. Make sure your crisis management team members have the support they need to devote sufficient concentration, energy, and time to the company's most pressing problem. One of the best ways to do that is to make sure the rest of the corporation attends to normal business activity.

The goal is to have the company manage the crisis, not vice versa. Every employee is an information conduit. Regardless of their positions on the organization chart, all the company's employees know friends, relatives, and neighbors who'll likely try to get the "inside skinny" on what's really happening at your crisis-plagued shop. The better informed you keep every employee, the better your chances at avoiding rumors and dissenting unnamed sources in speculative reports.

Keep your major customers (and sales people in remote locations) apprised of developments. Customers will look to their sales reps to supply answers and reassurance. In fact, when your organization finds itself in a public emergency situation, have the sales force initiate contact with customers to build confidence and head off rumors. (Early in the 1982 Tylenol crisis, McNeil Consumer Products Company, the Johnson and Johnson subsidiary that markets Tylenol, sent about 450,000 electronically printed messages by first class mail to distributors and members of the medical community to respond to questions raised by media coverage of the incident.)

During the acute crisis period, consider suspending all product advertising. This is standard procedure for airlines; they have standing orders for media outlets to pull any scheduled ads in the event of a plane crash. Even if your advertising delivers positive messages about your product or company, its very presence may remind people of your current front-page trouble.

Conversely, you may wish to increase advertising immediately after the crisis to reinforce positive information about your product or firm. The advertising messages may or may not directly address the crisis situation; this is a judgment call for management (and its communication consultants) to make based on the merits of a particular case. Johnson and Johnson officials suspended advertising for Tylenol within a day of news reports that linked cyanide-laced capsules to the deaths of seven people in Chicago. Less than two weeks later, the company placed full-page ads in major newspapers across the country offering to exchange Tylenol tablets for the now infamous capsules. And within three weeks, the company broadcast ads featuring the medical director of the Tylenol subsidiary who foretold of Tylenol capsules' return in tamper-resistant packages.

Remember Safety First. Journalists tend to ignore the warning that "curiosity killed the cat." Press cats are a breed whose bravado in chasing a story sometimes exceeds their common sense.

Expect pressure from reporters to personally inspect dangerous areas with news or dramatic value. If a reasonably equipped person can safely enter an otherwise dangerous area, anticipate the journalists' demands to view the site firsthand. Prepare to outfit reporters and photographers with necessary equipment (hard hats, gas masks, protective coverings) and provide a competent guide.

Or prepare to take a paternalistic stand and forbid access if that's what's necessary to ensure the press's safety. News media people don't respond well to paternalism. If you try to keep them out of an area, even for their own safety and well-being, they'll be suspicious. Some reporters are more than willing to risk their fannies in pursuit of the public's right to know.

Nonetheless, it is your property and your responsibility to avoid endangering the lives or safety of someone on your property.

Do not use safety as a smoke screen for hiding unpleasant revelations. The unpleasant secret will be revealed in a short time, anyway. Once you've hidden behind a bogus claim for protecting the press's safety while your only true interest was in protecting self-interest, you've crossed the point of no return for credibility.

Disarm suspicion by promising and scheduling (if possible) a visit to the area in question as soon as safety is not a problem. If entry to the forbidden zone must be restricted to highly qualified personnel, consider providing the press uncensored photographs made by your personnel. Provide both safety and disclosure in a credible fashion.

Maintain Information Quality. While in a crisis situation, prepare to provide the press the best information you can at the time. Try to answer the basic questions the news media need answered by following the rudiments of reporting: who, what, where, when, why, how.

Frame your information in the context of the public's interest in the situation. Explain what the crisis means to your constituents, not just the company (are your products safe, will shipments be impeded, are normal business activities proceeding?).

Provide full disclosure but sift for the relevant. Don't drown reporters in minutiae; rather, let them know minor details are available for the asking.

In the heat of the moment, be disciplined. Don't speculate, don't estimate, don't guess. Don't entertain hypothetical questions, don't be dramatic, don't place blame. Disseminate facts and disarm speculation and rumor the best of your ability.

If you don't have the answer to a question, say you don't, and in the same breath promise to get the answer.

Provide details as updates are available. Be timely, but make sure the information you pass along is correct. Double-check everything you can. To rephrase an old Associated Press slogan: Make right sure they get it from you first, but first get it right! Establish and keep to a briefing schedule to help the press avoid the stake-out mentality.

Keep the information as simple as possible. Highly technical information presents the press with difficulty even in optimum circumstances. The stressful environment of a crisis only heightens the need for complex or confusing information to be clearly understood. Your crisis communications plan should call for advance preparation of charts, diagrams, and explanations that can be distributed to the press quickly.

Admittedly, whether your role in the crisis is victim (such as Tylenol's, or as might be the case in a fire) or bad guy (as in a strike or contamination incident) affects the tone of the press coverage. But whatever role the company is initially assigned, your briefings ought to show human concern and strength touched by human vulnerability. The tone of your communications should reflect calm and confidence to reassure the public. Your goal is not only to provide information but to reinforce the organization's credibility, to allay fears, and to (re)build support.

Expect second-guessing. People want inordinate amounts of information in a crisis. The public appetite may be greater than your ability to feed it with official information. Critics, Monday morning quarterbacks, and speculators will dish out opinions and theories to meet the hunger. (The *Kansas City Star* won a Pulitzer Prize after paying an engineering consultant to comment on the cause of the tragic collapse of the Kansas City Hyatt skywalks.)

Pay attention to the discussion, but don't preoccupy yourself with trying to squelch it or control it. You can't. Be aware of what's being said, counter serious misinformation, and provide as much accurate information as you can. Place some faith in the public's ability to discriminate between the incredible and the indisputable.

CANDOR WINS PRAISE

Above all, be truthful. Be honest, be direct.

It would be difficult to find candor any more direct (or refreshing) than a statement made by Frank Agosti, manager of nuclear operations for Detroit Edison. Agosti made his comment following the early 1986 announcement that the Nuclear Regulatory Commission found serious safety violations concerning containment of radioactive material at an Edison nuclear facility. Those violations could have endangered workers. In good PR form, Agosti told the *Wall Street Journal* that the utility had reported the violations to the NRC and was correcting any problems that had not yet been corrected. He spoke as a concerned and credible human and not just as a corporate official when he admitted, "Violation of containment is about as bad as you can get . . . We should have been smart enough not to have done these kinds of things."[9]

Agosti's candid comment showed the kind of courage, remorse, and humanity that is so often missing from corporate responses to bad news. I believe such a response speeds the credibility rebuilding process light years ahead of defensive "yeah, but" statements from unnamed company representatives.

But did the company resent the candid remarks? Did speaking bluntly hurt Agosti's career?

"Not at all; I'm now vice-president of nuclear operations," he told me in a March 1987 interview. Candor, he said, is the best policy. "The bottom line is when you've let people down by making mistakes, either through omission or commission, you can't just say 'I misunderstood.' You have to take your lumps and then do a better job . . . Our company policy is to be a good neighbor. Honesty in the press—even when you're wrong—is part of that philosophy."

When a chair lift malfunctioned at the Keystone ski resort near Dillon, Colorado, in December 1985, skiers were thrown to the ground from as high as 40 feet. The accident injured 49, hospitalized 24, frightened more than 300 other skiers riding the lift, and made national news. The resort handled the crisis beautifully. It put into action an emergency plan that it drafted eight years earlier. A command post team gathered information about the injured, kept track of the hospitals they'd entered, and opened phone lines to the press and public to relay information. The press responded with accolades. Times Mirror's *Denver Post* ran a feature story titled "Crisis Management Pays, Keystone's disaster planning cut confusion." Scripps-Howard's *Rocky Mountain News* ran an editorial under the headline, "Response was Magnificent." It praised "those who helped in the (tragedy's) aftermath, including those Keystone officials who were so open with information."[10]

These are the success stories. I'm sorry to say that all news events aren't managed with such finesse. Interestingly, one of the best examples of how not to do it comes from a gaffe committed by none other than the 13,000-member Public Relations Society of America. In August 1986, Anthony Franco of Detroit resigned as president of the organization after being charged by the SEC with insider trading violations. In a page-one article, the *Wall Street Journal* observed in late September 1986 that "the PRSA never sent out a press release announcing the charges or the resignation. . . . Meanwhile, the Franco affair is being dragged out, and Mr. Franco and the PRSA are being dragged though the mud."[11]

The moral: Don't try to bury your bad news. The press will find it. Don't waste your time trying to sugarcoat bad news. The news media will strip the veneer and will expose the naked truth that lies beneath (and they'll be angry that you wasted their time in the process).

Reveal bad news in total. The slow drip, drip, drip of damaging facts piques public interest and surrounds the story in an air of a drama unfolding. Everyone loves a mystery. Solve it a little at a time and public interest grows with each small revelation (e.g., the Watergate scandal). Conversely, revealing all there is to tell right off the bat allows the media to tell everything in one shot. The resulting bang may be deafening for a brief moment, but then it's in one ear, out the other, and quickly forgotten in the face of noise from other news events. If there's nothing more to tell, there's nothing more to print.

Naturally, not every crisis can be put to bed simply by issuing a press release that says, "We goofed, we're sorry, we'll do better from now on." Sometimes the facts just aren't available to release in one shot; sometimes the problem is more systemic than incidental. Such was the case with Union Carbide. It suffered voluminous bad press related to its Bhopal, India, and Institute, West Virginia, disasters. "Oops, we're sorry" was not enough to keep the government investigators or a concerned public and press from asking many more questions than had been answered in company news releases. A year after Carbide's name was burned into eternal infamy for the world's worst industrial accident, three major business publications took a look at the company and found it wanting.

Forbes examined the rise in Union Carbide's stock price from under $33 per share right after the Bhopal incident to $60 a share just 11 months later. The magazine observed, "The action in the stock . . . has more to do with expectations of a takeover or a whole or partial liquidation than it does with a vote of confidence in management." The article concluded, "Give us a chance, Carbide management seems to be saying to shareholders, pointing to the vigor of its 'restructuring' effort. Too little, too late?"[12]

The *Wall Street Journal* also examined the state of Union Carbide one year later. It recalled how following the Bhopal tragedy that killed at least 1,750 people, Union Carbide's credibility was "quickly shattered . . . (when) a chemical cloud leaked from the company's Institute, W. Va., plant and 135 persons were injured." The article examined the company's management performance in light of unsettled, lawsuits, a possible takeover, poor morale, restructuring, and attempts to portray the company's troubles as being all in the past. "Even more telling," the article continued, "are the company's current perceptions of the Institute leak and of the plight of the Bhopal victims. In both instances, company officials now blame the media for what it terms public overreaction."[13]

Business Week, taking a one-year-later look at Union Carbide, observed that "Chairman Warren M. Anderson once said he would devote the rest of his career to resolving the problems caused by the [Bhopal] accident. Now, he says: 'I overreacted.' "[14]

Slick public relations, accusing the media of hysteria, or trying to retract earlier statements aren't enough to gloss over real problems that thwart public confidence. Having a good public reputation is still rooted in preventing tragedies, and, when they do implode upon you, handling them adeptly.

It bears repeating: There is no such thing as retroactive goodwill.

Rumors: A Crisis in Communications

What some invent the rest enlarge.

Jonathan Swift

A special and uniquely frustrating kind of crisis occasionally confronts an organization, and it's centered almost entirely on communications. It's the rumor, an unsubstantiated allegation that may be whispered along the grapevine or regarded as unchallenged truth even by responsible persons in positions of authority. Rumors can either constitute a crisis all by themselves or exacerbate the confusion and tension surrounding a larger crisis.

In the context of supplementing a bona fide crisis, rumors fill information voids. People have a need for information about important events. We want to know what happened or what it means. We're frightened of, or at least insecure with, an information vacuum. There is something comforting in learning more about serious events. (I admit to tuning around the radio dial desperately at 2:00 a.m. one morning seeking reports about an earthquake I'd just experienced in southern California. I'd already confirmed that my family and belongings were safe, but nevertheless I felt a compelling need to learn more about this experience that had just shaken up my sleepy household.)

When we lack information about something we consider important, we're in the dark. Most of us fear the dark because we imagine horrors lurking in the blackness. Information illuminates the dark; it delivers us into the comforting light of understanding. So we welcome information, any information about something that concerns us. Rumors spring up when real information is painfully absent. Speculation, innuendo, allegations, and even farfetched explanations seem more satisfying to us than nothing at all.

This human need for the reassurance of information is the reason that, in the face of a major tragedy, radio and television news anchors stay on the air in marathon talkfests, sometimes saying nothing more than, "We really don't know anything more than what we've been repeating for the last several hours."

The implication, of course, is that you should feed the press and public appetite for information when you face a crisis. When word of the event is released (intentionally or otherwise), it's quickly trailed by the dreaded information vacuum. A company in crisis faces a simple choice: fill the vacuum with your information, or let someone else fill it with theirs. Obviously, this should be no contest. But if you wait too long or offer too little news to fill the vacuum, other forces will rush to fill it.

Some rumors appear to embody spontaneous combustion—from out of nowhere and without warning they create a firestorm. These are the rumors we've all heard: about worms or rat meat in burgers at the local fast food outlet, about creepy creatures in bottles of soda or the pockets of clothing sold at a retail outlet, about glass slivers in packaged foods, about the satanists or religious fanatics who control a major corporation. Potentially devastating rumors like these often have their origins in bored or unstable people who tell a tall tale to amuse themselves or to stir things up. It may be a crackpot who starts the rumor, but if it's a news anchor who broadcasts it on "Eyewitness News," watch out!

Whether a rumor starts for entertainment or to fill an information void, once it circulates, it's difficult to recall or squash. This is especially true if the rumor has been legitimized by press coverage. Once a rumor has attained the status of news, it's no longer a rumor, it's half a step away from gospel truth. As T. K. Smith, vice-president of public affairs for Dow Chemical, observed, "even *minimal coverage* to an unsubstantiated claim" can generate "a significant level of public concern."[1]

This is because people ascribe credibility to reports they see or hear in the news media. "If it weren't true, they wouldn't say it," the old saying goes.

What course of action should a company follow once it finds itself the victim of a vicious rumor? The truth is that the experts are divided. One camp suggests ignoring the rumor and concentrating on counterpublicity to combat any impact the rumor may have. The risk of tackling the rumor directly is that you may alert people who've not heard the rumor to the problem you're denying. The impact may be to spread the rumor to a wider audience than would otherwise have heard it.

Say, for example, you make soap, and the rumor is that some people found rotten fish heads in your brand of soap and that these disgusting remains made some children contract an awful illness. Rather than call a press conference to deny the rumor (and thereby spread it), you might step up advertising that proclaims the purity of ingredients that go into your soap. You might also advertise testimonials showing your customers' great satisfaction with the soap.

This indirect approach never alerts the public to the existence of a destructive rumor. It puts its faith in the ability of a credible, positive message to outweigh one that's obviously farfetched and incredible.

The other camp of image experts says rumors should be defused clearly and publicly. This approach has you going to the media and saying, "Look, we've received several reports of a rumor about our soap. People have spread a ridiculous story that there are fish heads carrying a harmful bacteria embedded in the soap. Some versions of the lie claim that kids got sick from this stuff. Help us squash this terrible falsehood."

Both approaches to the problem can be appropriate. Your challenge as a manager is to find a balance between inaction, action, and overreaction. If you're staring a rumor problem in the face, I'd suggest you get a copy of *Rumor in the Marketplace*, an informative book by an authority on the effects of rumors on commerce, Fredrick Koenig of Tulane University.[2]

In the meantime, here is a summary of factors you and your communications advisers should consider when responding to a rumor.

The Origin of the Rumor. Track down the very first occurrence of the rumor that comes to your attention. Take every rumor report seriously. Ask for the help of the person who was kind enough to inform you of the rumor. Have somebody with an impressive title get on an airplane and diplomatically confront the accuser. Your concern and swift response will telegraph the gravity you're ascribing to the problem. A prankster likely will be dissuaded from targeting your company again. A rumor that's crushed immediately is a rumor that isn't a problem very long.

The Veracity People Assign to It. Find out how people regard the rumor. Do most people consider it a silly story, or does a significant portion of the rational population take it seriously? If the public reacts to the story as though it reflects reality, prepare to react quickly and seriously.

If the rumor originated with a local minister, teacher, politician, or other opinion leader, you'll have a tougher time convincing people that the story is nothing more than the ramblings of a kook. Try to persuade the offending party to retract the story. Get other opinion leaders in the community to assist by setting the record straight with their own constituents, perhaps writing them a letter, placing an article in a publication, or writing a letter to the editor on your behalf. The mission is to get enough debunking information into the public arena so that anyone hearing the rumor would feel like a fool to believe it.

If the rumor already found its way into the local press, you'll need to combat it there. Try to do this with editorial matter—a press conference, interviews, or the like. In most cases, you'll find the local press very cooperative (unless you've previously given them reason not to be). Even so, you may need to supplement this public relations effort with paid advertisements that reinforce the rumor-bashing message. In order to make this determination and to avoid embarrassing overkill, commission some opinion research. Keep working to defeat the rumor until you know it's gone.

When the rumor has been crushed, follow the antirumor campaign with positive, image-building messages that reinforce a desirable perception of your firm or product.

The Area of Circulation for the Rumor. Determine how widespread the problem is. Measure in terms beyond just geography. You'll want to know the degree of awareness among your significant publics. Commissioning opinion research to gauge the impact of the rumor could be a sound investment. (In 1984, Gerber Products responded to some reports of glass being found in its baby food by running special TV announcements. Television, with its wide consumer reach, served to publicize the reports rather than disarm them. Later, a spokesman assessed the effect by saying that "running TV ads just had a negative impact because it publicized something that few people knew about.")[3]

If by the time the situation comes to your attention it's pervasive or no longer very local in nature, you'll need to consider a wider reach for stomping out the rumor. Chasing down the origin of the rumor may be much more difficult. You may need to spend a fair amount of money to crush a far-flung rumor. To contain the impact of the rumor, restrict your response only to those areas where the problem has surfaced. Respond with a rifle, not a shotgun.

Do what must be done, spend what it takes, but spend wisely. It is your credibility, even your livelihood, that's at stake here.

The Existence of Press Coverage. If the news media have already given credence to the rumor by reporting it, you're no longer dealing with a rumor but a negative news story,. Your response must be swift, decisive, and appropriate. Don't waste time berating the press for contributing to the problem; rather, humbly ask for the media's help in setting the record straight.

Word of mouth has long been the most powerful form of advertising. It can work for you or against you. Don't hesitate to engage in some serious rumor-bashing should the need arise.

Soothing the Postcrisis Hangover

The corporate disaster becomes totally overshadowed immediately with the search for the guilty.

James E. Lukaszewski

The public seldom forgives twice.

Johann Kaspar Lavater

Handling communications during a crisis—gathering and issuing information, revising strategies, returning reporters' phone calls, and so on—
is hard work. After you've coped with the frenzy of the emergency, you
might be tempted to sit, catch your breath, and risk breaking your arm
patting yourself on the back.

But the reality is that you've accomplished only half of the crisis communications task. The job isn't done when the reporters stop calling.
Your challenge is to combat the negative publicity, generate positive
press coverage, and rebuild confidence in your company and products
in the minds of your various constituents. The postcrisis communications
job demands that you commit physically, psychically, and financially.
But, as the following examples demonstrate, the effort is critical to un-
doing the damage.

In July of 1984, a McDonald's restaurant in San Ysidro, California,
was the site of mass murder as a gunman brutally killed 21 people. The
tragedy devastated the small town and drew national news coverage.

Quietly, without seeking any media attention, McDonald's executives flew to the California border town to attend a funeral for some of the victims. Just as quietly, without telling even the local police (to assure that it drew no publicity), the company took down its sign in the middle of the night and closed its store. By doing this, McDonald's spared itself and the local community from having to live with a reminder of the great tragedy. The dignity displayed by the company drew praise from the public and press. Later, McDonald's opened a store just blocks from its former location, and sales exceeded those of its predecessor.[1]

In 1986, when tamper-resistant packages failed to prevent another cyanide poisoning linked to Tylenol capsules, Johnson and Johnson planned to spend up to $150 million to restore the Tylenol brand once again. It placed full-page ads in hundreds of newspapers across the country offering to exchange bottles of caplets for bottles of capsules. It again held press conferences and sent mailgrams and sales people to medical professionals to introduce them to the caplet form of Tylenol (which had been available for a few years). And, it again took its case to the television airwaves via interviews and—after some intentional delay, so as not to look insensitive—commercials to ask consumers to trust the Tylenol brand name and switch to caplets. J & J's credibility carried favor with Wall Street analysts who remained bullish on the company's stock, even in the face of huge expenses. The company also received words of praise from the FDA and positive publicity from the press as it repeated its challenge to endear an endangered brand to consumers.

SmithKline Beckman Corporation, maker of Contac, faced a similar challenge during 1986. It pulled its capsules from store shelves across the nation when it discovered that some bottles were contaminated with rat poison—the work of a man trying to affect the drug company's stock price. SmithKline reintroduced the product by offering a new caplet option and selling the medication in a new tamper-evident package. It launched the brand's renewal with a $40-million promotion campaign. (Contac had had total sales of about $60 million the year before.) Within months, sales rang in at their strongest pace in four years, ranking the drug as the nation's best-selling cold remedy.[2]

Sometimes, it takes a fair amount of time to put bad publicity and keen press interest behind you, especially if your dirty laundry keeps drifting toward center stage. Take, for example, E. F. Hutton. The company suffered severely negative publicity after pleading guilty, in May 1985, to charges of illegal check overdrafting some years before. Week after week, month after month, and then year after year, the papers dribbled out details of Hutton's troubles and trials.

The company tried to put the best face on the affair. It hired Griffin Bell, former attorney general in the Carter administration, to conduct an investigation into what the *New York Times* termed a "fraud scheme." Bell's law firm produced, and Hutton made available for the asking, a 184-page document that reviewed, with some candor, problems in the Hutton organization. Along with Bell's report, the firm distributed a 5-page, single-spaced news release outlining corrective action the company was taking. (In 1987, court papers revealed that Hutton paid Judge Bell $1,711 an hour for his 518 hours of work on the project. Bell's Atlanta law firm, King and Spaulding, billed Hutton $2.5 million for the investigation, including Bell's fee.)

Despite the attempt to polish up the company image, E. F. Hutton didn't find the government or press leading its cheers on the sidelines. In September 1985, the *Wall Street Journal* reported the findings of the Pennsylvania Securities Commission that hinted at a possible conflict of interest in Judge Bell's investigation of the company. His Atlanta law firm was advising Hutton in a securities offering. In November, *USA Today* ran a story titled, "Hutton works on its image." It noted, "Hutton brass is engaged in a quiet battle to overcome the blackened image it suffered" in its fraud conviction. And in the same breath it detailed "fresh cloudbursts" pouring down on the brokerage, which was under Securities and Exchange Commission investigation, and reported censure for problems besides the wire fraud.

A month later (we're into December now), the paper described E. F. Hutton as "scandal-plagued" and noted that "investigations into its check-overdraft scheme drag on." Those characterizations even found their way into a story about the brokerage firm's effort to help the American Red Cross raise badly needed funds. (And, no doubt, Hutton's sense of self-respect.) About a week later, the *Wall Street Journal* reported that the firm would post a fourth-quarter loss, despite the fact that many other brokerage firms were expecting "to report healthy profits." The article observed that, "The latest troubles come as the company is trying to recover from the public relations impact" of the guilty plea entered earlier in the year.

Adding insult to injury, syndicated financial columnist Dan Dorfman singled out the financial services giant in a December year-end wrap-up. He bestowed upon Hutton the distinction of "Worst Image" for "a series of fiascoes . . . "

In February 1987, Hutton made national news again when wire services picked up a damaging disclosure filed by the company at the SEC. The filing revealed that the company was under investigation by a federal grand jury in Providence, Rhode Island, for what the company claimed was the action of a "few individuals." A spokesperson contended that "the company is not in violation of any laws." Whether or not Hutton committed any wrongdoing, the case dredged up once again the PR muck of the mail-fraud conviction. Despite a spokesperson's statement that the latest investigation of the company was "totally unrelated to the cash management case of 1985," news reports of the item carried flashbacks to the scandal. More than a year and a half after the fraud scandal, Hutton was still haunted by its soiled image.[3]

GETTING OUT THE GOOD WORD

Not all business crisis recoveries require action as drastic as closing and relocating a facility, the withdrawal and reintroduction of a major product, or hiring a former United States attorney general. But regardless of the crisis you've faced, your public image needs polishing, if not repairs. This can be accomplished by generating press interest in post-crisis activity within your company, such as cleaning up or repairing the damage, improving procedures to prevent another crisis, your staff's rebound from the disaster, or other positive angles. If you do invite the news media to run postcrisis "puff" pieces, expect to face some tough questions relating to the original event. Use these interrogatories as a springboard for launching image-building answers. Speak frankly about the challenge the crisis presented to you and your staff. Point to the positive effects it catalyzed in your organization.

Follow the bad news with good no matter how grim the situation. If nothing else, generate some positive press by staging an event to express your gratitude to your employees, emergency workers, and customers (and hopefully the press) for all their help during the crisis. You might also step up corporate good works such as charitable contributions.

In addition to seeking some positive postcrisis coverage, you must expect and manage the lingering effects of a crisis. Just because the event no longer draws front-page coverage doesn't mean it's really gone away. For so long as there is one unanswered question or one significant doubt in the minds of your firm's constituents, the crisis hasn't been put to rest.

Make sure your postcrisis communications effectively address *perceptions* of your firm or product following a crisis. Don't assume your organization's constituents know all the positive things you and your staff know about the situation. They have a million more personally important things competing for their attention. To address perceptions you need to know what they are. This means conducting some opinion polling.

Within a week of the 1982 Tylenol tampering, more than 90 percent of the public had heard of the poisoning deaths, according to a Johnson and Johnson survey. But officials were surprised to learn that many consumers they surveyed didn't realize that only Tylenol *capsules* were involved in the fatal poisonings and that consumers were not aware that the company had not been implicated in the deadly contamination and that the tampering had been limited to the Chicago area. Even worse,

60 percent of those surveyed who previously took Tylenol thought it was unlikely that they would use the product again because of lingering fear. Additionally, consumers, early in the crisis, believed the company ought publicly to take a stand on the crisis.

Johnson and Johnson aggressively addressed those attitudes in letters and presentations to medical professionals, in consumer advertisements for Tylenol capsules, in media interviews by corporate representatives, in press briefings and news releases, in visits to Capitol Hill, and in shareholder, employee, and customer communications.

The strategy, of course, worked. Even after Tylenol sales reportedly dipped some 80 percent, confidence in the brand was restored. Consumer research showed marked improvement after the public relations blitz by J & J. The company reported that attitudes shifted to where 80 percent of those surveyed understood that Tylenol was tampered with *after* it left the drug maker's factory and that 90 percent now knew that tablets were not involved in the poisonings. The announcement of the tamper-resistant packaging also helped swing consumers' buying intentions. The company poll found that 77 percent of regular Tylenol users would "definitely or probably" purchase the analgesic in tamper-resistant packaging. History has shown that they did, and in record numbers. Tylenol rebounded from the Chicago deaths to the point where its post-poisoning market share exceeded the prepoisoning share.

DIE-HARD GHOSTS

A crisis never fully dies; it inevitably leaves behind a few ghosts to haunt you at the most inopportune times. Whatever struggle your company has survived, you must prepare to step back into the ring and wrestle the phantom of the crisis you thought you had just buried. For at least a short time, and maybe for a long while, the specter of Crises Past will haunt you through much greater than normal media inspection. News media attention to your postcrisis affairs is heightened a million-fold from precrisis, business-as-usual levels. Following a crisis in a given company or industry, the media pick up and play prominently stories that otherwise wouldn't qualify for the slightest mention.

For example, Kerr-McGee was cited by the Nuclear Regulatory Commission in 1985 for 15 violations of various rules over an eight-year period. But because the violations weren't considered serious and because they involved no fines, the company's infractions drew little attention—until early in 1986. That's when an accident at a Kerr-McGee plant in Oklahoma killed 1 worker and sent 110 local residents and workers to the hospital for treatment. News of the accident was reported in Sunday papers across the country, on January 5th. In the Tuesday, January 7, *Wall Street Journal*, an article ran under the headline, "Kerr-

McGee to Revise Some Plant Rules As Gas Leak Renews Concerns on Safety." The story contained both complaints about operating procedures at the Kerr-McGee plant as well as the company's pledges to make good. Overall, the firm appeared to make as good a situation out of the bad as it could.

But the next day, the same reporters who wrote the story about how Kerr-McGee planned to change safety practices and prepare for emergencies ran a story on the months-old NRC report concerning the violations (which in some cases had occurred years before). The article also reported a recent management change at the Oklahoma plant that was made because a previous manager didn't have the necessary qualifications.[4] Clearly Kerr-McGee had problems. The point is that they may have gone largely unnoticed but for a crisis that turned up national media scrutiny of the company.

A recent crisis heightens interest in a company or industry until the media either tire of kicking the dead horse or find a more lively target. When the press discovers a cold, every sneeze becomes news—until it discovers some other ailment to report. Journalists can't constantly harp about every imperfection in world. When one imperfection stands more prominently than usual because of some disaster or acute situation, journalists point to this outstanding occurrence. After the news media cover obvious, monumental features of the story, they turn their attention to more minute details that escaped notice until the crisis threw the public spotlight onto the whole area.

This crisis orientation to covering news events is consistent with Americans' general approach to problem solving. Problems compete for attention, and we ignore as many as we can until there's a crisis crying to be noticed. Given human nature, the system probably couldn't work much differently.

We may not like this approach to dealing with problems but if we are to handle crisis communications effectively, we must both admit and prepare to manage our human failings.

PART VII

FIGHTING BACK: WHEN PUBLIC WRONGS NEED RIGHTING

When men differ in opinion both sides ought equally to have the advantage of being heard by the public; and that when truth and error have fair play, the former is always an over-match for the latter.

Benjamin Franklin

Let Truth and falsehood grapple; who ever knew Truth put to the worse, in a free and open encounter.

John Milton

Fighting Fire with Fire

My pappy told me never to bet my bladder against a brewery
or get into an argument with people who buy ink by the barrel.
Lane Kirkland

The truth will emerge from free reporting and free discussion,
not that it will be presented perfectly in any one account.
Walter Lippmann

The best way to criticize bad news reporting is to confront
error with fact.

Reed Irvine

So it happens; you're a victim. The media "gotcha"! They went on the
attack or just plain misunderstood. Whatever the reason, mud adorns
your good name.

Intellectually, you know that most journalists, especially those toiling
for a daily publication or broadcast, work under severe deadline pressure. They frequently cover subjects they know little or less about; they
ply their trade alone, with little oversight and few checks on their work.
Mistakes are borne of such an environment. You understand this. Still,
you feel a need to respond. You know in your heart that striking back
isn't the appropriate response, but you don't want simply to turn the
other cheek, either. So what do you do?

This chapter examines several tactics for correcting errant press reports about your company.

Assess the Damage Dispassionately. Accept that you, the most interested party standing closest to the issue, are probably the worst judge of the infraction's proportion. Step back and view the misleading report with the disinterest of an outsider.

Gauge the erroneous coverage for its probable impact on the public's attention. An hour-long investigative piece on network television that's packed with accusations against your firm is not the same thing as the hint of innuendo in a couple of paragraphs in a minor newspaper story (even if the paragraphs find their way into the national news distribution system).

Differentiate between an unfavorable report and an inaccurate one; distinguish between the trivial and the meaningful. Honestly answer the following questions: Is your dissatisfaction with the story's balance or with its factual content? Is the balance unfair or just not the way you'd prefer to see it? (Balance is subjective and not suited to a correction or retraction, though it may justify a clarification.) How badly will this misinformation really hurt? Could it have a material effect on sales, your stock price, or general reputation, or is the infraction merely irritating or embarrassing? Who will really notice or care about the error?

Don't worry yourself unnecessarily. When it comes to important matters, the general population possesses a vast capacity for confusion that's reciprocated by the brevity of its memory. It's not that people don't try to pay attention, it's just that all of us get bombarded with thousands of pieces of data relating to hundreds of things every day. That's why advertising messages need to repeat and repeat and repeat to break through the mental clutter.

The bottom line: Most people won't see or hear the error that's so important to you. Of those who do see it, few will care, fewer will give it a moment's thought, and even fewer will retain any lasting (however minor) impression from the information. Many people distrust media reports, anyway.

Seek a few disinterested outsiders' opinions (not including your spouse's) to accurately gauge the impact of the offense. And then react proportionately as recommended below.

Tell the Press It's Mistaken. Immediately after spotting the error (or distortion) and assessing its relative importance, notify the offending press in a manner commensurate with the severity of the mistake's impact. The methods you might choose range from mailing a short, friendly letter to the errant reporter (in which you gently point out the oversight and ask that the information be noted for future reference) to paying a personal visit to the publication's CEO.

Many minor errors occurring in print publications are appropriately corrected with a "for publication" letter to the editor. You might attach a personal note explaining that you'd appreciate the editor's help in setting the record straight. (Letters to the editor can also serve as a forum for exposing viewpoints not receiving much play in the media. Many national and local publications print opinions from individuals and corporate representatives to enhance the public debate of important issues.)

A serious error, appearing either in print or on a broadcast, warrants a phone call directly to an editor immediately *after* you call the reporter who goofed. As a courtesy, advise the reporter that you plan to speak with an editor. Your goal is not to punish the reporter but to ensure a correction. By calling the reporter first, you help maintain a good businesslike relationship that will serve you well the next time the reporter writes a story concerning your firm. Be sure you actually make two calls. Reporters don't have authority to issue corrections (and probably won't rush to voluntarily embarrass themselves in front of their superiors). Talk with a decision maker but don't pressure, and don't start by calling the CEO or publisher even if he or she is a friend—that's annoying to the CEO and antagonistic to the editorial department.

When speaking to the editor, point out the errors and provide the correct information. Assume a tone of helpfulness; you understand everybody makes mistakes. You appreciate the deadline pressure the reporter was working under; you're attempting to help the publication maintain its integrity and reputation for accurate reporting. Don't waste time or psychic energy on placing blame or making demands. People whom you've insulted aren't inclined to be sympathetic toward you. Focus on the task of correcting the inaccuracies rather than shooting the messenger.

"Tell 'em your side of the story, and try to get them to at least acknowledge that you have a valid point—whether they agree with it or not," advises a veteran marketer. The objective is to persuade the publication to indicate in subsequent stories that there's another side to the issue.

Follow the call to the editor with hand-carried correspondence confirming your concern, your expectation of a correction, and ample information to assist the publication in setting the record straight. Offer your availability to assist in providing additional information or clarification.

You may encounter resistance to your suggestion for a correction. Story corrections are to journalists what product recalls are to capitalists. So getting a media outlet (especially a broadcast one) to (a) admit a mistake and (b) agree to publicly correct it can be a steep uphill battle. How many corrections do you recall seeing recently in your favorite newspaper or magazine? When was the last time you heard a radio or TV anchor apologize for a journalistic misstep?

Are the media infallible? Of course not. They just want the public to think they are. Corrections undercut credibility. So the press resists broadcasting self-incriminating information with the same intensity with which a manufacturer might resist recalling a slightly imperfect product.

You'll succeed in obtaining a public acknowledgment of an error in a published report—from most reputable news outlets—if you're willing to invest the requisite time and effort. Once it seemed impossible to pierce the tough veil surrounding network television news in order to present a correction or rebuttal. But in response to criticism, the networks are offering more opportunities to present views dissenting from those expressed in their news broadcasts. The best effort is ABC's "Viewpoint," which regularly examines media performance and opens up the airwaves to its aggrieved critics. The program debuted in July 1981, when a Kaiser Aluminum executive won the privilege of confronting Geraldo Rivera over a report on the network's "20/20" show. Kaiser claimed that the report contained unfair and inaccurate charges about aluminum electrical wiring.[1] (The more responsive atmosphere notwithstanding, the networks still aren't wide open to airing paid ads espousing opinions on controversial matters. See chapter 20.)

You might hope the correction you finally win receives the same prominence as the blunder. You'd hope in vain. Your chances of a prominent correction are about those of an ant halting a runaway steamroller. When the correction appears, brief and buried though it may be, write a short and sincere note of thinks to editorial management. This complimentary letter may well find its way to the newsroom bulletin board—everybody takes well to a little appreciation—furthering goodwill between your company and the news staff.

In the event of a serious slipup, the press organ that made the mistake might offer to run another entire story to clear up misconceptions (you might request this in lieu of a correction). The follow-up story, as it's known in the industry, might not appear the next day, and it might appear in a different section or on a different program than the original flawed report. Yet you might find this preferable to the lowly correction notice. Most likely, this avenue of redress gives you an opportunity to set the record straight in your own words and with more broadcast time or column inches than a correction.

Oddly, media executives say that when they offer such a forum to a complainer, they're often not taken up on the offer. "Lots of angry business guys call and demand their say," explains the manager of a talk-radio station, "but they never follow through. When we offer to put them on the air, they back out."

Why would people claiming to have suffered at the hands of the press resist the opportunity to set the record straight? Perhaps they're afraid to risk another foul-up, don't want to take the time to see the process through, or make unrealistic demands on the press (e.g., an hour of unedited airtime to state their case). Bernard Yoh of Accuracy in Media, a Washington-based media watchdog organization, told me, "There are so many cowards in business." Business people, he says, often don't urge the press to make corrections or represent their side of the story because they're afraid to tangle with the powerful media. "If you feel strongly that you've been wronged, do something about it! Fight for your rights. Even a mouse fights back when cornered!"

Of course, everyone would rather prevent errors or misperceptions than correct them. One of the best ways to do that remains to cooperate with the news media fully in the first place. Journalists are fond of pointing out that many errors they commit wouldn't have happened if they had received more cooperation from the subjects of their stories in the first place.

OPENING DEAF EARS

What if you can't get an editor even to acknowledge you've been wronged? First, consider the news editor's position. Why is he refusing you redress? Might he have a good point? If you earnestly consider the journalist's position and find it faulty, then try another avenue. Find out if there's an ombudsman or reader's representative who handles complaints, and plead your case to this arbiter. (Until July of 1983, you could take complaints of unfairness or inaccuracies to the independent National News Council. But, after 11 years of operating, it terminated its own existence. Members of the press, such as the *New York Times*, refused to cooperate with it, and the Council found itself ineffectual.[2] Accuracy in Media occasionally plays a role as an intermediary, but many news people regard the organization as more of an advocate for conservative causes than an independent arbiter.)

If you haven't yet, you might pay a personal visit to the newsroom of the agency with which you have a dispute. The visit need not be an angry or intimidating one. Contact the publication and suggest a meeting of minds to explore the issues. If you truly go into the session with a spirit of education rather than confrontation, chances are you'll find a fair hearing (if not a warm reception). If you encounter difficulty securing an appointment, just show up and demand the decency of a meeting. You won't be thrown out of the place.

The personal visit, expected or not, probably ranks, many reporters say, as the most effective method to gain attention from reporters and management. A flesh-and-blood appearance removes one from the abstraction of a story and forces journalists to recognize you as a person who feels wronged. (An Associated Press reporter recalls the impression made on him and his superiors by a visit from the angry subject of a story he'd written. The story concerned the divorce of an heir to a large corporate fortune. ("His coming down to the newsroom got our attention. Having him stand there looking right at me was a quick way to get action!")

If, after following all the steps above, you still lack satisfaction, then go ahead and contact senior management to register your complaint. And if you're still unhappy with the results after doing that, use other tactics to repair your reputation or advance your cause.

Go on the Offensive. Plead your case to competing media. Put out a release correcting the misinformation and hinting that you believe Channel 99's "Action News" maligned you. You'll hear from its competitors; with some glee they'll take your statement. With great care, emphasize the positive information you want disseminated and *not* the fact you're feuding with "Action News." The spat gets the other media's attention, but it's not the story. Your story is the story.

Find a columnist who'll write favorably about your mistreatment or put the matter into perspective. Don't try to buy or unduly influence a columnist, but at the same time, don't hesitate to provide relevant and helpful information to one. (Syndicated columnist William Donoghue, in expressing his personal opinion, gave the sagging reputation of E. F. Hutton a little boost in September 1985, after the firm pleaded guilty to wire fraud charges. Donoghue devoted a column to pointing out that Hutton paid millions in fines and reserved millions more for restitution. He called for "overzealous state and federal regulators" to get off Hutton's back and to stop worrying Hutton customers unnecessarily. "Why should customers be penalized after receiving years of sound, careful management and good, faithful service [from Hutton]?")[3]

If only a small or targeted audience might ascribe significance to the damaging news report (such as analysts or government authorities), consider reaching them directly rather than through the mass media. Good old U.S. mail is an effective tool for that. Following press reports about people finding glass fragments in its baby food, Gerber mailed reassuring letters to new mothers. General Motors in February 1987 mailed detailed letters to owners of its stock. The conglomerate responded to some stinging publicity over significantly smaller profits and charges that it was overly bureaucratic and losing market share. (The move was part of what *USA Today* called "a heavy public relations blitz" that also featured Roger Smith, GM's low-profile chairman, granting several media interviews.)[4]

Another way to counter unfavorable or inaccurate press is to become a publisher yourself! Our Constitution entitles any business to enter the marketplace of ideas. Distribute leaflets or a newsletter. Print your own newspaper or magazine.

Philip Morris Companies, America's largest manufacture of cigarettes

(Marlboro and others), turned to corporate publishing as a vehicle for its opinion. It created a quarterly magazine for smokers in July 1985, just a few months before the American Medical Association called for a ban on all tobacco advertising.[5]

Produce a video. Back in 1979, Illinois Power, an electric utility serving about a quarter of the state, was the subject of a "60 Minutes" report. As CBS filmed interviews with company executives, the utility video-taped the interviews, too. Al Adams, supervisor of Illinois Power's media relations, told me the company taped the interviews intending to use them as a vehicle to update employees on developments at a nuclear power plant the company was building.

After the "60 Minutes" segment aired, Illinois Power felt zapped. The company convinced CBS to air some corrections to its original broadcast, but it also produced a video rebuttal weaving its own material with CBS's. "60 Minutes: Our Reply" gave Illinois Power an outlet for disseminating *its* view of things.[6] The 42-minute program (which I found tedious and nitpicking) was shown to employees and shareholders and attracted considerable media attention. Several major corporations sent blank tapes to the utility to obtain a copy of the video. Adams says those requests are still coming in 1987. Now, in addition to corporations, colleges and high schools are requesting copies for journalism, business, and economics classes. CBS, by the way, notified the company that it wasn't thrilled with the wide distribution of the tape—in the thousands of copies—which contains portions of CBS's copyrighted program. It threatened to sue the power company but never did. Adams characterized the move as "trying to intimidate us."

The notoriety the company gained from standing up to "60 Minutes" didn't adversely affect relations with other media, Adams contends. "There was no decrease in inquiries . . . but I trust [reporters] were more careful."

Even if you aren't inclined to produce a show, consider providing television news operations with the video equivalent of a press release. Many firms do this. The tape may contain statements by corporate officials (some companies stage mock reports or interviews with an unidentified "reporter" paid by the company; I consider this ersatz journalism to be deceptive), footage of relevant events, and other appropriate material. Some radio stations would appreciate an audiotape equivalent.

Another effective technique involves using advertising as a medium to communicate your position. We'll examine that in chapter 20.

RETRIBUTION: BITING THE HAND YOU FEED

If the press stabbed you in the back you might want to launch a frontal attack to punish it. There are a few ways you might do that. You can deny information access to the media malefactor, you can apply economic pressure by canceling your advertising or boycotting the publication, or you could seek satisfaction by suing the publication for libel. We'll briefly look at the first options here and take up the issue of libel in a separate chapter.

Seeking retribution by denying information access to an offending publication only assures that your views won't be presented in a story about your affairs. News companies won't stop covering your company just because you won't talk to them. You'll succeed only in forcing the news agency to seek information from less informed (or less friendly) camps.

"If you pick a fight with a journalist, he's going to publish what he wants to. He's not necessarily going to publish things that would accurately depict your side of the story," advises a spokesperson for a large manufacturer.

Sociologist Herbert Gans adds a warning that "nothing whets journalistic hunger for a good story as much as being denied access, which may result in the scheduling of an exposé."[7]

Another classic response to perceived media abuse involves canceling your advertising (or threatening to cancel). Probably since the birth of the first ad-supported news medium, advertisers have sought to flex their economic muscles to influence editorial content or punish it. Mobil Oil Corporation, a modern-day example, has since late 1984 refused to grant interviews to *Wall Street Journal* reporters or to advertise in the paper. The outspoken oil giant cites displeasure over the paper's "emphasis, quality and character" in stories concerning Mobil as the reason for its protest.[8]

Louis Banks, former managing editor of *Fortune*, now of Massachusetts Institute of Technology's Sloan School of Management, suggests that threatening to withdraw your advertising from a publication probably won't accomplish much. Media editors, he says, can afford to be "contemptuous of business threats to pull advertising, for in today's thriving consumer market, there are other advertisers ready to take the space."[9]

The tactic not only fails to make the press kowtow to your wishes, it carries potentially serious consequences. "An eye for an eye" rings of justice, but it means spilling a lot of blood. While you inflict some small pain upon your nemesis you may well suffer additional injury.

For example, a columnist for *InfoWorld*, a personal computer magazine, reported some rumors in June 1985 alleging that Radio Shack planned to reduce prices on select computer models. The columnist also claimed that the chairman of Tandy Corporation, Radio Shack's parent, used profanity. Radio Shack's vice-president of advertising, David M. Beckerman, got angry and tried to get even. He wrote a strong letter to the company that owns *InfoWorld*, protesting what he termed a "classic case

of irresponsible, malicious destructive abuse of the journalistic privilege."

He declared that there was "not a single shred of truth" to the price
reduction rumors. After expressing his dissatisfaction with *InfoWorld*, he
concluded, "I have, therefore, instructed my Media Department to immediately cancel all contracts for advertising" in CW Communications
publications, publisher of the magazine, "regardless of group or geographic control. I have also instructed my Marketing Information Department to cease all communications with your publications."

The magazine company provided editors of *InfoWorld* with a copy of
the protest letter. The magazine published Beckerman's letter along with
a rebuttal immediately following it. The editors answered the charges
by asserting that readers "clearly understood" that the column in question contains the columnist's opinion and "insider gossip." They placed
blame for any hard feelings on "Tandy's policy of not responding to
queries" from the magazine's staff.[10]

Was the boycott effective? My calls to Beckerman's office were returned by Ed Juge, Radio Shack's director of market planning, who
handles press relations for the company. He was quick to distance the
incident from official Tandy policy. Juge declared "it wasn't the company, it as an individual executive within the company" who wrote the
letter to CW Communications. "He did it on a very personal basis."

Still, Juge explained, the whole story was considerably different from
the way it was presented in *InfoWorld*. Juge said Tandy is one of the
most responsive computer companies to press inquiries, and he accused
CW Communications of violating a trust. He claimed *InfoWorld* published
some information given to it by a representative of the magazine's parent
company who was, Juge declared, bound by a nondisclosure agreement
with Tandy.

"We viewed it not as an editorial problem; we viewed it as a breaking
of business agreements . . . It just so happened that when that editorial
broke, our vice-president of advertising got really upset on a personal
basis. He wrote a letter to [an executive of CW], not to the editor of the
magazine. [That executive] had that letter substantially altered—he
added things to it, as well as [took] things away from it—he sent it out
to *InfoWorld* and told them to publish it." The original correspondence's
references to the breach of confidence, Juge asserted, were removed in
the version published by *InfoWorld*.

Additionally, Juge said that at the time, Tandy was advertising in only
two CW Communications publications, and *InfoWorld* was not one of
them.

Juge provided me with a copy of Beckerman's original letter, and it
substantiates his allegations.

As for the effectiveness of Tandy's retaliatory strike, one measure might be the reaction from the computer-buying public. The published version of Beckerman's angry letter drew several letters from *InfoWorld* readers. Many reacted strongly and negatively to Tandy's move to cancel its advertising. The letters called Tandy's move "economic blackmail," an "attempt at censorship," an "irresponsible, malicious, and destructive action," a "cheap and dirty trick," a policy of "censorship, suppression and myopic self-interest," an act stemming from "information policies [that] closely resemble the Iron Curtain," "vindictive," "petty," "paranoid," "a serious mistake," "inept," and "the very worst of Tandy." (*InfoWorld* also printed a few letters supporting Tandy's action, saying the computer maker had the magazine "dead to rights in pulling Tandy's advertising.")[11]

Juge acknowledged that following the incident, Tandy also received "a fair amount of hate mail" at the company. "Every person who wrote to us objected. Some of them were just violently—violently—opposing our stand. I wrote them back and sent them a photostat of the original letter, and I pointed out some of the differences. I did not hear another word out of any of them. I've got to believe that when they saw what really happened it made a big difference in the way they looked at it."

Later, following negotiations between executives from the two embattled concerns, *InfoWorld* ran an unedited letter from Tandy without comment. Radio Shack resumed advertising in CW Communications publications about six months after striking them off its media buy list. The *Wall Street Journal* reported that the advertising boycott by Tandy cost CW Communications between $200,000 to $300,000.[12] But Juge says it was far, far less.

"We're on good terms with CW and *InfoWorld* today," Juge says. But he confesses that a year and a half after the affair there still are some aftershocks rumbling through the press community. The incident "left a bad taste in a lot of writers' mouths"; it still colors reporters' "willingness or unwillingness to cover us," as well as "the complexion of that coverage." Business journals occasionally run editorials critical of Tandy. "They remember" the ad boycott "but they don't remember our side of it."

Clearly, Tandy paid a price to extract its pound of flesh from CW Communications. Reacting to unfair treatment or negative publicity in the press by canceling your advertising probably satisfies a reflex to slap your adversary after you've been publicly kicked. But it's like firing a bullet through your stomach in order to hit the opponent riding on your back. While it may inflict financial pain on the faulty press outlet, it hurts you at least as much. After all, were you spending money with the publication because of altruism or because it served a profitable business purpose?

Another common form of retribution is the subscription boycott, where employees of a company mistreated by the press cancel their subscriptions to a publication. Workers might take such action following a request from corporate superiors or union bosses. T. Boone Pickens asked his Mesa Petroleum employees in Amarillo, Texas, to stop buying the local paper in early 1987. Later, after discussions with newspaper officials, Pickens withdrew the request.[13] Even more severe pressure may be brought to bear by staging a boycott of the publication's advertisers, as some activist groups have done.

Admittedly, if you take such punitive actions as a last resort, they can jar media managers into paying attention to what you're saying to them. However, you should recognize that applying economic pressure to a news outlet amounts to nothing less than a strong-arm technique. As the Tandy example points out, there can be severe negative reactions from the community, the buying public, following a power play with the press.

The media fraternity will note your actions. They may support their journalistic comrade by running stories critical of your actions. (This was the case in 1984 when unions at Bell Helicopter asked their employees to boycott the local Fort Worth paper. Dallas media editorially supported their Fort Worth neighbor.)[14] Economic reprisals against the press generate heat, but they won't warm your press relations.

If you're unhappy with media coverage you receive, invest the time and effort to win over the support of the media that displease you. You shouldn't be battling the news media; if you choose to fight you won't win by deploying economic firepower. The press will neither ignore your company in its news reports nor forget your retaliation. As Tandy's Ed Juge put it: "Working *with* [the news media] you stand a chance of doing some good. Diplomacy is always going to get you a little further than declaring war."

Advocacy Advertising: Feeding the Hand That Bites You

One thing is certain. The corporation has a right to state its views.

Herbert Schmertz

Our Bill of Rights . . . protects our right to state and print what is in our minds without interference. It does not give us the right to compel others to publish anything.

Editor and Publisher editorial

Some very prominent editors and publishers believe that freedom of speech and of the press belong only to professional journalists and not to those who would criticize them.

Quill editorial

Companies denied a fair hearing in the press, frustrated by an inability to focus media attention on a matter of importance to the corporation or wanting to portray their organization in a particular way, occasionally buy advertising to project their views. The paid advertisement provides a forum to present corporate pontifications without filtering or adulteration by meddlesome media editors.

Such nonproduct-oriented advertising is called by many names: image, corporate, institutional, identity, issue, or advocacy advertising.

I break such commercial corporate communication into three main categories: face, agenda, and rebuttal advertising.

What I call *face* advertising is what many people refer to as image or identity promotion. Image, to me, connotes something false or illusory, so I prefer not to use the term. Better to think in terms such as reputation or public perception. Face ads promote the corporation as a folksy corporate citizen, a great place to work, a concerned environmentalist, or as possessing other self-aggrandizing characteristics.

Critics of this kind of advertising are not hard to find. *Advertising Age* suggests that many corporate image ads look as if they're created by "refugees from some positive mental attitude symposium."[1] S. Prakash Sethi, who wrote a book on corporate advertising, describes institutional ads as "expensively and beautifully produced; . . . generally dull, bland, and self-serving," and "seldom taken seriously by anyone."[2]

Companies spend money on face ads to establish name recognition in the investment community, to boost employee morale, to aid recruiting, to inspire warm feelings for the company in the hearts of legislators or community groups, or to satisfy ego needs of corporate officials (much the way a company billboard sitting on the chairman's route to work does). You can find face ads hanging around the Sunday morning public affairs shows, adorning the publications of nonprofit organizations, filling up journalism trade magazines, attached to public broadcasting sponsorships, in newspaper business sections and commentary pages, and associated with other heady forums.

When General Electric and RCA got engaged in late 1985 they couldn't resist taking full-page ads in major publications to boast of their upcoming marriage. "Pardon our pride," read the headline over immodest copy in which the companies described themselves as "a pulse of progress and free enterprise."

The Chemical Manufacturers Association used face advertising to position its members as safety conscious. Manville Corporation, haunted by the asbestos troubles that forced it into Chapter 11, devised a $7-million face campaign featuring golfer Jack Nicklaus as corporate spokesman.[3]

E. F. Hutton, after admitting it committed felonies in the way it managed its money, used face advertising to say thank you to its customers and employees for their loyalty during the "trying times of these past few weeks." The full-page ads addressed the company's skeptics in both the public and private sectors by saying, "If you judge us on our merits, we are confident of your conclusions."

Agenda advertising promotes—directly or indirectly—a position on an issue the company would like to influence (but not elections, that's illegal!). Sponsorship of idea advertising dates back to early in this century; its current use indicates broad acceptance as a vehicle for mass persuasion.

R. J. Reynolds purchased ads in national publications in 1985 to counter growing antismoking sentiment. One ad, titled "Of Cigarettes and Science," disputed the claim that research proved cigarettes caused heart disease. ("It is an opinion. A judgment. But *not* scientific fact.") The ad drew heavy fire from critics, including the Federal Trade Commission.[4] The American Heart Association responded to "Of Cigarettes and Science" with an ad of its own, "The Science of Selling Cigarettes."

Another big tobacco company, Philip Morris, used agenda ads to rally feelings of patriotism for, are you ready, tobacco advertising! Using bold headlines, the cigarette seller posed these inflammatory questions: "Censorship? Here? In the USA?" The ad copy wrapped the lofty ideals of "free expression in a free market economy" and "freedom of speech" around tobacco advertising. It implored good citizens to stand up and protest "the abuse of a constitutional right by a few who would obstruct the flow of information in an attempt to bend human behavior to match their notion of the ideal, their concept of the acceptable." (Philip Morris correctly points to the danger of censoring the advertising of a legally produced and legally distributed product. But "obstruct the flow of information"? Read any absorbing cigarette ads lately?)

Sears ran ads featuring economist Alan Greenspan advocating banking deregulation before it launched its Discover credit card. The United Food and Commercial Workers union used biting local television ads to protest foreign-owned food stores.

Michigan National Corporation, a banking firm, used a television commercial—showing its employees gesturing defiantly—to influence public opinion on its battle against a takeover by bigger banker Comerica in 1985. Michigan National successfully kept its rival a competitor.

Joseph E. Seagram and Sons, the distiller, set out in 1985 to discourage an increase in what it considered discriminatory federal excise taxes. Seagram launched ads equating the alcoholic content of a bottle of beer, a glass of wine, and a shot of spirits. The "drink is a drink is a drink" series, according to company research, significantly affected public perceptions of the various alcoholic beverages. Through various media, the company took its message to schools, to Congress, and to the public at large. (The message also reached and aroused critics who pointed out that people's bodies react differently to the same amount of alcohol taken in different forms.)[5]

One of the great success stories in agenda advertising comes from an organization calling itself the U.S. Committee for Energy Awareness. The Committee is a coalition of electric utilities and other organizations with a financial interest in the electric industry, including suppliers (such as General Electric and Westinghouse), financial institutions, unions, and power plant architects. It spends millions (but won't reveal just how many millions) in advertising to bring its pronuclear and procoal message to the U.S. public. To get the word out, it buys TV time in news, public affairs, and sports shows on CBS, NBC, ABC, CNN, and local television in Washington, D.C. ("We want to make sure congressional leaders are seeing our commercials," says a spokesperson who adds that the Committee's messages "used to be on in prime time but it got too expensive.")

The Committee also places four-color ads in the major news magazines, as well as advertising in *Reader's Digest*, the *Wall Street Journal*, and other media.

"More nuclear energy means less imported oil," declares a committee ad in the June 1986 *National Geographic*. The ad addresses topics headlined "Electricity needed for economic growth" and "The proven safety of nuclear electricity." The ad closes with this tag line: "Information about energy America can count on."

Ed Aduss, vice-president for advertising at the Committee, told me he believes "strongly" that the ads are "benefiting the public because we're providing them with information that we think is vital for them to have." The industry promotion group does extensive advertising research to measure the effectiveness of its advertising. Aduss said the group is encouraged by public response to the campaign. "There's no question that public opinion of nuclear power and use of nuclear power to generate electricity is improving—not greatly, but slightly. We feel that the majority of the public are in favor of having nuclear power plants to generate electricity in the future . . . We do get a lot of response from the public, and it seems to be very favorable."

Aduss said he'd tell other companies wanting to disseminate their point of view to "conduct a strong corporate advertising or corporate advocacy type program," using a combination of advertising and public relations programs. "When I say strong, I mean it has to be a long-term investment in time, and it has to be a large financial investment. You have to be willing to spend millions of dollars a year—$20 million is not a figure that should be flinched at" for a national campaign. The ad executive says the time and money commitments need to be made for the long haul because "it's that patience and that constant wearing away [of old attitudes] and the constant presence of your message on your side of the story that's going to win the war for you." He adds that for the campaign to change people's opinions, "above all, you must tell the truth, and you must present the facts as they really are, good or bad."

The public relations component of an effective campaign, Aduss advises, must monitor what the news media report and must maintain good relations with journalists. "It's important that you supply them with information, because if [you] don't supply them with information, you know the opposition will!"

Of course, no matter how good your PR program, the news media will occasionally report information unfavorable to your company. You need to react, especially if you believe you've been maligned or misrepresented by media misinformation or misunderstanding. One way to assault the public misperception is to spend money with the adversary and buy a *rebuttal* ad. Rebuttal advertising offers corporations the opportunity to set the record straight by putting their money where their mouth is.

Here's a good example of this kind of advertising. The conservative media watchdog organization, Accuracy in Media, placed a full-page ad in the *Wall Street Journal*, May 31, 1983, proclaiming, "Dr. Edward Teller: 'I Was NOT the Only Victim of the New York Times'." The text of the ad took issue with a story in the *New York Times* regarding the relationship of physicist Teller (who counseled the White House on its Strategic Defense Initiative) and a publicly held firm in which Teller owned stock. In the ad, Teller suggested that "the *New York Times* story repeatedly asserted by innuendo and false statements that I had been *given* stock" in the company "and created the false impression that I had used prior knowledge of the President's protective defense proposal to inflate the value of some of the stock I own." The ad explained that the newspaper story was subsequently broadcast by Radio Moscow "with each misstatement and innuendo embellished." Teller then refuted the *Times'* allegations.

Below Teller's statement, AIM explained that Teller had circulated a news release to correct the "false statements," but the *Times* and other media ignored it. It noted that three weeks later, the *Times* published "on page D3 a brief story reporting that the White House had investigated and found no evidence of any impropriety" by Teller and no correlation between the stock price of the firm in question and the president's speech. The ad concluded: "Because of the exploitation of the *Times* story by Soviet propaganda and the failure of the *Times* to take adequate and timely action to undo the damage, Accuracy in Media has paid $72,531 for this advertisement." The ad also requested contributions to help defer the ad's cost.

Though AIM received contributions from around the world (many from journalists, it claims), Bernard Yoh, its director of communications, told me that the funds received by AIM covered only about half the cost. Still, he had no regrets about buying the ad. He said it was "our duty" to defend the reputation of Teller (whom he described as "a national treasure") against a "totally unjustified attack" by the *New York Times*.

Since the Teller ad ran, AIM has taken out other rebuttal ads in both national and local publications to contest other journalistic trespasses. Many other companies also use advertising to counter media coverage.

Bell Helicopter, a Textron subsidiary, placed an ad in the paper that offended it, the Fort Worth *Star Telegram*, after the paper ran an investigative series in 1984 questioning the safety of a helicopter rotor made by the company. Bell's response featured a drawing of a helicopter under the headline, "The Record Speaks for Itself." Citing government records, the ad defended the safety of the rotor system. The defense opened with, "Contrary to the allegations of the *Star Telegram* in its recent sensationalized series of articles regarding Bell Helicopter, the Bell two-bladed rotor system is NOT flawed by a design defect."

Ticor Title Insurance Company placed newspaper ads sporting the picture of the firm's chairman under the title, "Good news travels slow." The ad sought to separate the identity of Ticor Title from Ticor Mortgage Insurance Company, which was the subject of news stories in the fall of 1985 concerning possible loan defaults by a major customer.[6] The ad assured readers that the two Ticors were "distinct corporations, legally and financially" and that Ticor Title would not "suffer any losses, now or in the future, as a result of claims affecting Ticor Mortgage."

Defense contractor United Technologies took the media to task in a print ad titled "Where the Media Elite Stand," following an opinion survey of journalists working for large print publications and broadcast networks. The survey indicated liberal leanings in reporters and editors. The ad concluded: "At least now there's a scholarly confirmation of the ideological and political tilt of many of the folks who declaim daily, in print and on the tube, on the shape of the world."

Countering press reports with advertising may not undo the damage you believe you've sustained from media exposure, but it might mitigate it. The ad may reach fewer or greater numbers of people than were aware of the original coverage, but some people at least will get your side of the story. I think one could argue successfully that the type of person who reads issue-oriented advertising is the kind the advertiser wants to reach—the opinion leader or concerned citizen. Spending money to buy issue-oriented advertising may be the cost of maintaining your corporate self-esteem.

Frankly, I'd like to see more commercial messages that challenge our thinking or question press coverage of important issues and events. Such ads might grab attention with headlines such as:

• The Rest of the Story

• We Hate to Quibble, But . . .

• What Channel 99 News Didn't Tell You

• If You Must Know the Truth

• Allow Us to Shed a Little Different Light

• Let's Clear the Air

• This Is Fair Comment?

• What's *Really* News?

• WOOPS!

- Ye Shall Know the Truth
- To Err Is Human
- Fiction Might Read Better But...
- CORRECTION
- Another View
- The Other Side of the Coin
- All the News That's Fit to Correct
- You Deserve to Know More
- An Injustice Was Committed Here
- We Want You to Know
- We Beg to Differ
- The Answer You Get Depends on the Question You Ask
- There's More Than What Met Your Eye
- Half the Truth Is a Dangerous Thing
- Equal Time, Please

Rebuttal ads are most effective if they're humble and noncombative in tone. Their purpose is not to publicly flog the errant media but to impart correct information.

If you do play in the arena of public opinion, beware of overkill. Raising your corporate voice too loudly makes people suspect you're trying too hard. It recalls Shakespeare's words: Methinks thou dost protest too much. "Mobilitis" might describe the effect.

Mobil Oil is, as a *Wall Street Journal* editorial called it, "the nation's most outspoken corporate citizen." The company clearly ranks as the most prolific purveyor of promotion for a corporate agenda, and it spends millions and millions of dollars to earn the distinction (but says it doesn't take tax deductions for expenses incurred in spreading the corporate gospel).[7] Mobil espouses views on government, journalism, economics, the arts, and other subjects by buying advertising in a variety of media, writing letters to newspaper editors, patronizing public broadcasting and the arts, and sponsoring television productions.

Its feisty public affairs vice-president, Herbert Schmertz, gleefully participates in programs critical of the media, picks nits with journalists who cover the company, and writes a syndicated newspaper column. Schmertz, an attorney by training, even wrote a book on confrontation public relations. "We're a company that does not back off of an issue we believe in," the 1982 PR Professional of the year boasts.[8] (Roll over and play dead won't be found in the Mobil corporate playbook. The tenacious company cut off all relations with the *Wall Street Journal*, its president sued the *Washington Post* for libel, and it offers key executives a kind of reverse libel insurance—enabling them *to sue* for libel.)[9]

Many people find Mobil's incessant promotion of unsolicited opinion to be arrogant carping. It might not seem so, were there more voices in the corporate chorus.

ACCESS: DENIED

If you wanted to add your thoughts and voice to the public debate over important issues, you'd be welcome in many media quarters. But you might find something other than a red carpet awaiting you at the three major broadcast networks. They refuse to take money from many companies for issue-oriented advertising.

The networks, expressing concerns about fairness (or maybe appearances), refuse to run hard-hitting issue ads, even in some cases where a proponent offers to pay for its opponent's air time.

Planned Parenthood bought print ads in 1986 to take the commercial television networks to task for refusing to run programs or advertisements concerning contraceptive devices. ("They did it 20,000 times on television last year. How come nobody got pregnant?" the ads wanted to know.) The ads pointed out that "the television industry is very sensitive about people telling them what they cannot broadcast. But the TV industry itself feels free to censor content."

Mobil complained about the situation in 1980—"And now, the message the networks keep ignoring"—and again in 1983 in an ad titled, "The myth of the open airwaves." That ad, appearing in the *Wall Street Journal* (before Mobil's cold war with the paper), observed that the networks "refuse to air advertisements on 'controversial' issues, and have rejected Mobil advocacy commercials since 1974—despite evidence that public support for issue advertising is strong."

Kaiser Aluminum and Chemical Corporation published a booklet concerning corporate access to television in 1980. It argued that the networks' denying access to companies harmed society because "the public does not have the opportunity to hear what businessess—a significant, contributing force in today's society—might have to say on the pressing issues facing this country."[10]

W. R. Grace, trying to raise concern over the federal deficit with an emotional television spot, hit a brick wall at the networks in 1986. They refused to run the spot, citing its "controversial" nature.[11]

ABC, CBS, and NBC, all corporate giants themselves, don't erect roadblocks to a corporation's using their airwaves as an avenue for agenda advertising because they're necessarily antibusiness. Their reaction stems, in large part, from a piece of administrative law concocted many years ago at the Federal Communications Commission (FCC). The Fairness Doctrine, beneath its well-intending facade, holds frightening financial and political implications for broadcasters airing controversial opinions.

The Fairness Doctrine requires broadcasters licensed by the FCC (networks aren't, but their affiliated stations are) to "afford reasonable opportunity for the discussion of conflicting views on issues of public importance."[12] Translation: If a radio or TV station airs one side of a controversial issue, it's obligated to air opposing viewpoints. That's why radio or TV editorials always invite "responsible spokespersons with opposing views to reply to this station."

The implication for business is twofold. First, broadcasters and their networks tread very carefully when it comes to dedicating their air to controversial issues; they live in fear of opening the floodgates to a tide of requests to preempt precious air time in order to supply the public with contrasting viewpoints. The flip side of the coin is that the Fairness Doctrine offers businesses and others a mechanism to challenge broadcasters' lopsided presentations of issues. Phyliss Schlafly, the National Rifle Association, Mobil Oil, Accuracy in Media, and others at each end of the political spectrum have used the Fairness Doctrine as a lever to pry open broadcast programs to include their views to complement those of their ideological opponents or critics.[13]

While the Fairness Doctrine may occasionally serve as a hammer to hold over a "biased" broadcaster's head, it does more to inhibit the range of discussion concerning important issues than to encourage it. Hugh Carter Donahue, journalism professor at Ohio State University, put it succinctly: "Producers become timorous, reluctant to face conflicting demands for reply time and government complaints about fairness violations . . . Broadcasters purvey the uncontroversial to forestall the relentless stream of interest-group demands."[14] The *Wall Street Journal* voiced similar sentiment in a 1986 editorial saying that the Fairness Doctrine "breeds timidity" and pointed to the networks' quandary: "One commercial gets rejected because it is truly inflammatory and would surely call down the firestorm; the next is turned down because it is just a bit dangerous and running it would cause a lot of nagging irritation."[15]

So to hold back the potential mass of groups and individuals demanding their say, too, the networks simply avoid the whole matter by refusing to crack the door to controversy. (A small exception is ABC, which allows advocacy advertising spots to run in the half-hour period between midnight and 12:30 a.m. Opposing insomniacs are presumably welcome to reply.)

Because of the Fairness Doctrine's chilling effect on the public debate it was intended to spark, Mark Fowler, President Reagan's long-time chairman of the FCC, says the agency "concluded that the Doctrine was the wrong way to ensure the public access to diverse viewpoints" on stirring public issues. Fowler calls for the abolishment of the rule, terming it "an aberration in our tradition of free expression."[16]

In the Information Age, much has changed since 1969, when the Supreme Court upheld the constitutionality of the Fairness Doctrine, and legal challenges to it persist. Interestingly, the Supreme Court more recently also upheld the right of corporations to speak freely under the First Amendment and to use advertising as a means of exercising that right (*Bellotti v. Massachusetts*). Corporate citizens possess a right, perhaps even shoulder a duty, to speak on issues of the day, though no constitutional mechanism guarantees them an open forum, especially over network television.

But even the networks can be persuaded to air some agenda advertising while living within the Fairness Doctrine structure. The U.S. Committee for Energy Awareness, the publicity organ of the electric industry, places its television messages for "energy independence" on the networks. What's its secret to success? Ed Aduss, vice-president of advertising for the group, says, "We develop a commercial; we present it to the networks; if they have difficulties with it we revise the commercial after meeting and negotiating with them. The nature of our commercials is such that we're telling the truth and reporting the facts correctly." The changes made to appease the network censors amount to "word changes here and there, but nothing extensive by any stretch of the imagination." Aduss says the networks approve his scripts before production starts, and he doesn't object to their oversight. "They screen every spot. If you were putting a commercial together for jelly beans, you'd have to submit it to the same people who review our commercials. It's standard practice for all the networks and television stations, and it doesn't bother me at all."

Whether they cooperate or not, television networks aren't the only showcase for a company's agenda ads. Cable television offers a multitude of outlets, and many local stations have no qualms about running responsible spots. Even Grace's banned-on-network deficit trial commercial found a home at the CBS and ABC network affiliates in Washington, D.C.; it ran on CNN and the Financial News Network, as well. Additionally, the spot received air time on about 150 local stations belonging to the Association of Independent Television Stations gratis—in exchange for a mention in Grace's print ads.[17] Hundreds of ways exist to reach the minds of the public; network television is but a convenient one.

Opponents to advertisements featuring intellectual corporate messages argue that the practice gives control of public discussion to those with the deepest pockets. (The networks, afraid to point the finger at the Fairness Doctrine—for what if it were eliminated?—hide behind this argument in denying agenda advertising the opportunity to take its rightful place next to ads for denture cleaners, feminine products, and underarm spray.) The question is: Should the richest—who can afford access—speak the loudest on the important issues?

At first, that concern may "listen well." But financial control of the marketplace of ideas is not a compelling argument. For none of us, poor or rich, has the right of access to newspapers, magazines, radio or TV stations, networks, or cable systems. There's equality in that we are all equally unentitled. The fact is that freedom of the press exists only for those who own one or can afford to rent one. We can exert moral or intellectual influence on fellow citizens by becoming publishers ourselves. (Costs a dime at the local copy shop.) And we exert financial influence on the media by voting with our consumption of their products. (Don't like what you read? Don't buy it. Don't like what you hear? Change the station.) But we have no right to commandeer another's medium.

Many organizations that purport to represent the "liddle peeble"—who'd arguably have their voices drowned by the drone of big bucks' interests—are highly organized and sophisticated fund raisers. They're effective lobbyists of government agencies and the press. They would not be condemned to a ghetto of muted advocacy in a pay-as-you-go system of courting public opinion.

Besides, businesses wishing to buy agenda advertising don't want to strangle free thought or impose some sinister mind control over the populace. They just want to have their say in the public arena. This is a most defensible position.

Most important, if one has faith in the public's interest in important issues, one should have faith enough in the public's capability to recognize the intelligent from the inane. Seeing a slick ad proposing a dumb idea even many, many times won't force people to step in line behind bad policy. Citizens listening to conflicting voices may wander about confused occasionally, but they won't be misguided for long. There are too many outlets for opinion and information in this country for truth not to present itself clearly and quickly.

Mark Fowler, outgoing FCC chairman, places faith in an open marketplace of ideas. He contends that people who insist that the government restrict the free flow of information by enforcing the Fairness Doctrine assume "that the common man is too dimwitted to discern the truth among diverse voices, fair and unfair, moderate and extreme."

In other words, many paternalists feel compelled to watch out for poor old Joe Sixpack! But old Joe can think for himself and deserves to hear a robust and free flow of ideas from a diverse host of speakers.

Issue-oriented ads serve useful business purposes and enrich the quality of the discussion and debate essential to our republic. Businesses should embrace and vigorously exercise their right of free speech.

Filing Suit: Using the Law of Libel for Satisfaction

Too much checking on the facts has ruined many a good news story.

Roy Howard

If the press prints something that is blatantly untrue, unchecked, unfounded, and damaging to somebody, why shouldn't the press be as liable for a legal challenge as a doctor who makes a serious surgical mistake, as a business who cheats one of its customers—wittingly or unwittingly?

Ann Compton

Most libel complaints can be prepared in a couple of hours, at the cost of at most a few hundred dollars.

Atty. Martin Garbus

By chance, both of us were riding on a long ski lift up the side of a Colorado mountain one cold Sunday afternoon. During our chat, I mentioned to the trim, tanned skier that I worked for the Associated Press. "You don't want to know who I am," he replied. After some prodding, he told me he was Tony Herbert—former army Lt. Col. Anthony Herbert, who set some far-reaching libel law precedence in his suit against "60 Minutes."

Tony Herbert sued CBS after the network ran a story back in 1973 regarding Herbert's army career in Vietnam. While the details of the particular case are peripheral to our discussion of libel, Herbert's views of press accountability are central to it. On the way to the summit, Mr. Herbert told me he had nothing against the press. "I believe in a free press and its important role in our society. But I also firmly believe the press should be no different from anybody else—it should take *responsibility* for its actions, especially when they hurt someone. Why should the media escape accountability when everyone else has to be accountable for their actions?"

Herbert's comments about press responsibility seem reasonable. They might even inspire you to seek affirmation in a court of law should you find yourself or your company the subject of extremely embarrassing, unfair, or false news reports.

Unlike some of my journalistic friends, I believe you should have every right to sue a business (and surely, all of the major media are businesses) that sought to profit by maligning you. But at the same time, I believe you should have a clear understanding of the possible costs, to yourself and to society at large, that you face when directing your lawyer to "sue the bastards." That's what this chapter is all about.

Before examining the price you'll pay to seek redress from the news media in a court of law, I'd like to point out the critical components of a libel suit.[1] Libel laws vary from state to state, but fundamentally a libel in a published or broadcast report contains two basic parts: Identification and damage to reputation. To successfully charge a press outlet with committing a libel, you must establish that the news story in question clearly indicates that *you* are the subject of the purported libel, either by direct accusation or clear implication, and that the report was both false *and* harmful to you. The law generally takes "harm" to mean that your reputation was held up to public hatred, contempt, or disgrace or that the false report had some adverse impact on your social or professional standing.

Companies *can* sue for libel. A corporation "may collect general damages for libel when its reputation for honesty is impugned, its credit rating is questioned, or it is charged with fraud or mismanagement."[2]

News stories that are one-sided or biased are not libelous just because they might be unfair; your reputation must be *damaged* by *false* information. Likewise, inconsequential errors in fact aren't grounds for a libel suit. Libel is a gravely serious charge to level at a publication.

THE BURDEN OF FAME

If you or the activities with which you're involved are at all prominent, a court considering your libel suit may hold that you are a "public figure." Before assigning yourself to either the "famed" or the "obscure" column, beware that the courts boast an erratic record in determining who rates as a public figure, coloring this legal area in a deep shade of lawyer's gray.

As a public figure, you are not entitled to damages from a libel unless you can show that the news medium published the incorrect information either knowing it was false or with "reckless disregard" for the truth in not trying to verify the veracity of the information. This "actual malice" test goes back to 1964, when the Supreme Court, in *New York Times v. Sullivan*, sought to protect an earnest press—working in the public interest and in good faith—from frivolous lawsuits brought over inadvertent mistakes.

This rigorous test for libel of public figures left Israel's Ariel Sharon with a rather hollow victory over Time, Inc., in 1986. The jury in the Sharon case decided that *Time* magazine *had* printed false information about Sharon but did so without "actual malice," so technically there was no libel.[3]

If you are not qualified as a public figure by the court, you'll need to prove at least negligence on the part of the press to collect any punitive damages.

The test for actual malice places a tremendous burden of proof on you if you're deemed to be a public figure. You essentially have to prove the libeling publication defamed you on purpose. An easier task may be to define the universe and give three examples. It was Anthony Herbert's suit that established a landmark method for public figures to gather (or create) the kind of subjective evidence necessary to prove malice. His case validated examining the *intent* of journalists creating a news report. This so-called state-of-mind evidence can be crucial to a publicly prominent plaintiff suing a news agency. Much to the consternation of the news media (but probably to the credit of justice), the Supreme Court in 1979 upheld state-of-mind interrogation of reporters and editors (*Herbert v. Lando*).[4]

But the burden you face as a plaintiff goes beyond merely proving what exactly was inside the reporter's head when she framed the contested story. Not only will you need to prove the news agency acted terribly irresponsibly, you may need to prove the untrue allegation is in fact false! Unlike the presumption of innocence the law affords an accused murderer held by police, no universal "innocent until proven guilty" presumption is extended to you by the courts when it comes to challenging charges detailed by a television station or newspaper owned by Megabucks Media Corporation.

Michael McDonald, president of the Washington Legal Foundation (a conservative public-interest law firm that participates in important media cases), told me that news media reporting "a controversial issue of public importance" don't have to prove the truthfulness of their allegations. The Supreme Court took that position, as McDonald explains, "because there might be a possibility—if we place the burden of proving truth on a media defendant—that some truthful speech would be 'chilled' or deterred from getting out in public . . . The First Amendment compels that the burden has to be on the *plaintiff* to establish the falsity in a libel action, even if he's a *private figure*, not a public figure." [Emphasis mine.] McDonald estimates that about 90 percent of news reporting would qualify for this extraordinary protection from libel suits.

This means that if, say, you sell photocopiers or consulting services to the government and a newspaper alleges that you rigged a bid or bribed the purchasing agent of some agency, you may have to prove that you *didn't* in order to win a libel action!

If, after you've reviewed the tremendous legal constraints you face as a plaintiff in a libel action, you still covet vindication of your reputation to the point where you are willing to face the fight and want to file suit, there's more you need to know. Prevailing in the libel process is difficult and taxes one in many ways. Here's a summary of the libel liabilities you as plaintiff must prepare to endure.

THE COSTS OF VINDICATION

Forfeiting Your Privacy. Truth is an absolute defense for a publication accused of libel. The publication you sue will have legal license to closely comb your affairs in search of truth in order to defend itself. Filing a lawsuit alleging libel openly invites invasion of your privacy by a battery of attorneys and their journalist client.

"What most media organizations try to do once a suit's been initiated is use the discovery process to go through all sorts of business records or the records of the plaintiff trying to find corroborating evidence that they may have had no idea even existed," warns McDonald. The press tries to " 'postvalidate' the charges that they made."

This discovery process could result in the news outlet learning much more about you and your affairs than you might imagine in your worst nightmare. While pursuing their intense fact-finding expedition, your media adversaries are bound to discover information that may be unrelated to the matter at hand and which they otherwise might not ever have stumbled onto. (Though the press cannot search your records during a discovery process with the specific intent of fishing for new headlines.)

Media coverage of the libel action (a public matter because it's in the courts) just about ensures that whatever the offending medium originally reported that angered you so probably will be repeated widely and frequently by other press covering your libel action. You may also see coverage of any other juicy tidbits the discovery process laid bare, as they will be aired very publicly in the court room.

The upshot is that suing for libel just about guarantees that many more people will become much more aware of the false information, as well as other private information. The system works such that you may need to take a public mud bath to *try* to extract satisfaction from the party who threw mud in your eye.

You should also know that obtaining evidence from the journalists' camp may not be a very productive affair. No statute requires journalists to keep their notes or tapes of interviews or fact gathering ("Congress shall make no law . . . "). To the contrary, some states have enacted shield laws that protect journalists from having to reveal their "reliable" sources for news reports, and some reporters willingly go to jail rather than reveal their sources.

I've attended news industry seminars where reporters have been urged by press lawyers to destroy notes after filing a story to keep them from being subpoenaed in the future. Yes, the great proponents of the Freedom of Information Act and public disclosure of just about everything act differently where their own affairs are concerned. This ironic double standard is something you should recognize and consider when pondering a legal fight with the Fourth Estate.

Time. You can't just hand a libel suit off to your attorneys and ask them to keep you updated. You're going to spend time-consuming hours giving depositions, attending hearings, complying with requests for documents, and so on. As you might suspect, there's more than a briefcase full of legal maneuvers that the hotshot lawyers working for the other side (and maybe yours, too) can deploy to delay, drag out, and complicate the proceedings. Some libel cases have dragged on for nearly two decades.

Money. Chief Justice Warren Burger, writing a separate opinion to a 1985 Supreme Court ruling on a libel case involving a corporate plaintiff—*Dun and Bradstreet Inc. v. Greenmoss Builders, Inc.*—noted, "The burden that plaintiffs must meet . . . invites long and complicated discovery involving detailed investigation of the work of the press, how a news story is developed and the state of mind of the reporter and publisher. That kind of litigation is very expensive."[5]

Indeed, plan to spend huge amounts of money if you want the action to proceed beyond filing a nuisance suit (which some people file to get the attention of the uncooperative medium that harmed them). Legal counsel and court fees for jury trials or appeals can run into the hundreds of thousands and even the millions of dollars. That's real money to you; the news outlet may have its expenses paid by an insurance company from which it purchases libel coverage.

In fact, finding an attorney with experience or expertise in prosecuting libel cases may be difficult. "The economics of the situation tend to see to it that most of the good attorneys, most of the powerful firms, tend to gravitate toward the defense side," explains attorney McDonald, who's assisted in the Anthony Herbert and General William Westmoreland libel suits. "Newspapers are always around, they're always being sued for libel or invasion of privacy," so there's economic incentive for lawyers to make a career out of defending the media. Libel suits are initiated by individuals, many of whom are far from wealthy, from all over the country, with a wide variety of interests. The situation makes it difficult to spawn much of an industry for plaintiff's lawyers specializing in libel actions. The Washington Legal Foundation, in the nation's capital, makes referrals to qualified plaintiff attorneys and keeps files of resources for libel prosecutions.

Even reaching the out-of-court settlement stage may be very expensive and yield only a retraction, correction, or clarification by the errant medium—results you likely would've achieved with persistence and no costly libel action. After court action, your integrity might be faintly restored, if it's not further damaged by the concomitant publicity, while your pocketbook suffers intensely.

If you contemplate a libel action confident that the costs of publicly exposing your personal and business life, and your investment of time and money, will all be repaid when you win a huge damage settlement, think again. You might sue for millions, you might even leave the courthouse with a jury verdict that acknowledges that you *were* the victim of a false report, but you may still walk away without so much as a penny for your efforts.

"If you're facing the 'actual malice' standard [as a public figure], the media have . . . probably close to a 100 percent chance of winning the case at some point down the road," warns McDonald.

It's true that if you endure the process all the way through a jury trial you'd have about a 90 percent chance of winning, according to the recent experience of others. But you should be aware that a substantial portion of libel judgments against the news media are reversed on appeal.[6]

More sobering: only 1 *percent* of jury judgments in libel cases are ever paid, and to make matters worse, appeals and settlements vastly reduce the monetary sums winning plaintiffs really end up receiving, points out lawyer Martin Garbus.[7] Many huge jury awards you may recall reading about have been either thrown out or reduced substantially by an appeals judge.

The famed saga of William P. Tavoularas stands as a case in point. He was president of Mobil Oil and the target of some stinging accusations (concerning alleged nepotism) detailed in the *Washington Post* back in November 1979. He sued for libel and won a $2-million award from a jury. Then he lost it when the *Post* appealed. The appeals judge, in 1983, said that the *Washington Post* didn't act with actual malice and therefore did not libel public figure Tavoularas; ergo, jury award out. Then the

Mobil executive appealed and got his award back in April 1985, when a three-judge appeals court panel reversed the lone appeals judge. Then the award was set aside again, pending another appeal by the newspaper. On Friday the 13th, March 1987, the D.C. Court of Appeals ruled that there was no libel. Once again Tavoulareas, winner of a jury verdict, owner of million-dollar legal bills, left the courthouse with nothing but one last hope, that the U.S. Supreme Court might agree to review the case. McDonald of the Washington Legal Foundation doubts that it will.[8]

This libel game, like most, pinged and ponged, passed go several times, and cost both sides a fortune. The bottom line: just because a jury says you should be paid a million dollars (or two) doesn't mean you'll get anything even close. Or anything, period. And a good chunk of whatever judgment you might eventually receive—a decade or so later—is already long spent.

Given the fiscal and emotional realities of libel actions, filing suit against a media outlet—even one you believe has wronged you terribly— can only be considered as the course of last resort. There are other, less taxing, and in the long run more effective methods to seek redress (see previous chapters). Admittedly, they may not hold the same potential for moral victory that vindication by a jury may seem to deliver. But they may, in fact, save you further loss of reputation, agonizing years of distraction, and significant sums of money.

CHILLING EFFECT OR NECESSARY CHECK?

Deciding not to sue for libel after being treated unfairly probably won't scratch your itch for revenge, and it may strike you as a grand, moral cop-out. After all, shouldn't the press be accountable for what it does? Other organizations who serve society—by making tranquilizers, toasters, or toys; by building bridges, driving trucks, healing the sick, or even counseling litigants—face stiff tort liability for their actions. It would seem fair to expect the press to face similar responsibility.

The press enjoys tremendous constitutional protection to pursue truth in our democracy. Our laws and customs favor a vigorous press. Without question, our individual freedom and the integrity of our democracy is enhanced by a free and aggressive press. (I recall attending a press club luncheon where the executive editor of a large daily paper, half in jest and with some pride, told his audience, "Two pending libel suits by policemen prove the newspapers in this town are aggressive!")[9]

Despite the favoritism our society affords the news media and the bravado with which they pursue their trade, they do not and should not enjoy absolute impunity to pursue character assassination for fun and profit. As with all privilege, responsibility should follow in equal measure.

194 Fighting Back

Don't wait for the press to seek you; when they come looking, it's too late for casual introductions. Initiate a personal relationship with members of the press, for they are a direct and powerful link to all your significant publics. Heed these wise words from Harold J. Corbett, senior vice-president of Monsanto Company:

If we [business people] talk to the general public at all, we talk *at* them—not with them. We give a speech—or place a corporate advertisement—or publish a pamphlet—or issue a press release. At best we may send representatives to talk with people when a problem arises. And when the meeting is over we congratulate ourselves on having had a dialogue and retreat to our offices . . . What people don't understand they fear—and that which is feared is often rejected. If people don't know what we do and why—not just chemical companies, but all companies—then how in the world can they make reasonable judgments about our behaviors?"[1]

Monitor the news media (consider subscribing to a computerized news service to help you track coverage relevant to your business). Let the press know, in a helpful way, how it's doing in covering your industry. Understand that humans, even journalists, make mistakes. Point out errors and suggest new angles for future stories. Recognize outstanding journalistic efforts by sending your compliments.

Meet reporters and editors in their offices to discuss your industry and your company. Don't offer to visit only when you have a message to sell or are in search of ink. Visit key media organizations periodically. Go expecting to meet tough questions with honest answers. Let the conversation work two ways; ask the journalists for their observations and thoughts about your industry—you may discover misconceptions or learn something of value from their outsiders' perspective.

Offer to aid reporters by providing background information or your perspective on industry issues.

Send a company representative to journalism industry meetings—to learn, not to lobby, and to establish or renew contacts.

Insist that your media relations personnel deal humbly and forthrightly with news organizations.

Codify in writing your company's commitment to honesty in public communications.

Help the Press Do a Better Job. Business and the press occasionally and necessarily relate to each other as adversaries; any other approach could only disserve the nation. But more often than being combative, the relationship resembles that of bees and flowers. The flowers may complain about those darn bees constantly buzzing about, and the bees may resent having to cater to the flowers, but the flowers would surely die out without the bees, and the bees would surely starve without the flowers.

Toward a Better Understanding: Closing Thoughts on Improving the Business/Media Relationship

Civilization and profits go hand in hand.

Calvin Coolidge

Humility can sometimes head off humiliation.

Broadcasting editorial

What we must aim for is eradication of editorial rudeness and cynicism.

Editor and Publisher editorial

Business stands to gain much from improved press coverage of its activities, and it stands in an ideal spot to influence change in the way the press shapes that coverage (really!). It follows then, that business ought to take the initiative. Throughout this book, I've offered advice on how to work with the media in a more constructive way. Some additional suggestions follow.

IMPRESSING THE PRESS

Actively Seek Productive Press Relations. Recognize the legitimacy of the news media's interest in your activities (they represent the public you serve), and recognize the opportunity this interest presents you. Rather than gripe about how the press doesn't understand the first thing about your business, take affirmative action to correct the situation.

Don't wait for the press to seek you; when they come looking, it's too late for casual introductions. Initiate a personal relationship with members of the press, for they are a direct and powerful link to all your significant publics. Heed these wise words from Harold J. Corbett, senior vice-president of Monsanto Company:

If we [business people] talk to the general public at all, we talk *at* them—not with them. We give a speech—or place a corporate advertisement—or publish a pamphlet—or issue a press release. At best we may send representatives to talk with people when a problem arises. And when the meeting is over we congratulate ourselves on having had a dialogue and retreat to our offices . . . What people don't understand they fear—and that which is feared is often rejected. If people don't know what we do and why—not just chemical companies, but all companies—then how in the world can they make reasonable judgments about our behaviors?"[1]

Monitor the news media (consider subscribing to a computerized news service to help you track coverage relevant to your business). Let the press know, in a helpful way, how it's doing in covering your industry. Understand that humans, even journalists, make mistakes. Point out errors and suggest new angles for future stories. Recognize outstanding journalistic efforts by sending your compliments.

Meet reporters and editors in their offices to discuss your industry and your company. Don't offer to visit only when you have a message to sell or are in search of ink. Visit key media organizations periodically. Go expecting to meet tough questions with honest answers. Let the conversation work two ways; ask the journalists for their observations and thoughts about your industry—you may discover misconceptions or learn something of value from their outsiders' perspective.

Offer to aid reporters by providing background information or your perspective on industry issues.

Send a company representative to journalism industry meetings—to learn, not to lobby, and to establish or renew contacts.

Insist that your media relations personnel deal humbly and forthrightly with news organizations.

Codify in writing your company's commitment to honesty in public communications.

Help the Press Do a Better Job. Business and the press occasionally and necessarily relate to each other as adversaries; any other approach could only disserve the nation. But more often than being combative, the relationship resembles that of bees and flowers. The flowers may complain about those darn bees constantly buzzing about, and the bees may resent having to cater to the flowers, but the flowers would surely die out without the bees, and the bees would surely starve without the flowers.

Mobil executive appealed and got his award back in April 1985, when a three-judge appeals court panel reversed the lone appeals judge. Then the award was set aside again, pending another appeal by the newspaper. On Friday the 13th, March 1987, the D.C. Court of Appeals ruled that there was no libel. Once again Tavoulareas, winner of a jury verdict, owner of million-dollar legal bills, left the courthouse with nothing but one last hope, that the U.S. Supreme Court might agree to review the case. McDonald of the Washington Legal Foundation doubts that it will.[8]

This libel game, like most, pinged and ponged, passed go several times, and cost both sides a fortune. The bottom line: just because a jury says you should be paid a million dollars (or two) doesn't mean you'll get anything even close. Or anything, period. And a good chunk of whatever judgment you might eventually receive—a decade or so later—is already long spent.

Given the fiscal and emotional realities of libel actions, filing suit against a media outlet—even one you believe has wronged you terribly—can only be considered as the course of last resort. There are other, less taxing, and in the long run more effective methods to seek redress (see previous chapters). Admittedly, they may not hold the same potential for moral victory that vindication by a jury may seem to deliver. But they may, in fact, save you further loss of reputation, agonizing years of distraction, and significant sums of money.

CHILLING EFFECT OR NECESSARY CHECK?

Deciding not to sue for libel after being treated unfairly probably won't scratch your itch for revenge, and it may strike you as a grand, moral cop-out. After all, shouldn't the press be accountable for what it does? Other organizations who serve society—by making tranquilizers, toasters, or toys; by building bridges, driving trucks, healing the sick, or even counseling litigants—face stiff tort liability for their actions. It would seem fair to expect the press to face similar responsibility.

The press enjoys tremendous constitutional protection to pursue truth in our democracy. Our laws and customs favor a vigorous press. Without question, our individual freedom and the integrity of our democracy is enhanced by a free and aggressive press. (I recall attending a press club luncheon where the executive editor of a large daily paper, half in jest and with some pride, told his audience, "Two pending libel suits by policemen prove the newspapers in this town are aggressive!")[9]

Despite the favoritism our society affords the news media and the bravado with which they pursue their trade, they do not and should not enjoy absolute impunity to pursue character assassination for fun and profit. As with all privilege, responsibility should follow in equal measure.

The threat of libel action serves as a powerful incentive for the news media to exercise care in reporting. No honest reporter or editor who's plied his trade at a publication that's been sued for libel will tell you that the libel suit didn't affect his work.

Journalists say the intimidating impact of a libel suit, or the very threat of one, has a chilling effect on serious journalism. Others, especially those on the receiving end of cavalier press coverage, call it a dose of accountability. Both camps are correct. The question of whether we should have an immune or accountable press is one of degree. The Supreme Court wrestles with this very question regularly and with inconsistent results. A free and aggressive press has been instrumental—no, make that indispensable—to our thriving democracy. But libel law stands as a check on the checkers, a sobering influence on an institution that may otherwise become intoxicated (and then abusive) with its own power and success.

If you're considering a libel action, talk to a competent attorney (and maybe your banker) to weigh the pros and cons.

After consulting your lawyer and before filing suit to financially penalize the press for its imperfections, thoroughly and honestly examine your fortitude and conscience.

The news media live on information; business thrives in accord with its reputation. By carefully choosing how and what information it feeds the press, business can constructively affect the type and tone of the information the press consumes and in turn disseminates. When the news media receive cooperation, they're more likely to nourish positive perceptions about business.

Release news to the press when you have something of interest to say, and then say it effectively.

Train your managers to answer questions from the media effectively.

Include your engineers, scientists, and technicians in your public relations effort. They can be a powerful source to help spread the truth about your industry. The public ascribes much more credibility to people of science than silver-tongued spokespersons. Use this to your advantage not only to respond to press inquires but to initiate them. Westinghouse and Dow Chemical have used this approach with great success. Journalists deeply resent slick, hard-sell press agentry maneuvers, but they receive with open arms thoughtful, competent, and frank assistance to help them understand scientific and technical complexities. Professor Dorothy Nelkin watches the way journalists wrestle with technical issues from her vantage point at Cornell University's Program on Science, Technology, and Society. She observes that, "When information is complex, disputed and politically sensitive, reporters pressed by deadlines tend to rely on preselected news, especially if it seems to be based on scientific authority . . . Sources best organized to provide well-packaged facts have an unusual degree of power."[2]

Make a long-term investment in press relations by positively influencing young news people. Offer to meet college journalism classes. Let budding reporters and editors meet a real executive face to face. While you're there, explain your industry and views on the relationship between the press and business. Establish a scholarship or tuition aid package for journalism students who agree to take business or technical courses.

Sponsor a fellowship for a working journalist to go back to school and study business, economic, or scientific issues.

Contribute to national not-for-profit organizations that work to improve journalists' understanding of business and economic issues.

Following these suggestions surely will improve your company's stature within the journalism community. Improving the perception of business-the-institution among the press corps, as well as society at large, requires broader actions as well.

BEYOND MEDIA RELATIONS

It goes without saying that the best way to avoid negative publicity and to foster a positive reputation is to be a law-abiding and ethical corporate citizen. The formula for positive public relations for your individual corporation includes significant portions of these key elements: responsibility, accountability, accessibility, and honesty.

In addition to gaining by enhancing your own firm's reputation, you have a vested interest in the public's general attitude toward business. Even if your company stands as a sterling example of corporate citizenship, it can find its reputation tarnished by the corrosive actions of others in the business community. A lone neat house on a dilapidated block can't restore the reputation of the neighborhood simply by standing there.

Business will claim a higher standing with the press and the public when business leaders *champion* ethical behavior.

To truly affect public opinion on the positive role of commerce in our capitalist society requires business managers to assume an exemplary and publicly visible role of moral leadership and, beyond that, to commend good works by others and, most important, to vocally condemn unethical trespass by others. As author S. Prakash Sethi states:

The case of business is poorly served when corporate spokespeople concentrate their fire on corporate critics but refuse to speak out against businesspeople [sic] and business practices that are illegal or that are considered socially irresponsible. By refusing to take a public position against corporate wrongdoers they invite criticism against all businesses and convey the image of business as a monolithic entity.[3]

I would offer the following as an example of a missed opportunity to move beyond carping at the press—and blaming everyone else—in order to account for ethical deficiencies in business.

Sanford McDonnell, chairman of McDonnell Douglas, gave a speech entitled, "People, Profits, and Ethics" in early 1987 at Dr. Robert Schuller's Crystal Cathedral in southern California.[4] In the address, sprinkled with quotes from Montesquieu, Benjamin Franklin, George Washington, and others, McDonnell suggested that schools, religious institutions, and homes in the United States were defaulting on their moral responsibilities to educate youths about important values. He charged that the deterioration of ethics in the United States was the fault of selfish special interest groups (no mention of any specific group), apathetic voters, and dependency by "far too many people who have their hand out to entitlements."

The chief executive officer of the $12.66-billion-dollar company shamed his audience of business people: "We've done a great job of voting ourselves largess from the public treasury, haven't we? Last year, 45 percent of our national budget were 'entitlements'—which are sacrosanct." (An odd, perhaps perverse, condemnation from the leader of a company that grabbed $8.4 billion from the public trough in 1986 alone.)[5]

What about business and ethics? McDonnell noted the recent attack on the defense industry. "We're being accused of all sorts of skullduggery. We've gotten to the point where the average person in the street feels that the chief executive officers in the defense business lie awake every night figuring out how they can gouge the public out of another $435 hammer."

McDonnell said the $435 hammer was a "case of ethics and values," but not for the defense industry. He alleged that a "congressperson" misrepresented the invoice for the hammer. The widely reported accusation that a hammer cost taxpayers $435 constituted, McDonnell claimed, "unethical behavior" on the part of Congress and the press. Another ethical lapse by Congress and the news media was the report of a $7,000 coffee pot, which McDonnell said was really a coffee maker that the commercial airlines actually bought at a higher price than the defense department.

In response to a question I posed to him, McDonnell acknowledged that the press had a "definite" and "appropriate" role as a "watchdog" over business. McDonnell called the news media the "most powerful educators that we have in America." But he quickly added that they were "filling the minds and hearts of our young people with all sorts of trash" and were "not living up to . . . standards and codes of ethics that the rest of us are trying to live up to."

If there were ethics problems in business—outside the press—McDonnell seemed oblivious to them. He chose not to mention the felonies and other ethical disgraces committed by brethren business people. McDonnell stood before an audience of people who paid $14 each to hear a discussion on business ethics, and he ignored the convictions for defense fraud at companies like General Electric, Rockwell, GTE, and lesser lights.[6] (A company spokesperson told me in March 1987, that McDonnell Douglas isn't aware of any investigation concerning its own contracting activities.)

Speeches by executives that ignore or soft-pedal the role business plays in the erosion of American ethical values (and where else but in business is this erosion most evident?) or that point the accusing finger at the news media, religious institutions, schools, social programs, and everywhere *but* business do little to inspire confidence in business's moral integrity.

To its credit, McDonnell Douglas adopted a code of ethics in 1983 and has since 1984 trained over 25,000 of its 100,000 employees "to always take the high road" and to avoid increasing the bottom line by "cutting ethical corners." The company also sponsors a program in St. Louis grade schools to "bring character back into our public schools again."

Maybe in a future speech McDonnell will complement those actions by moving past rhetorical platitudes and forcefully condemning not welfare mothers but those in business who've taken the low road, cut ethical corners, and robbed business people everywhere of a rightful presumption of ethical character.

A move closer to the mark was made by Thomas G. Pownall, chairman and CEO of Martin Marietta Corporation. He wrote a syndicated commentary in late 1985 that also addressed the loss of public trust in the defense industry.[7] He too had a high opinion of his business: "Never has so much money been spent by so many people with so little dishonesty." He too addressed a Rodeo Drive–priced hammer (though he referenced a bargain variety that cost only $363), "of which there was one," while pointing out that "more than 6,000 were bought for less than $8." He didn't lay blame for the defense fraternity's woes at the feet of an unethical press.

Significantly, Pownall called for higher standards among his own in the defense business. "We must hold ourselves more accountable than ever, and expect others to hold us strictly to account." He also called for defense managers to impress upon their employees the expectation for the highest ethical standards. Pownall stopped short of condemning bad behavior in his ranks, but he did summon attention to improving the industry, a forward march in the right direction.

Business needs executives to lead by example, to speak out for what's right, and to denounce unacceptable behavior by others. It would be delightful to open local papers and see full-page ads proclaiming messages such as "Where We Stand on Ethics at Acme" or "Such Behavior Hurts Us All," over an ad rejecting the illegal conduct of a member of the business community.

Business delivers useful, powerful, and wonderful forces to our society. It deserves a fair hearing in the press and the respect of the public it serves.

Enhancing confidence in business requires the business community to deal forthrightly with the public it serves and to stand up for accountability.

Notes

Some works cited in the notes employ abbreviations. These include:

A. A. News	*Ann Arbor News* (Ann Arbor, Mich.)
Ad Age	*Advertising Age*
AP	Associated Press
E&P	*Editor & Publisher*
L.A. Times	*Los Angeles Times*
NYT	*New York Times*
O.C. Register	*Orange County Register* (Santa Ana, Calif.)
Rocky	*Rocky Mountain News* (Denver, CO)
UPI	United Press International
U.S. News	*U.S. News & World Report*
WJR	*Washington Journalism Review*
WSJ	*Wall Street Journal*

In the interest of space, authors' first names are abbreviated. In some references, I've listed a representative sample of sources cited for documentation. The select bibliography lists some additional significant sources, but neither list is complete.

I don't cite individual notes for the sources from which I've derived information regarding the Johnson and Johnson Tylenol crises. Rather, I'm listing below the sources from which I compiled the pertinent facts used throughout this book.

TYLENOL REFERENCES

AP, "Cyanide deaths prompt company to pull capsules," *Rocky*, Feb. 18, 1986, 3.

"Communication guides Tylenol's comeback," *Communication World*, Mar. 1983, 1, 8.

P. Guy and C. Glickman, "J & J uses candor in crisis," *USA Today*, Feb. 12, 1986, 2B.

"Johnson & Johnson tries ads to revive sales of Tylenol," *WSJ* Oct. 25, 1982, 35.

A. Kates, "J & J stock rebounds," *USA Today*, Feb. 19, 1986, 1B.

N. R. Kleinfield (*NYT*), "Tylenol: an image problem of the worst kind," *A.A. News*, Oct. 8, 1982, C1, C2.

D. Kneale, "Tylenol rival's ads have a sharper tone in wake of tragedy," *WSJ*, Dec. 9, 1982.

S. Koepp, "A hard decision to swallow," *Time*, Mar. 3, 1986, 59.

K. McCoy, "New finds spark Tylenol ban in N.Y." *USA Today*, Feb. 14, 1986, 3A.

K. Miniclier, "Nation gets Tylenol warning," *Denver Post*, Feb. 14, 1986, 1, 17.

B. Powell, "The Tylenol rescue," *Newsweek*, Mar. 3, 1986, 56.

"Death of woman linked to tainted capsules," *WSJ*, Feb. 11, 1986, 2.

R. L. Rundle, "Johnson & Johnson shares post strong rise, but some analysts question Tylenol's future," *WSJ*, Feb. 19, 1986, 59.

C. Skrzycki, "Tampering with buyers' confidence," *U.S. News*, Mar. 3, 1986, 46–47.

S. Siwolop and C. S. Eklund, "The capsule controversy," *Business Week*, Mar. 3, 1986, 37.

"Switching to caplets," *Fortune*, Mar. 17, 1986, 8.

The Tylenol Comeback, Johnson & Johnson special report, 1983.

UPI, "Tylenol poisoning suspected in death," *Denver Post*, Feb. 11, 1986, 1, 8.

M. Waldholz and D. Kneale, "Tylenol's maker tries to regain good image in wake of tragedy," *WSJ*, Nov. 12, 1982, 1, 14.

———, "For Tylenol's manufacturer, the dilemma is to be aggressive—but not appear pushy," *WSJ*, Feb. 20, 1986, 25.

———, "Tylenol maker mounting campaign to restore trust of doctors, buyers," *WSJ*, Oct. 29, 1982, 21.

INTRODUCTION

1. "Importance of image," *WSJ*, Aug. 12, 1985, 19.

2. T. Wainwright, "Beyond advertising," *Ad Age*, Sept. 15, 1986, 67.

3. W. Guzzardi, Jr., "How much should companies talk? *Fortune*, Mar. 4, 1985, 67.

CHAPTER 1. OMNIMEDIA

1. AP, "Gastric bubble not a proven weight-loss method," *O.C. Register*, Dec. 19, 1986, B15.

CHAPTER 2. CORPORATE AMERICA: UNDER THE MICROSCOPE

1. *O.C. Register*, Jan. 13, 1987, E3.

2. J. F. Awad, *The Power of Public Relations* (New York: Praeger, 1985), 18.

3. C. Koshetz, "We're stocking up, with care, on the market," *USA Today*, Dec. 5, 1985, 1B.

4. W. L. Chaze, "What America thinks of TV," *U.S. News*, May 13, 1985, 67.

5. "The myth of the crusading reporter," Mobil Corp. advertisement in *WSJ*, Nov. 1, 1983, 24.

6. Quoted in Johnson & Johnson special report, *The Tylenol Comeback*," 1983, 4.

7. Published by Addison-Wesley, Reading, Mass., 1986.

8. J. Greenwald, "Let's make a deal," *Time*, Dec. 23, 1985, 42–47; C. Blaine, "3rd-quarter mergers are near record," *USA Today*, Oct. 29, 1985, 1B; "Deals top '85 action," *USA Today*, Dec. 23, 1985, 4B; C. Timberlake (AP), "GE, RCA come full circle from friends, to foes, and merger," Dec. 16, 1985; B. Abrams, "General Electric to acquire RCA for $6.28 billion," *WSJ*, Dec. 12, 1985, 3; T. Hall and D. Hertzberg, "Philip Morris today begins $120-a-share tender bid for $5.75 billion acquisition of General Foods Corp." *WSJ*, Sept. 30, 1985, 3.

9. E. Goodman, "Whoops! Here we go on another New Year!" *Rocky*, Jan. 2, 1986.

10. "Mergers and acquisitions for '86," *Institutional Investor*, Jan. 1987, 110–11; " '86, a year in review," *O.C. Register*, Dec. 28, 1986, K5.

11. "For better or for worse? The biggest restructuring in history winds down," *Business Week*, Jan. 12, 1987, 38.

12. "Cargill feeds sales, hits top of list," *USA Today*, Nov. 4, 1985, 1B; L. Pittel, "Behind the paper curtain," *Forbes*, Nov. 18, 1985, 128–66; L. M. Mesdag, "The 50 largest private industrial companies," *Fortune*, May 31, 1982, 108–14.

13. "Nightline," ABC, Nov. 21, 1986.

14. C. Blaine, "Japanese invest more in the USA," *USA Today*, Sept. 13, 1985, 1B.

15. "For better or for worse," 38.

16. R. I. Kirkland, Jr., "We're all in this together," *Fortune*, Feb. 2, 1987, 27.

17. AP, "More defense contractors face inquiries," *O.C. Register*, Feb. 22, 1987, N14.

18. *Washington Post*, "Drug money laundering targeted," *Denver Post*, Aug. 29, 1985, 8B.

19. A. Etzioni, "Corporations that play dirty may take a bath," *Rocky*, Nov. 19, 1985, 39.

20. C. Amory, "Worst business news," *Parade*, Jan. 5, 1986, 5.

21. R. Ricklefs, "Executives and general public say ethical behavior is declining in U.S." *WSJ*, Oct. 31, 1983, 27.

22. R. Lacayo, "Setting off the smoke alarm," *Time*, Dec. 23, 1985, 56.

CHAPTER 3. ACTION NEWS: THE LIFE OF JOURNALISTS

1. Department of Labor, "Rules and Regulations," sect. 541.304, (f)(1),(2).

2. J. Kalter, " 'I don't think he will ever be totally at peace with himself,' " *TV Guide*, Jan. 3, 1987, 28.

CHAPTER 4: GOOD, BAD NEWS!

1. Gallup Poll commissioned by Times Mirror Co., "Media Poll," *USA Today*, Jan. 16, 1986, 6A.

2. M. J. Robinson and M. E. Clancey, "Network news, 15 years after Agnew," *Channels*, Jan./Feb. 1985, 38.

3. P. Donahue, *Donahue: My Own Story* (New York: Simon and Schuster, 1979), 124.

4. E. Peer, "Business vs. the media," *Newsweek*, Oct. 12, 1981, 108.

5. "NBC Nightly News," Mar. 3, 1983.

6. "Tom Brokaw, off camera," NBC advertisement in *WSJ*, Mar. 18, 1985, 33.

7. "TBS cuts back 'Good News' show," *Multichannel News*, Nov. 7, 1983, 17.

8. "Turner to axe 'Nice People,' " *Multichannel News*, Dec. 5, 1983, 20.

9. *The World Almanac and Book of Facts, 1987* (New York: Newspaper Enterprise Association, 1986), 771, 337; "Death on the road," *WSJ*, Apr. 14, 1982, 1; "Americans are dying for better gas mileage," United Services Automobile Association advertisement in *WSJ*, Jan. 14, 1982, 17.

10. "Concorde emergency forces Boston landing," *O.C. Register*, Jan. 18, 1987, A24.

CHAPTER 5. DIVINE RIGHT

1. W. H. Phillips, "A report to *The Wall Street Journal*'s readers," editorial, *WSJ*, Jan. 4, 1982.

2. "The right to know," Gannett advertisement, *E&P*, Dec. 5, 1981, cover.

3. H. Thomas, "Keeping an eye on the presidents," *E&P*, Jan. 19, 1985, 48.

4. H. Simons and J. A. Califano, Jr., *The Media and Business* (New York: Vintage Books, 1979), 128.

CHAPTER 6. OBJECTIVITY AND THE PARALLLAX FACTOR

1. "The view from the trenches," *Broadcasting*, Nov. 15, 1982, 96, in an interview with *Broadcasting* editors.

CHAPTER 7. THEY LEAN LEFT, RIGHT?

1. E. Diamond and S. Bates, "How accurate is the network news?" *TV Guide*, Feb. 27, 1982, 8.

2. H. J. Gans, *Deciding What's News* (New York: Vintage Books, 1980), 92.

3. Published by Arlington House, New Rochelle, N.Y.

4. M. J. Robinson and M. E. Clancey, "Network News, 15 years after Agnew," *Channels*, Jan./Feb. 1985, 34–39.

5. J. Friendly, "Reporter's notebook: Surprising profile of a journalist," *NYT*, May 13, 1983, A16.

6. J. Chancellor, W. R. Mears, *The News Business* (New York: Harper and Row, 1983), 41.

7. H. J. Gans, "Are U.S. journalists dangerously liberal?." *Columbia Journalism Review*, Nov./Dec. 1985, 32.

8. "In defense of business reporting," *Broadcasting*, Nov. 21, 1983, 50. Scheffler made the remark during a Boston University conference on business and the news media.

9. A. R. Hunt, "Media bias is in eye of the beholder," *WSJ*, July 23, 1985; J. P. Cain, letter to the editor, *WSJ*, Aug. 9, 1985; J. Weisman, letter to the editor, *WSJ*, Aug. 16, 1985.

CHAPTER 8. CHAMPIONS OF THE PROLETARIAT

1. W. Smith, "Business and the media," speech delivered before the Third Annual Business and the Media Luncheon of the Public Relations Society of America and Press Club of Cleveland, September 17, 1985.

2. D. Finn, *The Business-Media Relationship* (New York: AMACOM, 1981), 46.

3. E. Bark, "Two pains in the tube we won't miss," *Denver Post*, Nov. 17, 1985, 4. Bark, of the "Dallas Morning News," was quoting a remark made by Rivera during a 1981 conference on journalism at Princeton University.

4. M. L. Stein, "Improving credibility," *E&P*, July 13, 1985, 9. Davies' remarks came during a Future of Journalism seminar at Linfield College in Oregon, June 1985.

5. Page A8.

6. "Behind the rise and fall of Air Florida," *Business Week*, July 23, 1984, 122.

7. "News Analysis," *Broadcasting*, Sept. 26, 1983, 97. Chancellor spoke the words in accepting an award at a 1983 convention of the Radio-Television News Directors Association.

8. "Cartoonist Conrad wields mighty pen, *Times Mirror Today*, Winter 1987, 3. The publication is a quarterly for shareholders and employees of the multibillion-dollar media conglomerate.

9. J. E. Roper, "News groups oppose changes in FOIA," *E&P*, June 28, 1986, 11–12.

10. E. Efron, "The media and the omniscient class," in *Business and the Media*, ed. C. Aronoff (Santa Monica, Calif.: Goodyear Publishing, 1979), 24–25.

11. "Briefings," *Columbia Journalism Review*, Jan./Feb. 1982, 68. The remark came in a review of *Business and the Media* by Kevin Phillips.

12. J. Friendly, "Reporter's notebook: Surprising profile of a journalist," *NYT*, May 13, 1983, A16.

13. D. Hill, "Life on the bottom rung," *Washington Journalism Review*, Jan./Feb. 1987, 20.

14. "Radio-Television News Directors Assoc. salary survey," *Broadcasting*, Feb. 3, 1986, 56.

15. "Print profits rebound," *USA Today*, Jan. 13, 1986, 1B; A. B. Block, "39th annual report on American industry: Communications media," *Forbes*, Jan. 12, 1987, 99–100. *Forbes* reported that the five-year median average return on equity for large communications and media companies was 19.1 percent; the net profit margin for the companies was 7.3 percent in 1986.

16. D. Schaaf, "King of American opinion polls, George Gallup has a few

opinions of his own about the public image of American business," *Ozark*, Dec. 1982, 10.

17. "A challenge to media," *E&P*, Oct. 27, 1984, 6. In an editorial, *E&P* quoted Bennack regarding a national survey of "the American public's knowledge of business and economy," sponsored by Hearst.

18. W. A. Henry III, "American Institutions and the Media," Gannett Center for Media Studies, Columbia University, Nov. 1985.

19. F. Barnes, "A conversation with Jane Bryant Quinn," *WJR*, July/Aug. 1982, 24.

20. T. K. Smith, speech to American Chemical Society's Central Regional Meeting, Bowling Green, Ohio, June 3, 1986.

21. AP, "Media bamboozled on oil supply story?" *A.A. News*, Mar. 4, 1982; J. Weisman, "What TV *didn't* tell us about the energy crisis," *TV Guide*, Mar. 6, 1982, 4–12; "Media Institute lobs another brick at oil coverage by TV networks," *Broadcasting*, Oct. 11, 1982, 72–73.

22. G. Brandon, "News media 'exonerated' for problems in TMI stories," *E&P*, July 18, 1981, 20. Sandman's comments came during a conference on nuclear energy and the media in Reston, Va.

23. "A move to improve high-tech reporting," *USA Today*, Sept. 22, 1983, 2B.

CHAPTER 9. WHAT *IS* PUBLIC RELATIONS?

1. Newscast, WMHE FM, Toledo, August 7, 1980.

2. "Dow goes all warm and fuzzy," *USA Today*, Oct. 15, 1985, 2B; R. Rice, "Dow Chemical: from napalm to nice guy," *Fortune* May 12, 1986, 75.

3. P. Caesar, "Cause-related marketing: the new face of corporate philanthropy," *Business and Society Review*, Fall 1986, 15–19; "Altruistic Marketing," *Fortune*, Nov. 25, 1985, 7; P. Maher, "What corporations get by giving," *Business Marketing*, Dec. 1984, 80–89.

4. B. Abrams, "NRA tries to soften its image with 'laid back' advertising," *WSJ*, Feb. 4, 1982.

5. G. Pitts, "Ronald McDonald houses given free MCI long-distance service," *Denver Post*, Dec. 16, 1985, 2E; "Big Mac attacked," *WSJ*, Sept. 12, 1985, 33; "McDonald's Food: The facts . . . " McDonald's Corporation, 1987; "Balance," McDonald's Corporation, advertisement in *TV Guide*, Mar. 14, 1987, 13.

CHAPTER 10: KAMIKAZE PUBLIC RELATIONS

1. "Killer cars," "West 57th Street," CBS, Sept. 3, 1985; "Group seeks new Ford probe," *USA Today*, Sept. 10, 1985, 1B; "Fords in reverse," *Consumer Reports*, Sept. 1985, 520–23; "Nine firms win readers' poll," *USA Today*, Oct. 23, 1985, 2B; J. Flint, "39th annual report on American Industry: Automotive," *Forbes*, Jan. 12, 1987, 71.

2. "Oh, those flacks," *APME Guidelines*, 1969, 42–44.

3. "A reporter who doesn't want to be used must consider the sources of his stories," *WSJ*, Sept. 5, 1985, 23.

4. A. Sanoff, "Business strikes back against the press," *U.S. News*, Oct. 26, 1981, 57.

5. D. Finn, The *Business-Media Relationship* (New York: AMACOM, 1981), 20.

6. "The news from Disney World," *New York Times*, Oct. 8, 1986, A34; A. Prendergast, "Mickey Mouse journalism," *WJR*, Jan./Feb. 1987, 32–35.

7. W. Guzzardi, Jr., "How much should companies talk?" *Fortune*, Mar. 4, 1985, 66.

8. D. Finn, *Business-Media*, 10.

CHAPTER 11. TAKING RESPONSIBILITY FOR PR: WHOSE JOB IS IT, ANYWAY?

1. D. Finn, The *Business-Media Relationship* (New York: AMACOM, 1981), 65.

2. "Marketing" column, *WSJ*, July 8, 1982, 17.

3. J. F. Awad, *The Power of Public Relations* (New York: Praeger, 1985), 62.

4. "Notable and quotable," *WSJ*, Nov. 8, 1984, 30, quoting Grant's observation in *Leaders Magazine*, Oct./Nov. 1984.

5. C. Low, "Lawyers bill clients for 'media time,' " *E&P*, Mar. 9, 1985, 8. Low's article was reprinted from the February 7, 1985, *Los Angeles Daily Journal*.

6. H. F. Myers, "Mobil's Marathon loss, its second in 6 months, is tied to its blunders," Jan. 8, 1982, 1.

7. "CBS refers its lawsuit questions to PR firm," *Broadcasting*, Oct. 24, 1983, 75.

CHAPTER 12. THE MEDIA ARE COMING, THE MEDIA ARE COMING!

1. "TV criticized at media seminar," *Broadcasting*, Nov. 15, 1982, 93.

2. L. M. Mesdag, "The 50 largest private industrial companies," *Fortune*, May 31, 1982, 114.

3. J. F. Peltz (AP), "Insider scandal heightens dispute over when to disclose merger talks," *O.C. Register*, Mar. 1, 1987; D. Galant, "Can we talk?" *Institutional Investor*, Jan. 1987, 55–57; S. Raabe, "SEC steps up disclosure enforcement," *Rocky Mountain Business Journal*, Aug. 12, 1985, 1–4.

4. L. D. Boccardi, "A comment on 'no immediate comment,' " *Prose & Cons*, October 19, 1981, 1. *Prose & Cons* is a publication for AP editorial employees.

5. P. Guy, "Wall street wonders, 'Where's Crazy Eddie?' " *USA Today*, Jan. 13, 1987, 2B.

6. P. H. Dougherty, "J.W.T. suspends executive," *NYT*, Feb. 4, 1982, 41.

7. J. Pryor, "What went wrong in Albuquerque," *Electronic Media*, July 11, 1985, 1, 30.

8. "Airline executives: Skies still friendly," *Denver Post*, Jan. 5, 1986, 12A.

9. D. B. Hilder, "Aetna life unit sues Marvin Davis over oil projects," *WSJ*, Aug. 6, 1985, 3.

10. "A heartbeat away," "20/20," ABC, Jan. 1, 1987.

11. "Burger King not chicken of no. 1," *O.C. Register*, Jan. 13, 1987, E2.

12. B. Thomas (AP), "Walt Disney studio has changed dramatically since his death 20 years ago," *O.C. Register*, Dec. 15, 1986; "Disney welcomes competition from Spielberg," *O.C. Register*, Dec. 5, 1986.

13. S. Widener, "How Coors won friends and influenced '60 Minutes,' " *Denver Post Magazine*, Oct. 16, 1983, 10–37; "Turnabout," *Broadcasting*, Apr. 11, 1983, 185; S. Richard, letter to the editor, *WSJ*, Sept. 13, 1982.

14. M. Z. Levy, "Playboy Guide interview: Mike Wallace," *Playboy Guide to Electronic Entertainment*, Fall/Winter 1981, 26.

15. "People" column, *Cincinnati Enquirer*, Dec. 17, 1981, A3; "In Brief," *Broadcasting*, Dec. 21, 1981, 88.

16. "60 Minutes," CBS, Sept. 28, 1981. The program examined its own editorial methods.

CHAPTER 13. "SIR, A MR. MIKE WALLACE IS HERE TO SEE YOU"

1. H. Carr, "Communicating during a 'crisis,' " speech delivered at Public Relations Society of America Chapter, Vancouver, B.C., Dec. 2, 1986.

2. E. Frankel, "Learning to conquer 'Mike' fright," *WJR*, July/Aug. 1982, 32.

3. W. Westmoreland, letter to the editor, *Broadcasting*, Feb. 15, 1982, 22; "Apology," *Broadcasting*, Feb. 8, 1982, 94; "Westmoreland returns fire," *Broadcasting*, Feb. 1, 1982.

4. "Media scan," *CableVision*, Nov. 16, 1981, 66, quoting remarks by Baker in an *NYT* interview.

5. "Programs for Business," information brochure, Foundation for American Communications, 1985.

6. "The Mary and Bill story," *Time*, Oct. 27, 1980, 80.

7. *Broadcasting*, Feb. 15, 1982, 105.

8. L. M. Katz, "A hostile interviewer won't get information," *USA Today*, Nov. 13, 1984, 11A. Interview with Mike Wallace.

9. Thomas appeared before the last annual convention of Associated Press Broadcasters in Washington, D.C., during the first week in June, 1981. Since leaving Moral Majority, Thomas has become a columnist for the Los Angeles Times Syndicate and comments for National Public Radio. For additional insight into Thomas's jaded view of the press, see P. D. Young's *God's Bullies: Power Politics and Religious Tyranny*, Holt, Rinehart and Winston, 1982; excerpted in *Quill*, June 1982, 24–30.

10. H. Cox, *The Seduction of The Spirit* (New York: Simon and Schuster, 1973), 10.

11. H. Thomas, UPI, " 'Off-record' talk haunts politicians," *A.A. News*, Nov. 15, 1981, F12.

12. S. Strasser, "Jesse Jackson and the Jews," *Newsweek*, Mar. 5, 1984, 26; "Belatedly, Jackson comes clean," *Time*, Mar. 12, 1984, 27.

13. AP, "Candidate lashes gays on live mike," *Denver Post*, Oct. 26, 1985.

14. W. A. Henry III, "On and off the record," *Time*, Aug. 27, 1984, 52; G. Skelton, "Reagan wants to curb government and arms," *L.A. Times*, Aug. 24, 1984, 1, 11. After Skelton's formal interview with Reagan, he asked him if the president was going to joke anymore during mike checks. Skelton quotes the president as saying, "No, now that I know that the security of the nation is at stake when people eavesdrop . . ."

15. T. Schwartz, "Wallace taped in ethnic remark," *NYT*, Jan. 12, 1982, C15; D. Henninger, "The anchorman chronicles: Wallace gets an A," commentary, *WSJ*, Jan. 19, 1982.

CHAPTER 15. PLANNING FOR THE UNTHINKABLE

1. B. Rudolph, "Coping with catastrophe," *Time*, Feb. 24, 1986, 53.
2. R. F. Littlejohn, *Crisis Management: A Team Approach* (New York: AMA Management Briefing, American Management Associations, 1983), 24–25.
3. "Union Carbide plant leaks gas; at least 100 hurt," *WSJ*, Aug. 12, 1985, 8.
4. T. Roth and F. Rose, "Union Carbide says plant safety system wasn't geared to track gas that leaked," *WSJ*, Aug. 14, 1985, 3.

CHAPTER 16. COMMUNICATING CONTROL AMID CHAOS

1. S. Fink, *Crisis Management* (New York: AMACOM, 1986), 92.
2. H. Carr, "Communicating during a 'crisis,' " speech delivered at Public Relations Society of America Chapter, Vancouver, B.C., Dec. 2, 1986.
3. F. Kessler, "Tremors from the Tylenol scare hit food companies," *Fortune* Mar. 31, 1986, 59; "J & J and Gerber deal with crises," *Dun's Business Month*, Apr. 1986, 22; P. Strnad, "Gerber ignores 'Tylenol textbook,' " *Ad Age*, Mar. 10, 1986, 3; C. Skrzycki, "Tampering with buyers' confidence," *U.S. News*, Mar. 3, 1986, 46–47; S. Koepp, "A hard decision to swallow," *Time*, Mar. 3, 1986, 59. All references to Gerber are drawn from these sources.
4. B. Ingersoll, "Merrill Lynch censured by SEC over fraud case," *WSJ*, Sept. 12, 1985, 8.
5. B. Meier, "Carbide pledges immediate alert on toxic leaks," *WSJ*, Aug. 19, 1985, 5.
6. K. Anderson, "Stray parentheses corner banker," *USA Today*, Sept. 9, 1985, 2B.
7. W. C. Symonds, "How companies are learning to prepare for the worst," *Business Week*, Dec. 23, 1985, 74; B. Rudolph, "Coping with catastrophe," *Time*, Feb. 24, 1986, 53.
8. D. Rotbart, "Marathon oil executives sharply criticized for not building better takeover defenses," *WSJ*, Nov. 17, 1981.
9. J. Bussey, "Violations cited at Detroit Edison nuclear facility," *WSJ*, Jan. 13, 1986, 8.
10. J. Sanko and S. Chawkins, "Keystone chairlift collapses; 49 hurt," *Rocky*, Dec. 15, 1985, 1; J. Sanko, "Investigators mum on cause of lift collapse," *Rocky*, Dec. 16, 1985, 1; G. Lurie, "Collapse of ski life probed," *USA Today*, Dec. 16, 1985, 3A; "Response was magnificent," editorial, *Rocky*, Dec. 17, 1985, 68; P. Bulman, "Crisis management pays," *Denver Post*, Dec. 19, 1985, D1.
11. J. Lipman, "PR society receives some very bad PR—from its ex-chief," *WSJ*, Sept. 26, 1986, 1.
12. A. D. Frank, "Shark Bait?" *Forbes*, Nov. 18, 1985, 114–19.
13. B. Meier and J. B. Stewart, "A year after Bhopal, Union Carbide faces a slew of problems," *WSJ*, Nov. 26, 1985, 1.

14. "Bhopal, a year later: Union Carbide takes a tougher line," *Business Week,* Nov. 25, 1985, 96.

CHAPTER 17. RUMORS: A CRISIS IN COMMUNICATIONS

1. T. K. Smith, speech to American Chemical Society's Central Regional Meeting, Bowling Green, Ohio, June 3, 1986.
2. Published by Auburn House, Dover, Mass., 1985.
3. P. Strnad, "Gerber ignores "Tylenol textbook,' " *Ad Age,* Mar. 10, 1986, 3.

CHAPTER 18. SOOTHING THE POSTCRISIS HANGOVER

1. J. F. Love, "McDonald's hits 'big leagues,' " *O.C. Register,* Nov. 3, 1986, D1. Excerpted from Love's book, *McDonald's: Behind the Arches.*
2. J. Persinos (*Orlando Sentinel*), "Contac no longer feels the chill," *O.C. Register,* Dec. 15, 1986, D6.
3. A. Pasztor, "Hutton again says it failed to give documents to U.S.," *WSJ,* Aug. 15, 1985, 10; "E. F. Hutton execs waiting for prober Bell's ax to fall," *Denver Post,* Aug. 29, 1985, 8B; S. McMurray, "Hutton's report on check overdrafting to implicate about a dozen employees," *WSJ,* Sept. 4, 1985, 4; AP, "Hutton chief: implicated employees to be punished," *Denver Post,* Sept. 5, 1985, 2C; news release, E. F. Hutton Group, Sept. 5, 1985; G. B. Bell, King & Spalding, "The Hutton Report," Sept. 4, 1985; M. Osborn, "Investigation exonerates top Hutton execs," USA Today, Sept. 6, 1985, 1B; "Hutton being advised by Bell's law firm in offering, panel says," *WSJ,* Sept. 9, 1985; "SEC orders E. F. Hutton to pay back $1 million," *Rocky,* Oct. 30, 1985, 87; A. L. Adams and J. Friedman, "Hutton works on its image," *USA Today,* Nov. 4, 1985, 7B; "Hutton aids Red Cross disaster-relief efforts," *USA Today,* Dec. 10, 1985, 2B; S. McMurray, "E. F. Hutton to post 4th-quarter loss; problems at securities unit are cited," *WSJ,* Dec. 16, 1985, 7; D. Dorfman, " '85 market scene had its heroes, villains," *Rocky,* Dec. 17, 1985, 21B; "Restitution by Hutton in millions," *Denver Post,* Jan. 2, 1986; AP, "Bell paid $1,711 an hour for Hutton prove," *O.C. Register,* Feb. 1, 1987, n. 15; "Hutton's accounts target of new probe," *O.C. Register,* Feb. 20, 1987, C3.
4. UPI, "Worker dies in nuclear plant blast," *Rocky,* Jan. 5, 1986, 2; P. Johnson, "Ruptured N-tank was overfilled," *USA Today,* Jan. 6, 1986, 3A; AP, UPI, "Kerr-McGee uranium spill scrubbed up," *Rocky,* Jan. 7, 1986, 4; J. Dahl and L. P. Cohen, "Kerr-McGee facility was cited by NRC 4 months ago for 'excessive' violations," *WSJ,* Jan. 8, 1986, 6.

CHAPTER 19. FIGHTING FIRE WITH FIRE

1. *Broadcasting,* July 27, 1981, 145.
2. A. Radolf, "National News Council folds," *E&P,* Mar. 31, 1983, 9.
3. W. Donoghue, "E. F. Hutton investment advice not at issue," *Denver Post,* Sept. 1, 1985, 4F.

4. D. Carroll, "GM's beleaguered chairman fights back," *USA Today*, Feb. 12, 1987, 1B.

5. T. Hall, "Philip Morris Cos. magazine promotes pro-smoking issues," *WSJ*, July 24, 1985, 6; D. Sperling, "Doctors: ban all ads for tobacco," *USA Today*, Dec. 11, 1985, 1A.

6. "Fighting fire with fire, television style," *Broadcasting*, July 14, 1980, 58.

7. H. J. Gans, *Deciding What's News* (New York: Vintage Books, 1980), 118.

8. "Boycott by big business," *E&P*, Dec. 15, 1984, 10; T. Griffith, "Getting back at the press," *Time*, June 9, 1986, 81.

9. L. Banks, "Why the media look less fearsome," *Fortune*, Oct. 14, 1985, 207.

10. "Letters: Tandy pulls its ads," *InfoWorld*, Aug. 5, 1985, 6.

11. "Letters: Tandy Redux," *Infoworld*, Aug. 26, 1985, 6–8.

12. E. Bean, "Passing on reviews," *WSJ*, June 16, 1986, 19D.

13. T. FitzPatrick, "T. Boone takes on the press," *WJR*, Mar. 1987, 10.

14. M. K. Guzda, "Shedding a negative light on big business," *E&P*, May 12, 1984, 10.

CHAPTER 20. ADVOCACY ADVERTISING: FEEDING THE HAND THAT BITES YOU

1. E. Fitch, "Image ads more than glad tidings," *Ad Age*, Mar. 10, 1986, 42.

2. S. P. Sethi, *Advocacy Advertising and Large Corporations* (Lexington, Mass.: Heath., 1977), 8.

3. C. R. Milsap, "Manville fights image woes with $7 million of ads," *Business Marketing*, Dec. 1984.

4. S. W. Colford, "RJR ruling may 'open up' issue advertising," *Ad Age*, Aug. 18, 1986, 6.

5. L. Cecere, "Seagram fights for equality for distillers," *Ad Age*, July 21, 1986, S11–S12.

6. "Ticor proposal aimed at EPIC's problems," *Denver Post*, Sept. 12, 1985, 3D.

7. S. W. Colford, "Deduction change could hurt issue ads," *Ad Age*, Mar. 3, 1986, 70.

8. L. Winer, "Herb Schmertz,' *View*, Nov. 1983, 60.

9. "At Mobil, executives get libel protection," *WSJ*, Feb. 24, 1983, 27.

10. "At Issue: Access to Television," Kaiser Aluminum & Chemical Corporation, Oakland, Calif., 1980, 1.

11. L. E. Phillips, "LM, Grace press nets," *Ad Age*, May 5, 1986, 4; *Broadcasting*, Feb. 3, 1986, 40.

12. D. M. Gilmore and J. A. Barron, *Mass Communication Law* (St. Paul, Minn.: West, 1974), 802.

13. H. C. Donahue, "The Fairness Doctrine is shackling broadcast," *Technology Review*, Nov./Dec. 1986, 44–52; "Fowler Play," editorial, *National Review*, Nov. 21, 1986, 30–31.

14. H. C. Donahue, "Fairness Doctrine shackling broadcast," 46–47.

15. "Controversial Grace," editorial, *WSJ*, Feb. 4, 1986, 26.

16. M. Fowler, "The fairness doctrine can hurt," *Broadcasting*, Mar. 3, 1986, 67. Fowler's remarks originally appeared as a commentary in the *Washington Post*, Feb. 25, 1986.

17. "INTV members to air Grace deficit spot," *Broadcasting*, Aug. 11, 1986, 60; J. Nelson-Horchler, "A 'controversial' ad?" *Industry Week*, Feb. 17, 1986, 20–21.

CHAPTER 21. FILING SUIT: USING THE LAW OF LIBEL FOR SATISFACTION

1. *Primer on the Law of Political Broadcasting and Related Doctrines: The Broadcaster's Responsibilities under the Communications Act. The Law of Libel, Slander and Privacy* (Washington, D.C.: Gardner, Carton & Douglas, 1983), 31–48; D. A. Lieberth, *A Media Survival Kit for Ohio Reporters and Editors*, Associated Press Society of Ohio, 1980, 18–19; D. M. Gilmore and J. A. Barron, *Mass Communication Law* (St. Paul, Minn.: West, 1974), 180–286.

2. Ibid., 188.

3. B. Kantrowitz, "Time and CBS: still arguing their cases," *Newsweek*, Nov. 10, 1986, 10.

4. L. Denniston, "The libel case that won't quit," *WJR*, May 1986, 14.

5. J. E. Roper, "A whittling away of media libel protection?" *E&P*, July 6, 1985, 12–13.

6. M. L. Stein, "Limited public figures—a problem in libel cases," Aug. 10, 1985, 17; "Mobilspeak," editorial, *WSJ*, Apr. 28, 1983, 28.

7. M. Garbus, *Publishers Weekly*, Sept. 5, 1986, 34.

8. Phone conversation with M. McDonald, Mar. 16, 1987; "The Mobil man tells his tale," *Time*, Dec. 23, 1985, 53; "$2 million libel verdict against *Washington Post* is reinstated," *E&P*, April 13, 1985, 11; "Judge clears *Post* in libel suit," *Broadcasting*, May 9, 1983, 44–45.

9. Sigma Delta Chi luncheon, Denver Press Club, Mar. 16, 1983.

CHAPTER 22. TOWARD A BETTER UNDERSTANDING: CLOSING THOUGHTS ON IMPROVING THE BUSINESS/MEDIA RELATIONSHIP

1. H. J. Corbett, "The Best of The Thieves," speech delivered to the Oklahoma Jaycees, Stillwater, Okla., Feb. 16, 1985.

2. D. Nelkin, "The scientist as P.R.," *Journalist*, Winter 1985, 16–17.

3. S. P. Sethi, *Advocacy Advertising and Large Corporations* (Lexington, Mass.: Heath, 1977), 327.

4. S. N. McDonnell, "People, Profits, and Ethics," Possibility Thinkers Luncheon, Garden Grove, Calif., Jan. 16, 1987.

5. According to a McDonnell Douglas spokesman in St. Louis, Mar. 16, 1987.

6. "Rockwell ordered to give to charity," *Rocky*, Dec. 15, 1985, 102; R. S. Greenberger, "General Dynamics temporarily barred from new U.S. work after indictment," *WSJ*, Dec. 4, 1985; E. T. Pound, "Investigators detect pattern of kickbacks for defense business," *WSJ*, Nov. 14, 1985, 1; UPI, "Rockwell sus-

pended in fraud case," *Rocky*, Nov. 1, 1985; AP, "Firm admits illegal look at defense budget," Sept. 11, 1985, 17.

7. T. G. Pownall, "Defense industry wounded by loss of public's trust," *Rocky*, Dec. 13, 1985, 103.

Selected Bibliography

These works, along with those cited in the notes, form the core of my research, outside personal interviews. Space does not allow for a full disclosure of all the articles and books that helped shape my thinking. *Broadcasting* magazine has been especially useful over the years with its excellent coverage of industry events and meetings.

Aronoff, C. E., ed. *Business and the Media*. Santa Monica, Calif.: Goodyear, 1979.

Bland, M. *Executive's Guide to TV and Radio Appearances*. White Plains, N.Y.: Knowledge Industry, 1981.

Capelin, J. "How to manage a crisis." *Architectural Record*, August 1985

Colson, C. "The state must deal in deceit." *Orange County Register*, March 8, 1987.

Corrado, F. M. *Media for Managers*. Englewood Cliffs, N.J.: Prentice-Hall, 1984.

Coulson-Thomas, C. J. *Marketing Communications*. London: Institute of Marketing, 1983.

"Crisis Management." Seminar. Denver Chamber of Commerce, November 19, 1985.

Cutlip, S. M., and A. H. Center. *Effective Public Relations*. Englewood Cliffs, N.J.: Prentice-Hall, 1978.

DiBacco,, T. V., "The businessman flees history." *Wall Street Journal*, November 30, 1981.

Dorfman, H. "Fighting the Fairness Doctrine." *The New Leader*, November 17, 1986.

Garbett, T. F. "Today's trends in corporate advertising." *Business Marketing*, August 1985.

Goldstein, T. *The News at Any Cost*. New York: Simon and Schuster, 1985.

Gorden, R. L. *Interviewing*. Homewood, Ill.: Dorsey Press, 1975.

Hilton, J., and M. Knoblauch. *On Television!* New York: AMACOM, 1980.

Hogan, B. "Corporations and the press are now in business." *Washington Journalism Review*, July/August 1983.

Howard, C., and W. Matthews. *On Deadline, Managing Media Relations*. New York: Longman, 1985.

Huber, P. "The press gets off easy in tort law." *Wall Street Journal*, July 24, 1985.

Lamb, R., and W. G. Armstrong, Jr. *Business, Media, and the Law*. New York: New York University Press, 1980.

"Learning to shine on TV." *Business Week*, January 19, 1981.

Lukaszewski, J. E. "Corporate and private sector communications responsibility." Speech to Annenberg School of Communication, Washington, D.C., October 10, 1986.

MacDougall, A. K. *Ninety Seconds To Tell All*. Homewood, Ill.: Dow Jones Irwin, 1981.

Murray, T. "FACS aids industry public relations effort." *Media Memo*, November 7, 1983.

Murray, T. "Just the FACS, ma'm." *Media Memo*, October 24, 1983.

"Name your villains." *Wall Street Journal*, November 19, 1981.

Pines, W. L. "How to handle a PR crisis." *Public Relations Quarterly*, Summer 1985.

Rickover, H. G. "Getting the job done right." *New York Times*, November 25, 1981.

Salant, R. "The press of business." *Channels*, July/August 1985.

Schmertz, H. *Corporations and the First Amendment*. New York: AMACOM, 1978.

Seldes, G., ed. *The Great Thoughts*. New York: Ballantine Books, 1983.

"Should private opinions get air time?" *Nation's Business*, August 1979.

"Smith finds fault, progress in business reporting." *Broadcasting*, May 4, 1981.

Stevens, C. W. "K mart has a little trouble killing those phantom snakes from Asia." *Wall Street Journal*, October 20, 1981.

Swearingen J. E. "Responsibility in Journalism." Speech delivered at the Conference on the Responsibilities of Journalism, University of Notre Dame, November 22, 1982.

Webster's New Twentieth Century Dictionary. 2nd ed. New York: Simon and Schuster, 1983.

Will, G. "Stockman profits from irrational economics." *Rocky Mountain News*, August 8, 1985.

Index

About the Author

DONALD W. BLOHOWIAK learned to speak the languages of journalism and business while in editorial and marketing management positions with some of the largest communications companies in America. He has served the Associated Press, Hearst, Multimedia, Times Mirror, a venture of Tele-Communications, Inc., McGraw-Hill and Telecrafter Corp., in addition to consulting for other firms. His broad background includes posts in radio, television, cable television, news wire services, electronic information services and book publishing, in posts ranging from reporter to company president.

Blohowiak currently directs advertising and public relations for a major New York publisher. An award winning speaker and debater, he is a graduate of the University of Wisconsin at Milwaukee.